Standard Deviations

*Chance and the
Modern British Novel*

Standard Deviations

Chance and the
Modern British Novel

Leland Monk

STANFORD UNIVERSITY PRESS, STANFORD, CALIFORNIA

1993

Stanford University Press, Stanford, California
© 1993 by the Board of Trustees of the Leland Stanford Junior University
Printed in the United States of America

CIP data appear at the end of the book

For Jay—

"again, still, always"

Acknowledgements

It is perhaps always the case that in our intellectual lives we happen upon people, books, and ideas simply by chance that end up influencing our thinking for the rest of our lives. The narrative of this study about chance in narrative tends to enact what it in other ways tries to resist, leaving out of the story it tells the countless random accidents that made its telling possible in the first place. I would therefore like here to remark the sense of excitement, uncanniness, and strange pleasure occasioned by the many chance encounters with people and texts that influenced this work. I would also like to express my gratitude to the friends and associates who contributed to this project and whose assistance was never haphazard: to Catherine Gallagher, for guiding and encouraging this study from its awkward initial stages; to David Lloyd, for always knowing what the next step was; to Neil Hertz and D. A. Miller, whose writings and teachings helped me to think and write about novels at crucial moments when I thought I had nothing to say; to the late Joel Fineman, who taught me how to take seriously the play of the proper name; to my colleagues at Boston University, especially the poker players; and to John Bishop, Mary Ann O'Farrell, Robert Newsom, and Jim Porter, who read and improved earlier versions of various chapters. But most of all I would like to thank Jay Baer, who gave me a chance.

Contents

Toute Pensée émet un Coup de Dés.

Stephane Mallarmé

Standard Deviations

Chance and the
Modern British Novel

Introduction:
"Chance Is the Fool's Name for Fate"

In the 1934 movie *The Gay Divorcee*, starring Fred Astaire and Ginger Rogers, Ginger's character plans to stage an affair in order to provide grounds for a divorce from her husband. Her lawyer, played by Edward Everett Horton, arranges for her to rendezvous with a paid corespondent who will pretend to be her adulterous lover. Horton chooses as the password by which she will know the man a phrase from one of Fred's shows that has tickled his fancy: "Chance is the fool's name for fate." Fred has already met and fallen in love with Ginger; when he sees her again he by chance repeats the phrase to her, and she becomes furious that (so she thinks) the man she was falling for is also the man she is paying to play the part of her lover. Fred repeatedly makes a fool of himself trying to win her back until the misunderstanding is cleared up and they dance off together in the moonlight to the sound of "The Continental."

The chance repetition of this phrase about chance moves the story along nicely in *The Gay Divorcee*. In this study I will be tracing the way chance is represented in certain narratives and in the process affects the form of that narrative.

1. chance is   2. the fool's name   3. for fate

If we bear in mind how foolishly Fred behaves when he's on the outs with Ginger, we can see how this phrase encapsulates the most rudimentary and shopworn narrative, the Hollywood storyline:

1. boy meets girl   2. boy loses girl   3. boy gets girl

But if boy and girl are *meant* to be together (as Fred and Ginger always are), can we even say that their meeting is a chance meeting? It would seem that the story of boy meets girl leaves nothing to chance. If, as I will argue, chance *always* takes on a necessarily fateful quality once it is represented in narrative, are we foolish even to speak of chance?

Chance is *not* fate, though the word has a tendency to drift in that direction. Chance (from the Latin *cadere*, to fall) can mean a totally haphazard event (the fall of the dice) or an opportunity (your turn to throw the dice) or a lucky break (the fall of the dice that wins the game). Fate, on the other hand, refers to events that fall out in a manner predetermined by a higher power (the loaded dice of the gods). What seems like chance to us, throwing the dice, becomes a way of divining our fate (from the Latin *fatum*, the gods' sentence). We take our chances, we throw the dice, we read our fate. Once the dice are thrown the element of chance in their fall tends to be effaced by the fate we read in them. This being the case, there seems to be no way to negotiate our way from a necessarily fateful reading (of the dice, of a text) back to an original and clearly recognizable instance of chance.

Still, the effacement of chance by our reading of fate leaves a residual trace inscribed in the structure of that reading, and this is where the middle term in Edward Everett Horton's felicitous phrase becomes helpful. "Chance is *the fool's name* for fate": the phrase does not equate chance with fate, nor does it say that the concept of fate subsumes the concept of chance; rather, it says that fools call fate "chance," while implying that anyone who calls fate "chance" is a fool. Calling something by a particular name then becomes an occasion for name-calling. What do fools and name-calling have to do with chance and fate?

The Fool, of course, is a figure with a rich historical and literary heritage. The Fool is traditionally a person on the periphery of an established order, able by his marginality to give expression to alternative modes of speaking and being. At times of crisis, the Fool often becomes a token victim by virtue of his expression or embodiment of traits identified as "other" and considered (for whatever reasons) a threat to the stability of the established order. The system then purges itself of those unwanted traits by identifying and containing them in the figure of the Fool and expelling him, usually in a public ritual involving banishment or execution.[1]

In retracing the contours of chance inscribed in and hollowing out the fateful reading of a text, name-calling and Fools—verbal aggression and the scapegoat mechanism—will guide the inquiry. I will be looking at the way certain characters in a novel who are some-how associated with chance are vilified and victimized and so seem to carry a burden greater than that warranted by their ostensible shortcomings. By questioning the abuse such characters receive, I will delineate the traces of chance that the excesses of their ultimate fate tend to write off. Giving these fated figures a second chance will then help to articulate the role chance played in the development of modernist narrative forms.

F. R. Leavis, writing in *The Great Tradition* about Joseph Conrad's novel *Chance*, observes, "[T]he theme indicated by the title, inge-niously exploited as it is in the mode of presentation, has no essential relation with the main theme: chance plays no notably different part from that it must play in any story offering a novelist a study of human nature." [2] This passage is remarkable for what it leaves unexamined, not just about the novel *Chance* but about chance in the novel. Leavis points out that chance is an essential element in any novel—at least a novel that purports to study human nature—and so, he implies, it goes without saying. Leavis's remarks are typical: for reasons that I consider in some detail, literary and critical studies usually dismiss, discount, or altogether ignore the subject of chance. *Standard Devia-tions: Chance and the Modern British Novel* spells out what tradi-tionally goes without saying about chance in the novel by examining what Leavis considers only incidental in Conrad's work: namely, the way a concern with chance affects the novel's "mode of presenta-tion." This project traces the theme of chance in the British novel from the late-Victorian to the modern period in order to demonstrate its influence on the development of modernist narrative forms.

The history of thinking about chance is in general a history of its marginalization. Democritus and Epicurus, the two great atomists of the Greek philosophers, took chance seriously and found a place for it in their cosmologies. Of the two, Epicurus is the more important for this study. In order to escape the strict determinism of Democritus's atomic theory, Epicurus claimed that a chance "swerve," or *clinamen* (as his disciple Lucretius called it), was an essential feature of atomic motion.* *Standard Deviations* adopts Epicurus's theory (with some

---

*Harold Bloom adopts the Epicurean/Lucretian term *clinamen*, which in the archi-tectonics of his system of poetic influence signifies "the trope-as-misreading, irony as a dialectical alternation of images of presence and absence, or the beginning of the defensive process." Bloom's *clinamen*, which describes one of the possible dynam-

modifications) and applies it as a model to various discourses about chance because it effectively eludes the usual metaphysical treatment of chance.

Metaphysical thinking is organized by a series of mutually exclusive and contradictory categories that are defined by their logical opposition. Implicit in the duality and contrariety of metaphysics and essential to its operation is the prioritizing of one term and the consequent devaluation of its logical opposite. Necessity and contingency, determinism and indeterminism, order and randomness are all particular instances of the binomial structure of metaphysical thought. Traditionally and consistently, the former terms of these pairings have been exalted while the latter terms have been relegated to a marginal and denigrated position. Chance and its cognates have been systematically suppressed in Western science and philosophy in the service of order, certainty, and necessity in order to assure metaphysics a cognitive and conceptual mastery over reality.* Of course, chance has been marginalized not simply because of some covert and pervasive metaphysical conspiracy but because it is by its very nature eccentric in relation to a central paradigm of action and thought; chance inhab-

---

ics between the poet and his precursor, will not directly influence this study because Bloom (exemplifying the usual critical treatment of chance) disregards what is for Epicurus and Lucretius the swerve's defining characteristic—its chance nature. Bloom comes to the term by way of Coleridge, who was much more receptive to the operations of chance. Objecting to the obtrusion of the moral sentiment in explanations of *The Rime of the Ancient Mariner*, for instance, Coleridge said the cause of the poem should be as adventitious as the genie's killing of the merchant in the *Arabian Nights* simply because the date pit the merchant threw down a well happened to put out the eye of the genie's son. For Bloom's use of *clinamen*, see *Poetry and Repression*, pp. 16–17.

*William Beatty Warner insightfully discusses the relation of chance to metaphysics in *Chance and the Text of Experience*. Warner's project is similar to mine insofar as he sets out to release the question of chance "from under the sway of a text, understood as a metaphysical noncontingent locus of truth and authority" (p. 301). He examines critical moments in the "master texts" of Freud, Nietzsche, and Shakespeare in order to reinsert the contingent historical aspects represented in the author's "life-writing" (bio-graphy understood as a text of experience that is not considered simply subordinate to or background for the master texts). He therefore thematizes chance as a necessary element in the author's life and writing, which has been effaced by the process of canonization. My approach differs from his in arguing that the effacement of chance is a structural feature of *all* narratives; and my historical interest focuses not on a writer's life (which Warner seems to endow with some transcendental access to the chance-laden Real in the form of "experience") but on a period during which novelistic narratives attempted to represent chance in specific ways and for specific reasons.

its the periphery of whatever frame of power-knowledge is in place, simultaneously defining and transgressing the borders or limits that constitute that frame.* The metaphysical treatment of chance establishes and ensures the integrity and propriety of what it is opposed to by re-presenting chance's differential structure as a binary opposition structured by the logic of identity. The self-identical realm of order, certainty, and necessity is therefore made possible by the active suppression of what is thought to be its logical opposite: chance.

Epicurus's atomic theory provides the model for this analysis of chance in narrative because it both grants a positive, formative, creative status to chance and insists that the resultant configuration of atoms is organized according to regular and recognizable patterns. Chance and ideas of order are therefore not mutually exclusive or logically opposed. The chance "swerve" of the atom is for Epicurus an unaccountable variable in an otherwise normalized system; there is an element of inertia in the atom's usually uniform motion that prevents the occasional fortuitous fluctuation from initiating an interminable chain reaction of change. When atoms aggregate as the result of the *clinamen*, they form increasingly complex and stable entities. This is how I see the permutations and fluctuations of chance in narrative as giving rise to increasingly complex, innovative, and eventually stable (that is, conventional) narrative forms.

The sense of what constitutes an atomic entity—an elementary, fundamental, and indivisible unit—in the novel will change in the course of my argument just as it changes over the course of time. In the Victorian period, it is the novelistic character that has the status of an individual and indissoluble atom in the operations of narrative; but in the modern period, as I will show, this sense of the character as a basic unit of novelistic meaning is gradually supplanted by a self-conscious preoccupation with the proper name. The propriety of the proper name with respect to common nouns grants it the status of an elementary and indivisible entity in the linguistic field. My application of the Epicurean-Lucretian *clinamen* to the development of

---

*I use Michel Foucault's term "power-knowledge" here to refer to discursive formations that enforce a regimen of action and thought, both determining and policing what can and cannot be said. The discourses that work to efface or account for chance in this study are not simply and solely concerned with epistemological matters; they also represent systems of power that make what counts as knowledge possible and knowable in the first place.

post-Victorian narrative forms will therefore focus with increasing intensity on the atomic nature of the proper name in order to analyze the swerves of chance in the modern novel.

This project asks three questions about chance and the modern novel: Why did British novelists become intensely interested in chance beginning in the latter part of the nineteenth century? How did they thematize it in their fictions? And what effect did the novelistic treatment of chance have on modernist narrative forms? Three related and overlapping aspects of chance are therefore considered in three representative novels. The chapter on George Eliot's *Middlemarch* considers the advent of a qualitatively new understanding of chance in the English novel. The chapter on Joseph Conrad's *Chance* examines the most rigorous and extended meditation on chance and narrative in British fiction. The chapter on James Joyce's *Ulysses* articulates the limits and formal consequences of the modern novel's interest in chance.

The historical line of thought in this study examines three time periods when chance became an overt concern for writers and thinkers and considers the aesthetic forms of novels that were responding to that concern in relation to major innovations in the sciences. A discussion of the rise of the novel and the contemporaneous discovery of probability theory considers why and how the emerging genre mediated between providential and aesthetic impulses in narrative, taking Daniel Defoe's *Robinson Crusoe* as an exemplary case. The analysis of *Middlemarch* and its relation to nineteenth-century evolutionary theory examines the way Eliot's fiction broke with a providential aesthetic and replaced it with a realist aesthetic informed by scientific principles. The discussion of *Chance* and the theories of quantum physics (as well as, to some extent, psychoanalysis)* that were being formulated at the time of its writing considers the way Conrad's modernist aesthetic called into question a kind of scientific causality in narrative. In analyzing simultaneous scientific and novelistic interests in chance, I am not making claims for direct influence of one on the other. Joseph Conrad almost certainly did not read the theoretical work of quantum physicists; and although George Eliot read

---

*I realize that to characterize psychoanalysis as a science is problematic at best. I do however consider its own claims to scientific status—especially regarding the topic of chance—an important instance of the prevalent scientism I analyze in relation to Conrad's work.

Darwin's *The Origin of Species* with interest, she did not immediately acknowledge the importance of chance in the theory of natural selection. The concurrent writings of the novelists and scientists examined in this study indicate that they were responding, in their own ways, to an epistemic crisis during which notions of certainty were destabilized by the insistent and anomalous appearance of chance phenomena.

Standard Deviations considers three distinct epochs in the history of chance. Although chance and its relation to that-for-which-it-is-the-other has a recognizable structure, the meaning and experience of chance varies according to the operant frame of power-knowledge it is defined by and against. The historical frameworks of alterity in this study correspond roughly to the distinctions chance versus Providence (a generally theological debate), chance versus necessity (the latter being for the most part scientific—that is, causal—necessity), and chance versus fate (an opposition having generally to do with narrative). The three movements of this study proceed in what might at first seem to be a dialectical progression: the explanatory power of Providence is destabilized by a chance that materializes for the most part in and as a scientific discourse, and the viability of the scientific frame of reference is in turn called into question by a chance the saliencies of which are characterized by an overt concern with narrative. What makes this account not exactly dialectical is the way the problematics of narrative (chance vesus fate) underlie and underwrite the other epochs; the providential and the scientific discourses can then be understood as particular kinds of narrative—what Jean-François Lyotard calls master-narratives [3]—which dictate the specific ways chance is effaced in the stories they tell.

The statistical term "standard deviation," which gives this study its title, refers to the degree of variability in a set of data, a measure that is useful in determining whether or not those findings are the result of "mere chance." Scientists are always dealing with chance but they must filter out its influence as much as possible in order to make calculated predictions about the outcomes of events. In most scientific inquiry, chance is treated as a kind of non-sense; determining the standard deviation of the data therefore helps to determine in quantifiable terms to what extent the experimental results make sense. The statistical use of standard deviations is not concerned with making sense out of chance itself, so such calculations will not directly inform this study of chance in the modern novel. But the interpenetration of stability and disruption that the term suggests—deviations from what is considered standard, the standardization of deviancies—conveys the way a concern with chance introduces a new sense of random and contingent experience into narrative, a sense that is inevitably assimilated to novelistic notions of order and design. That is to say, "standard deviations" aptly describes the oxymoronic nature of the phrase "chance in narrative." As I will show, it is in the nature of narrative to render chance as fate so that "what happens" in a story becomes indistinguishable from the more evaluative "it was *meant* to happen." A thoroughgoing analysis of chance in the modern British novel therefore requires a kind of double vision that focuses both on (what is at least purported to be) a random and contingent event and on how that instance of chance is put to work in order to generate an ordered, coherent, fateful reading. *Standard Deviations* examines moments in several novels that the text explicitly labels chance occurrences; just what is at stake in that claim is then clarified by tracing the way the aleatory elements in the novel are expunged in the course of the narrative.

The two trajectories in this study of chance in the modern novel suggested by the "standard" and the "deviations" of the title do not simply operate as a neat pair of contraries that allows the convenient separation of subject matter into tidy categories. There is after all something deviant about the phrase "standard deviations" itself as it is being used here that destabilizes such a binary logic. I am not therefore interested in describing anything like "pure" chance in the novel or celebrating moments of "radical" "subversive" "freedom" that stand out in opposition to the normally determined, conventional, and humdrum operations of novelistic narrative. It is certainly true, as this study will demonstrate, that the desire and effort to represent chance is potentially disruptive; but the disruptions occasioned by ostensible chance events in narrative are always and already in the process of being recuperated by *some* sense of formal coherence and design. The instance of chance proves to be a revealing site for interrogation because it challenges an already established system of epistemic and narrative order; at the same time, it helps to formulate a new kind of order and integration that leaves nothing to chance.

Stephane Mallarmé published in 1897 his poem *Un Coup de Dés jamais n'abolira le Hasard*, a prolonged meditation about (among other things) chance and its relation to literary mastery. If I were to date the beginnings of a truly modernist interest in chance, it would be with this poem. In the Preface to *Un Coup de Dés*, Mallarmé explained: "Tout se passe, par raccourci, en hypothèse; on évite le récit" ("Everything happens, by foreshortening, as a hypothesis; narrative is avoided").[4] The poem stretches across 21 pages and uses different type sizes and an innovative distribution of words on the page to elaborate a series of image-clusters from segments of the core sentence that is the poem's title. These experimental typographical and topographical techniques both illuminate and frustrate the desire to make the poem tell a linear and coherent story. Mallarmé understood that, though a throw of the dice will never do away with chance, narrative will; another title for the poem might be *Le récit toujours abolira le Hasard*.

Although I would say that, finally, no novelist actually manages to represent chance in narrative, there is a history to the ongoing attempt to do so, with specific historical explanations about how and why novelists in the British tradition responded to this challenge. My account of chance in the modern British novel has some affinities with the argument of George Levine's book *The Realistic Imagination*. In that work Levine argues that "realism" is an ongoing process in which successive writers recognize and reject earlier notions of what was considered "real" that have come to seem a mere literary convention; a new imagination of "the real" then emerges and diverges from earlier and established realistic notions. Although Levine does not mention Jacques Lacan, "the real" is for both writers that which cannot be represented in language; but Levine argues that successive attempts to do so account for major developments in the English novel during the nineteenth and early twentieth centuries. Similarly, and in a way that is not just an analogy, I would say that chance marks and defines a fundamental limit to the telling of any story: *chance is that which cannot be represented in narrative*; but the efforts of British novelists to do just that from the late-Victorian to the modern period resulted in major innovations in narrative form.

I need hardly point out that this study is thoroughly implicated in the paradoxical nature of its subject matter. My critical project, to relate a coherent narrative about chance in the modern British novel, is subject to the same formal constraints as the works it examines.

Whether or not there is, after all, anything like chance in this book about chance I will leave to the reader to decide. In any case, I have found the paradox of "standard deviations" a generative one. And if this study concludes that there is in fact no such thing as chance in narrative, its operating premise is the conviction that without chance there would really be no stories to tell.

The argument of *Standard Deviations* addresses three areas of interest. The first is *a general history of ideas*; I provide an overview of the philosophical, scientific, and (as evidenced in the novel genre) * literary thinking about chance from the pre-Socratics to postmodern art. The second area is *literary history*, in which I consider why and how late-nineteenth- and early-twentieth-century British novelists' unprecedented interest in chance influenced modernist narrative practices. The third area is *narrative theory*, where I argue that chance is an essential feature of *all* narratives. This last is the strongest and most far-reaching claim I make. As I have said and as I will show, chance is that which cannot be represented in narrative; as such, it marks and defines a fundamental limit to the workings of *any* narrative. Epicurus's atomic theory of the *clinamen* provides a theoretical framework for the analysis of a chance that, though more or less obscured, always informs the operations and effects of narrative in whatever historical period, discipline, or compositional form it appears. Chance is the unrepresentable Other of narrative; in order to gain a more comprehensive understanding of what narrative is and

---

*It is beyond the scope of this study to consider in any detail the literary prehistory of the novel's treatment of chance, although there is certainly much to say on the subject. As I have suggested, chance *always* gets read as fate, and this inevitability is characteristic of *any* narrative. I have decided to focus almost exclusively on novelistic narrative, however, and especially those works in the British tradition in which chance first becomes a matter for serious regard. I do so because, as I demonstrate in the particular analyses of these works, the subject of chance cannot be adequately comprehended without sustained attention to the larger intellectual and historical forces that help to constitute its local and specific meaning, which is always defined diacritically as well as diachronically. Examining earlier genres that deal with chance (Homeric epic, fabliaux, the plays and poetry of Shakespeare, or pre-novelistic picaresque, to name a few) would no doubt be revealing; but such an enterprise would either result in a capacious overview of the "theme" of chance over time or require the imposition of a transhistorical and archetypical understanding of chance onto the material to make it manageable. Both a thematics and a typology of chance would obscure precisely what I think makes chance such a compelling topic for study: its historically specific oppositional structure.

how it works, we could not do better than to ask: what is chance? As an initial response to that question, which must always be answered in the particular, here is a summary of the argument developed in more depth and detail in the chapters that follow.

Chapter 1 of this work provides a history of thinking about chance in philosophy, science, and the novel. It begins by considering three Greek philosophers—Democritus, Aristotle, and Epicurus—who consider the meaning and importance of chance. The theories of Democritus and Aristotle provide models for understanding how most subsequent thinkers have considered chance phenomena. But it is Epicurus's atomistic theory of the *clinamen* that serves as the model for this study because it provides a theoretical framework for understanding the paradoxical nature of representing chance in *any* narrative. The chapter then considers the place and importance of chance in genetics and quantum physics, the two sciences for which chance is currently a central concern. The chapter concludes by considering the role chance played in the origins of the English novel, taking Daniel Defoe's *Robinson Crusoe* as an exemplary case. The generic premises of the novel formulated at the beginning of the eighteenth century are related both to the discovery of probability theory in the sciences at that time and to the period's intense concern with Providence in theological debates. I argue that the new genre we call the novel, probability theory, and the providential discourse that emerged in the early 1700s are all attempts to redefine literary, scientific, and religious ideas of certainty that had been called into question by the eruption of new forms of chance.

Chapter 2 examines a new understanding of chance in the English novel as it materializes in George Eliot's later fiction, especially *Middlemarch*. It relates her use of chance to a similar emphasis on—and discomfort with—the subject in Charles Darwin's evolutionary theories. For both Darwin and George Eliot, the agency of chance challenges the idea of a providential design informing the worlds they describe; but as a final explanation for the way things happen in life, it makes both writers very uneasy. The chapter focuses in particular on the character John Raffles in *Middlemarch*, who, as his name suggests, embodies Eliot's concern with the problem of chance. I show how the introduction of Raffles into the plot of *Middlemarch* represents a dramatic break with the conventional use of coincidence in the novel (especially in Dickens) as a sign of God's Providence at work in the world. I then show how, in the end, Eliot works to purge the novel of chance by getting rid of Raffles, who is found morally despicable and unworthy of sympathy. Expelling Raffles from *Middlemarch* then helps to define a sense of novelistic coherence and design based not on providential notions but on a secular humanist moral order informed by sympathy. The chapter concludes by briefly considering how the naturalist novel at the end of the nineteenth century used its own sense of chance to challenge the idea of a moral universe such as is depicted in Eliot's fiction, replacing that sense of narrative order with one based on scientific principles.

Chapter 3 relates Joseph Conrad's novel *Chance* to the theoretical formulations of quantum physics and psychoanalysis. It is in particular the way chance calls into question established notions of causality that unites the literary, scientific, and psychoanalytic understanding of chance in the early years of the twentieth century. Conrad challenges the usual understanding of causality in narrative (based on scientific principles) by beginning *Chance* as though it were a naturalist novel tracking the grim fate of its protagonist in a deterministic universe, and then by allowing a new kind of chance to intervene, providing an alternative to the seemingly inexorable cause-and-effect progression of naturalism's narrative practices. While Conrad's novel repudiates a sense of novelistic order based on the scientific laws of causal necessity, it eventually yields to a kind of *aesthetic* determinism; it illustrates the way chance is always and inevitably rendered as fate because, despite its strenuous resistance, it ultimately capitulates to this narrative imperative.

Chapter 4 considers the modern novel's most successful representation of chance, in James Joyce's *Ulysses*. The chapter begins by examining a theme *in* the novel (consubstantial becoming transubstantial paternity) and a critical approach *to* the novel (informed by that theme), both of which work to efface all traces of chance in *Ulysses*. The various meanings attached to the word "throwaway" (both the name of a racehorse and a piece of paper read and discarded by Leopold Bloom) together formulate an "aesthetic of the throwaway" in *Ulysses*, an aesthetic different from the transubstantial aesthetic that occupies most criticism of the novel. The throwaway aesthetic represents a kind of chance that is not necessarily effaced by the novel's narrative operations. I argue that the transubstantial aesthetic represents not just the usual way of thinking about chance in *Ulysses* but also the standard way of thinking about chance in *any* novel. The deviations of the throwaway aesthetic in *Ulysses* then figure another way of thinking about chance in the novel (*any* novel) that might possibly resist narrative assimilation. For reasons I spell out more completely in the Conclusion, *Ulysses* marks a limit to the representation of chance in narrative; from the vantage of this limit point it becomes possible to read other novelistic narratives in terms of a logic and aesthetic informed by a receptiveness to the operations of chance.

The Conclusion briefly considers the importance of chance in postmodern art. Although interest in chance has intensified in the postmodern period, I argue that the structural limit to the representation of chance in narrative defined by Joyce's *Ulysses* has not been, and probably cannot be, surpassed by subsequent literary efforts.

One of the stories I tell in this study concerns chance's role in the development of narrative forms during the transitional period from the Victorian to the modern novel. I have therefore included an Appendix at the end of this volume that considers the place and importance of chance in the work of two exemplary novelists, Thomas Hardy and Henry James. Although these writers are not integral to my argument about chance in the modern novel, I include this material to fill in the history of chance's influence on narrative practices from George Eliot to Joseph Conrad. The analysis of chance in Hardy (by my account, the last Victorian novelist) and James (the first modern novelist) shows how their interest in the subject contributed to the generic shifts at the turn of the century that made the modernist experiments of Conrad and Joyce possible.

Starting with George Eliot, and with *Middlemarch* in particular, a new and distinctive interest in chance emerged in British fiction, and subsequent novelists, in their own ways and for their own purposes, continued explicitly to thematize the subject in their work. Of course they did not succeed in representing chance "itself." Joseph Conrad's novel *Chance* clearly illustrates the textual and theoretical problems involved in the paradoxical attempt to depict chance in a narrative that gives order and design to novelistic experience. It is not until James Joyce's *Ulysses* that a narrative mode manages to convey a kind of chance that does not necessarily yield to an altogether fateful reading. Joyce's work goes as far as any novel can, marking a limit point to the representation of chance in narrative. The movement from high realism to high modernism in the British novel is then in part a story about writers in that tradition for the first time taking chance seriously.

CHAPTER ONE

Taking Chance Seriously:
Philosophy, Science, the Novel

Werner Heisenberg tells a story about a skiing and mountain-climbing vacation in 1933 with Neils Bohr and his son Christian, Felix Bloch, and Carl Friedrich von Weizsäcker. One evening the group played a game of poker, during which they resumed an earlier, freewheeling discussion about the nature of language. In analyzing why and how some of the players managed to out-bluff the others, Neils Bohr suggested: "Perhaps our ability to convince others depends on the intensity with which we can persuade others of the force of our own imagination." This theory was subsequently confirmed when Bohr won a great deal of play money betting on what he thought was a flush: "When it was all over, and he proudly showed us his fifth card, it turned out it was not of the same suit, as he himself had wrongly thought. He had mistaken the ten of hearts for a ten of diamonds." [1] A few days later they played poker again, and Bohr suggested that they try the whole thing without cards.

The attempt was made, but did not lead to a successful game, whereupon Neils said: "My suggestion was probably based on an overestimate of the importance of language; language is forced to rely on some link with reality. In real poker one plays with real cards. In that case, we can use language to 'improve' the real hand with as much optimism and conviction as we can summon up. But if we start with no reality at all, then it becomes impossible to make credible suggestions." [2]

The scene Heisenberg describes, several quantum physicists playing a game of chance and philosophizing about the nature of language, is interesting for several reasons. In the first poker game, the expressiveness of language is linked with the power of the imagination to represent (or convincingly misrepresent) what chance deals out. In the second poker game, the players discover that language must have some basis in reality; and it is chance, the dealing out of actual cards, that provides access to that reality by giving language something credible to talk about and bet on.

It is tempting to raise the stakes in this anecdotal poker game and theoretical discussion about the nature of language by dealing in alongside the men who revolutionized classical physics some players who knew something about language and its relation to *meta*physics: Ludwig Wittgenstein, for instance, who was familiar with language games; or Friedrich Nietzsche, who with his *amor fati* knew the importance of play and said we must learn to love what fate deals out to us; or Jacques Lacan, who would want to distinguish between the *imaginary* freedom of the game played without cards and the delimited possibilities at the *symbolic* level of the game played with an actual deck of cards (which, like the unconscious, is structured like a language); or Martin Heidegger, who might want to compare the dealing out of real cards to the "It gives" he speaks of in "Time and Being," which sends Being as presencing and determines its destiny. Of course, these thinkers might not be too eager to ante up in the physicists' linguistic game of chance because they all—each in his own way—understood that when one thinks about language in order to question metaphysics one is always playing against the house and by its rules.

This chapter will examine various theories of chance, focusing in particular on their relation to metaphysics; it will discuss the relevance of chance to current scientific inquiry (including quantum physics); and then it will analyze the imaginative and interpretive processes involved in the representation of chance in language, specifically in the novel form. As the philosophical poker games suggest, a certain playfulness will be one aspect of this study's effort to take chance seriously.

Philosophy

Although chance (*tyche*) is initially mentioned by the Greek philosopher Empedocles, it is first consistently thematized by the atomists Leucippus and Democritus in the fifth century B.C.[3] But they considered chance only to deny its existence. One of the few surviving fragments from Leucippus states: "Nothing occurs at random, but everything for a reason and by necessity."[4] According to Aristotle, the atomists described a completely deterministic world (the result of the motion and collision of atoms); they believed that "nothing happens by chance, but that everything we ascribe to chance or spontaneity has some definite cause."[5] We are not always able to discern the cause, however; those who "believe that chance is a cause" do so because "it is inscrutable to human intelligence."[6] According to the early atomists, when we designate or experience something as chance, we do so simply because we are ignorant of its determinant cause.

While asserting that all things are necessarily determined on earth, Democritus claimed that chance (*automaton*) was responsible for the original creation of "the heavenly spheres and all the worlds, . . . i.e. the motion that separated and arranged into present order all that exists."[7] The word *automaton* is variously translated as "the spontaneous" or "the automatic" and means, literally, "self-moving." Events brought about by *automaton* have no prior or determining cause; they are instead self-caused. The apparent contradiction in Democritus's philosophy—affirming the importance of a kind of chance (*automaton*) in his celestial cosmogony while denying chance (*tyche*) in terrestrial matters—is no doubt his method of escaping the infinite regress of determinism that results when one attempts to trace all causes back to their original impetus.

Aristotle (384–322 B.C) was in other ways and in other places concerned with the problem of a first cause and self-generated motion, but in Book II of his *Physics* he takes issue with Democritus's polarized account of chance, which relegates it to the heavens, leaving the world below completely and causally determined. For Aristotle, the two forms of chance (*automaton* and *tyche*) both exist in our everyday experience, and are as real as other forms of causation. They are alike in that they are both causes of effects that happen *incidentally*; they are different in that chance as *automaton* operates in the realm of *nature* ("both in the lower animals and in many inanimate objects") while the chance called *tyche* operates in the realm of the *mind*. *Tyche* is experienced by agents capable of moral action and is predicated on deliberate intention. "Thus an inanimate thing or a lower animal or a child cannot do anything by chance [*tyche*], because it is incapable of deliberate intention."[8] An example of *automaton* would be a stone's falling and striking a man as he walked beneath it, provided that the stone did not fall for the purpose of striking him (it was not for instance dropped by his enemy with evil intentions). An example of *tyche* would be a man's going to the marketplace to make a purchase and there meeting an acquaintance who owes him money; his collection of the debt then happens *incidentally* to his original reason for going to the marketplace. As these two examples make clear, chance (of either kind) for Aristotle consists not in the occurrence of a completely *un*caused event in an otherwise determined system, but instead in the concurrence of two causal sequences (the falling of a stone with the walking of a man; the shopping of a man with the shopping of a debtor) in an event of some consequence. The Aristotelian analysis clarifies the notion of a chance event as a *co-incidence*.

The two models of chance provided by Aristotle and Democritus offer a framework for understanding most of the theories and analyses of chance put forth since the Greek philosophers. And by far the most pervasive has been the Democritean model which defines chance (if it exists at all) in opposition to a deterministic world of compulsory and invariable causality. Bertrand Russell, for instance, summarized much of what others have said about chance by defining it simply as an event whose cause is unknown.[9] A standard way of accounting for the experience of chance is to attribute it, as does Democritus, to our limited knowledge: according to Pierre Simon de Laplace, for instance, problems of chance "entirely disappear for the sound philosophy that sees in them but an expression of our ignorance as regards the real causes."[10]

The view of chance that considers it merely a function of our ignorance of the determining causes of a phenomenon ignores the sense of chance as being not an obscurely caused event but an absolutely *un*caused event. The existence of such events, sometimes called "pure" chance events, has been affirmed by a minority of thinkers on the subject (including Charles Sanders Peirce and William James).[11] As pragmatic as Peirce's and James's claims about the experience of chance may be, however, instances of "pure" chance are impossible to prove because we can never determine whether an event is totally uncaused or whether new evidence might eventually illuminate the hitherto uncomprehended cause. *The Encyclopedia of Philosophy* therefore concludes its entry on chance:

It would thus appear that any event whose cause has not yet been discovered may be viewed either as a pure chance event that possesses no cause or as a complex event whose cause is as yet unknown but may eventually be discovered. It is this difficulty—that one situation can be so interpreted as to support two contradictory theses—that lies at the heart of the philosophical problem of chance.[12]

This is in fact a false problem, and it arises from a particular kind of metaphysical thinking. We have already seen how Democritus's philosophy entails both of these senses of chance: in terrestrial terms, chance is ascribed to occurrences of whose determining causes we are simply ignorant; and in celestial terms chance exists as the original and enabling *self*-caused event that saves the deterministic system from the problem of infinite regress. In the Democritean system, either chance is chimerical or the physics of mechanical determinism leads to a metaphysical sense of a "pure" chance event with no determinant cause.

Necessity and chance, determinism and indeterminism, order and randomness, and so on, are simply particular instances of the binomial structure of metaphysical thought. As Friedrich Engels observes:

Another contradiction in which metaphysics is entangled is that of chance and necessity. What can be more sharply contradictory than these two thought determinations? Common sense, and with it the great majority of natural scientists, treat necessity and chance as determinations that exclude each other once for all.[13]

Metaphysics is a system of thought organized by a series of mutually exclusive and contradictory categories that are defined by their logical opposition. Implicit in the duality and contrariety of metaphysics's binary logic and essential to its operation is the prioritizing of one term and the consequent devaluation of its logical opposite. Traditionally and consistently, starting with Democritus, order, determinism, and necessity have been exalted while chance has been relegated to a marginal and denigrated position, a ranking that assures metaphysics a cognitive and conceptual mastery over experience. To affirm the existence and importance of "pure" chance events then is merely to invert the hierarchical structure of dualistic thought without altering its metaphysical presuppositions.

In the Aristotelian model, necessity and chance do not necessarily exclude each other. A chance event for Aristotle is one in which two objects, both following the natural and necessary laws of their respective causes, come together. A few theorists have attempted to escape the metaphysical dilemmas of the Democritean system by following Aristotle's example. John Stuart Mill, for instance, in response to the notion of chance as itself a form of causality, observes: "It is incorrect to say that any phenomenon is *produced by chance*; but we must say that two or more phenomena are *conjoined* by chance." [14] Similarly, Antoine Cournot remarks: "The *combination* or the *encounter* of other events pertaining to mutually *independent* series are those which we name *fortuitous* events or result of chance." [15] Cournot goes on to argue that, even if the Laplacian ideal of reducing natural causes to a known quantity were possible, there would still be chance because there would always be crossings of independent series. Chance, then, does not arise exclusively from our ignorance, nor does it necessarily decrease (or disappear) as our ignorance is diminished.

The Aristotelian model provides an understanding of chance that grants it an objective existence and experiential reality. It also manages to avoid the strict logical opposition of chance and necessity which leads to many of the false problems that have occupied thinkers about chance. But the Aristotelian model and theory of chance as *coincidence* does not sufficiently consider why and how chance events can themselves give rise to a new understanding of order and design. Which brings us to the third Greek philosopher to take chance seriously, whose thinking on the subject provides the model for this study of chance and the modern British novel.

There is a tendency to equate or confuse the work of Epicurus (341–270 B.C.), the other great atomist of the Greek philosophers, with that of Democritus. In his doctoral dissertation *The Difference Between the Democritean and Epicurean Philosophy of Nature*, Karl Marx tries to rectify the tendency to conflate the two thinkers. Epicurus adopted many of Democritus's ideas regarding the nature of atoms; but his most important modification of Democritean atomism was to introduce the idea of chance as an essential feature of atomic motion. Marx explains:

Epicurus assumes a threefold motion of the atoms of the void. One motion is that of a fall in a straight line, the second comes from the atom deviating from a straight line, and the third is established through the repulsion of the many atoms. The assumption of the first and last motion Democritus has in common with Epicurus; the declination of the atom from the straight line differentiates them.[16]

Epicurean atoms are the elementary and indivisible constituents of matter, which by nature fall downward in the void in a parallel motion at uniform speed; but if this were a comprehensive account of atomic motion then no collisions would take place and there would be no change in the universe. Occasionally, though, there is a deviation or declination—the term usually used is "swerve"—in an atom's downward motion. Epicurus's follower Lucretius (?98–55 B.C.) explained that, as the atoms are falling in the void, "at quite indeterminate times and places they swerve ever so little from their course, just so much that you can call it a change of direction."* This swerve, or *clinamen* (as Lucretius called it), causes collisions with the other atoms, which then generate further perturbations in the downward trajectory of surrounding atoms; the result is a general ferment of atoms, which eventually aggregate, forming objects and, ultimately, whole worlds.

Introducing the possibility of oblique motion into the straight lines of atomic trajectory breaks with what Lucretius calls "the bonds of fate" (*fati foedera*); the *clinamen* then explains how human beings have moral freedom of choice in a world not completely and causally determined:

> Again, if all movement is always interconnected, the new arising from the old in a determinate order—if the atoms never swerve so as to originate some new movement that will snap the bonds of fate, the everlasting sequence of cause and effect—what is the source of the free will possessed by living things throughout the earth? [17]

The atomic swerve defuses the logical problem of infinite regress ("the everlasting sequence of cause and effect") and makes human choice possible. Cyril Bailey explains: "[T]he act of volition is neither more nor less than the 'swerve' of the fine atoms which comprise the mind. The fortuitous indeterminate movement of the individual atoms in the void is in the conscious complex (*concilium*) of the mind transformed into an act of deliberate will." [18] It is important to note that the Epicurean swerve of the atom is not due to an external force or any qualitative change in the atom itself. It takes place "nec regione certa nec tempore certo" ("neither at a determinant place nor at a fixed time") but spontaneously. [19] Chance, which in Democritus's cosmology was marginal and metaphysical in relation to a deterministic world of atoms in motion, is essential to the structure of the Epicurean atom.

---

*Lucretius, *Nature of the Universe*, p. 66. Most of what we know about the Epicurean "swerve" comes from Lucretius. No texts on the subject by Epicurus are extant.

This does not mean that the universe is a series of completely random occurrences. The swerve is an unaccountable variable in an otherwise normalized system; there is an element of inertia in the atoms' natural tendency to fall in a uniform downward motion that prevents the occasional fortuitous fluctuation from initiating an unlimited chain reaction of change. When atoms aggregate as the result of the *clinamen* they form increasingly complex and eventually stable entities (what Lucretius calls a *concilium*).[20] Changes in the combination of atoms eventually occur in regular sequences that constitute a new principle of order. It is thus not possible (to use Lucretian examples) for an animal to be half man and half horse, for a tree to grow in the sky, or for a man to be large enough to wade across the sea.[21] There is order to our experience, and that order is formed and facilitated by the successive aggregation of atoms originally made possible by an atom's occasional and idiosyncratic swerve.

Epicurus's atomic theory provides the model for this study of chance in narrative. There are three phases in the operation of the *clinamen* that I will be adopting and adapting for my own purposes: first there is the normalized motion of atoms in a system that operates in an orderly and regular fashion; then there is the atomic swerve of chance, which deviates from the standard operating procedure of the system, thereby breaking with what Lucretius calls "the bonds of fate"; and finally there is the resultant aggregate of atoms, which incorporates the disruptions initiated by the swerve of chance and stabilizes into a new and more complexly organized system. In narratological terms, these three phases correspond first to a narrative form that normally works (as do all narratives) to efface or assimilate any sense of chance in the stories it tells; then to the introduction of a new kind of chance that can no longer be accommodated by the established narrative system; and finally to a resultant new representational mode that absorbs the anomalous sense of randomness and contingency, constituting in the process a more complex narrative form that again leaves nothing to chance. The appearance and effects of the *clinamen* in narrative always entail both an affirmation and a denial of chance. The *affirmation* of chance breaks with the historically specific bonds of fate constructing and constricting narrative experience at the time (a deviation from standard narrative practice); and the *denial* of chance helps to constitute an innovative, complex, and finally stable (in other words, conventional) narrative form from which all sense of the aleatory has been expunged (the standardization of deviancies).

The standard deviations of the Epicurean *clinamen* described above provide a theoretical framework for the analysis of chance in any narrative. Chance is an essential feature of atomic motion in Epicurus's theory, and (though narrative theory has given the subject scant attention) it is also intrinsic to the operations of narrative. Chance is the unrepresentable Other of narrative; as such, it marks and defines a limit to the workings of *any* narrative. Epicurus's atomic theory of the *clinamen* provides a theoretical framework for analyzing the historically specific oppositional structure of chance, a structure that, though more or less obscured, always informs the operations and effects of narrative in whatever time or form it appears.

Epicurus's atomic theory conceives of chance as a positive, formative, creative force while insisting that there is order and regularity in the world. These defining features also make Epicurus's system pertinent and applicable to the narrative framework of recent theories in genetics and physics, the two sciences for which chance is currently an essential factor. I will briefly consider how in these disciplines an originally random and variable phenomenon eventually and inevitably yields to norms and patterns that obey scientific laws; that is, I will examine in scientific terms how and why, given the original and ineluctable importance of chance, it is impossible (invoking those Lucretian examples) for an animal to be half horse and half man (genetics) and for a tree to grow in the sky (physics). I will then consider the status and constraints of chance in fictional narratives where, in the case of Lemuel Gulliver, for instance, it is altogether possible for a man to be large enough to wade across the sea.*

Science

Genetics is a branch of biology and replicates on a microcosmic and chromosomal level the similar interaction of chance and design evident on a macrocosmic and phylogenetic level in the theory of

---

*Michel Serres considers the Epicurean *clinamen* in a way amenable to this chapter's analysis of chance in philosophy, science, and the novel, as is suggested by the title of a collection of his essays in English. See Serres, *Hermes: Literature, Science, Philosophy*, especially the essay "Lucretius: Science and Religion," pp. 98–124.

evolution. The development and survival of species is the result of the complex interaction of chance variations and the laws of natural selection. These variations occur as the result of mutations in the genetic sequence and structure of a DNA segment. "We call such events accidental," observes Jacques Monod, the Nobel Prize-winning geneticist who has tried to relate recent genetic research to larger philosophical issues.

They [genetic mutations] are random occurrences. And since they constitute the *only* possible source of modifications in the genetic text, itself the *sole* repository of the organism's hereditary structures, it necessarily follows that chance *alone* is at the source of every innovation, of all creation in the biosphere. Pure chance, absolutely free but blind, at the very root of the stupendous edifice of evolution: this central concept of modern biology is no longer one among other possible or even conceivable hypotheses. It is today the *sole* conceivable hypothesis, the only one that squares with observed and tested fact.[22]

Monod's tone is a bit declamatory here, and he goes on to make some rather dubious philosophical and ethical claims about the importance of such assertions; but his work clearly demonstrates how chance is, quite literally, a *sine qua non* of genetic operations and evolutionary development. His book *Chance and Necessity* explains why and how initially random mutations eventually result in prodigiously stable and enduring species. On the genetic level, the process of DNA replication is almost completely invariant:

The initial elementary events which open the way to evolution in the intensely conservative systems called living beings are microscopic, fortuitous, and utterly without relation to whatever may be their effects upon teleonomic functioning.

But once incorporated in the DNA structure, the accident—essentially unpredictable because always singular—will be mechanically and faithfully replicated and translated: that is to say, both multiplied and transposed into millions or billions of copies. Drawn out of the realm of pure chance, the accident enters into that of necessity, of the most implacable certainties.[23]

Likewise on the macrocosmic, evolutionary scale chance variations become subject to the normalizing and stabilizing laws of natural selection: "In effect, natural selection operates *upon* the products of chance and can feed nowhere else; but it operates in a domain of very demanding conditions, and from this domain chance is barred."[24]

The problematics of chance in the science of genetics were already for the most part inscribed in the evolutionary theories of Charles Darwin in the second half of the nineteenth century. Much of the research in genetics has been a process of substantiating and working out the mechanisms of Darwin's theory of natural selection, which I discuss in conjunction with George Eliot's fiction in Chapter 2. The particular relevance of Epicurean atomism to recent work in genetics is the way chance is affirmed as an essential and constitutive factor in the most elementary and fundamental operations ("at the very root of the stupendous edifice of evolution," Monod says) while the chance-initiated genetic variations necessarily stabilize into normative patterns.

Chance has played an even more decisive role in recent research in physics, and again the Epicurean model is applicable and pertinent.[25] In particular, the set of formulae logically derivable from the assumptions of quantum theory known as the Heisenberg uncertainty principle have challenged the traditional assumptions of classical physics about the deterministic structure of the universe and the viability of strictly causal explanations of phenomena. The uncertainty principle applies to the instantaneous coordinates of the momentum and position of an electron or other subatomic element: if one of these coordinates is measured with great precision (say the given position of an electron at a given time) it is not possible to obtain simultaneously a precise value for the conjugate coordinate (in this case, no measurement can assign a precise value to the momentum, and hence the velocity, of the electron at that time). The results of the formula Heisenberg developed to express this relationship indicate that it is a reciprocal one: the more accurately the position is calculated, the less accurately the momentum can be calculated, and vice versa. Without precise simultaneous measurement of both coordinates the behavior of an individual subatomic particle or process is impossible to determine or predict; it is, then, a matter of chance.*

---

*When Werner Heisenberg places the ideas of quantum physics in relation to the Greek atomists he (quite rightly) associates Democritean atomism with the mechanical determinism of classical physics (see Heisenberg, *Physics and Beyond*, p. 133); but when he discusses the atomism of Epicurus he does not just omit but—perhaps out of some anxiety of influence—denies its most distinctive feature, the chance "swerve": "The Epicureans, too, adopted the essential concepts of the atomic theory, and appended to it an idea which was to play an important part in natural science at a later date: the idea of natural necessity. According to this theory, the atoms are not thrown

The incommensurable nature of exact measurements for the position and velocity of a particle is not a function of inadequate measuring instruments—a margin of error that could conceivably be erased with the development of more sensitive instruments—but an essential and relational feature of subatomic measurement (one that may very well be a result of the unaccountable effects of that measurement, an unavoidable by-product of the interaction between object and observer). Nor is incommensurability a function of inadequately formulated physical laws, so that we might expect further research eventually to yield heretofore unacknowledged laws that will explain the unaccountable fluctuations and perturbations observed. There is no known cause for such variations, and moreover, the evidence indicates that the laws of causality simply do not apply to the phenomena of quantum physics. David Bohm explains in *Causality and Chance in Modern Physics*:

> [T]he renunciation of causality in the usual interpretation of the quantum theory is not to be regarded as merely the result of our inability to *measure* the precise values of the variables that would enter into the expression of causal laws at the atomic level, but, rather, it should be regarded as a reflection of the fact that no such laws exist.[26]

There is a fundamental and absolute limitation to a definition of the state of things at the subatomic level. According to Heisenberg—and most quantum physicists agree—this limitation makes it not just unlikely but impossible that the element of chance in subatomic research will ever be eliminated.[27]

The inapplicability of causal explanations to much of quantum theory indicates a certain limit to the representation of subatomic phenomena. Similarly, the dual nature of electron behavior marks a limit to traditional modes of representation in physics: depending on the circumstances and formulation of the experiment, electrons can be understood to behave either as waves or as particles; neither interpretation can provide a comprehensive explanation of electron behavior. Wave theory and particle theory are both partial analogies adopted to describe and conceptualize experimental results. The wave and particle models, like the laws of causality, take their bear-

---

together arbitrarily, at random, like dice, nor set in motion by forces such as Love or Hate, but their paths are determined by natural laws, or by the working of blind necessity" (Heisenberg, *Nuclear Physics*, p. 4).

ings and structure from classical physics and break down at the level of subatomic quantum theory.[28]

Chance calls into question the laws of causality in subatomic phenomena; but this does not result in the abandonment of scientific inquiry even though physics had previously been premised on the idea of a deterministic universe. Although the findings of quantum theory indicate the completely fortuitous character of individual particles and processes at the subatomic level, a large number of observations yield results that, in a statistical aggregate, show a regular mean behavior. It is thus possible to establish the *statistical* properties of certain subatomic events based on the *probability* of their behavior. The laws of causality are replaced by the laws of probability. The formulae and scientific uses of quantum theory incorporate and quantify the element of chance that is an essential feature of subatomic phenomena.

Again, the "swerve" of the Epicurean atom is an effective model for understanding the way chance operates intrinsically and essentially on the subatomic, microscopic level in quantum physics without precluding order, regularity, and predictability on the macroscopic level. Not only do regular patterns emerge in statistical compilations of microscopic observations; but further, as Ernest Nagel points out,

the indeterministic behavior of the subatomic elements postulated by quantum theory . . . is not exhibited in any experimentally detectable behavior of *macroscopic* objects. Indeed, the theoretical indeterminism as calculated from quantum mechanics in the motion even of molecules, to say nothing of bodies with larger masses, is far smaller than the limits of experimental accuracy.[29]

Some physicists uncomfortable with the Epicurean prioritizing of chance in quantum theory have voiced their objections in familiar Democritean terms by asserting that what seems like chance to our limited understanding is merely a function of our ignorance. Albert Einstein, for instance, resisted the abandonment of causality and deterministic thinking in quantum physics. In conversation with a colleague, Heisenberg agreed that Einstein "rejects quantum mechanics, simply because chance plays a fundamental part in it."[30] In explaining his objections to the fortuitous nature of quantum physics, Einstein wrote to Max Born:

You believe in the God who plays dice, and I in complete law and order in a world which objectively exists, and which I, in a wildly speculative way, am trying to capture. I firmly *believe*, but I hope that someone will discover a more realistic way, or rather a more tangible basis than it has been my lot to find. Even the great initial success of the quantum theory does not make me believe in the fundamental dice game.[31]

Heisenberg and his associates had no trouble accepting the fundamental game of dice—or poker. The experimental poker games and theoretical discussions about the nature of language with which this chapter began indicate their blithe acceptance of the fact that chance offers us access to the physical and material reality out of which we try to make sense.

The final area of current theoretical work for which the Epicurean model is especially pertinent has precisely to do with the place and importance of chance in language. It is in fact in specifically Epicurean terms that Jacques Derrida critiques the linguistic theories of Jacques Lacan.[32] What Derrida objects to in Lacan's "Seminar on 'The Purloined Letter'" is that Lacan both affirms the atomistic nature of the letter (its indivisibility and integrity) and denies the element of chance in the letter's itinerary (Lacan concludes his "Seminar" with the summary statement "a letter always arrives at its destination").[33] Arguing against such atomistic destiny, Derrida uses the Epicurean-Lucretian concept of the *clinamen*, the always possible and hence structurally defining element of chance in an atom's makeup, to describe chance's influence on the movement and meaning of any linguistic unit. The force and implications of Derrida's Epicurean argument will be elaborated in Chapter Three in relation to the linguistic entity with an atomistic nature in modernist narrative, namely: the proper name.

When Lacan discusses the thematics of chance, it is more often than not in Aristotelian terms. He adopts the terms *automaton* and *tuché* (the French spelling of *tyche*) from Aristotle's *Physics* to explain a particular kind of causality associated with repetition. He observes in his explanation of repetition in *The Four Fundamental Concepts of Psychoanalysis*: "It is a question, then, of revising the relation that Aristotle establishes between the *automaton*—and we know, at the present stage of modern mathematics, that it is the network of signifiers—and what he designates as the *tuché*—which is for us the encounter with the real."[34] The *automaton* is that which repeats, comes back; Lacan translates Freud's term *Wiederholungszwang* not as repetition *compulsion* but as repetition *automatism*, which emphasizes both the unreflective and (by way of Aristotle) the fortuitous nature of that which is repeated: "What is repeated, in fact, is always something that occurs . . . *as if by chance*." [35] Lacan's reference to "the present stage of modern mathematics," which allows us to understand the *automaton* as "the network of signifiers," refers specifically to the laws of probability that govern the permutations of repetition.* Just what is repeated is determined by what Lacan calls the *tuché*, the encounter with the real.

"The real is beyond the *automaton*, the return, the coming back, the insistence of the signs, by which we see ourselves governed by the pleasure principle." [36] The encounter with the real, which is the beyond of the pleasure principle, is always and essentially the *missed* encounter. Lacan's model for the missed encounter is the psychoanalytic trauma, in which the real occurs as something unassimilable (e.g., a sexual experience that has no significance for the child at the time but that informs and infuses later analogous experiences with sexual energy once the subject becomes capable of sexual affect, thereby determining the character of successive conscious sexual fantasies). The (by definition missed) encounter with the real is not recuperable for the conscious mind because it works to structure the unconscious: the eruption of the real in an unassimilable form results in a rupture between perception and consciousness, which is how Lacan defines the unconscious—"*the between perception and consciousness*." [37] The *tuché*, the encounter with the real, is knowable only by its effects, by the automatistic repetitions that have an apparently accidental origin and determine all that follows.

"What is repeated, in fact, is always something that occurs—the expression tells us quite a bit about its relation to the *tuché*—*as if by chance*." [38] The expression also tells us quite a bit about Lacan's understanding of chance. The dual nature of the encounter with the real both admits and does away with chance: *what* is repeated is fortuitous and accidental; *that* it is repeated is necessary and determined. It would seem then that Lacan's Aristotelian version of chance is not so far from the Epicurean model I have been tracing in the philosophical and scientific accounts of chance: an originally fortuitous

---

*See the first editor's note to Lacan's "Seminar on 'The Purloined Letter' " (p. 39), which, in a similar context, refers to "Lacan's speculative effort to reinterpret Freudian 'overdetermination' in terms of the laws of probability."

occurrence gives rise to (in this case, psychological rather than scientific) law and order. Lacan even concludes his discussion of *tyche* and *automaton* by invoking the Epicurean "swerve": "If development is entirely animated by accident, by the obstacle of the *tuché*, it is in so far as the *tuché* brings us back to the same point at which pre-Socratic philosophy sought to motivate the world itself. It required a *clinamen*, an inclination, at some point."* But how much room for chance is there in Lacan's revealing phrase "*as if by chance*"?

Of course, when Lacan discusses and reworks for his own purposes the meaning of the word *tyche* he is not just referring to Aristotle's *Physics* but (no surprise, and certainly not by chance) to Oedipus, whose self-proclaimed epithet in Sophocles' play is "child of *tyche*."[39] Oedipus is also, more literally, the child of Laius, whom he killed, and Jocasta, with whom he enjoyed sexual relations. He describes himself as "child of *tyche*" immediately before discovering that he has already fulfilled his destiny, while fleeing the oracle that predicted he would murder his father and marry his mother. Oedipus's affirmation of *tyche* then turns out to be just one of the threads in the unfurling of his fate (*moira*).

The law and order consequent to Jacques Lacan's sense of chance is that of Oedipus Tyrannus. The scene in Sophocles's play that begins with Oedipus's assertion of his parentage as "child of *tyche*" and culminates in the blinding realization that the Delphic Oracle has been fulfilled enacts the shift from chance to fate that is repeated in Lacan's discussions of repetition. Discussing repetition automatism in the repeated scenarios structured by the movement of the letter in Poe's "The Purloined Letter," Lacan concludes: "[T]he displacement of the signifier determines the subjects in their acts, in their destiny, in their refusals, in their blindnesses, in their end and in their fate.... Here we are, in fact, yet again at the crossroads at which we had left our drama."[40] If for Freud all roads lead to Rome, city of fathers,†

---

*Lacan, *Four Fundamental Concepts*, p. 63. Lacan's chronology is wrong here: the *clinamen* was introduced by Epicurus only after and in response to Aristotle's criticisms of Democritus. Lacan is apparently attributing the term to Democritus since he goes on to discuss the Heideggerian wordplay of the genuinely *pre*-Socratic Democritus. Lacan seems to be falling into the same confusion that prompted Marx to write a doctoral dissertation distinguishing between the atomistic philosophies of Democritus and Epicurus.

†See "Politics and Patricide in Freud's *Interpretation of Dreams*," chap. 4 of Carl E. Schorske's *Fin-de-Siècle Vienna*, pp. 181–207. Schorske argues that Freud's reformist

then for Lacan all roads lead to the crossroads, the *coincidence* of the three highways leading to Delphi, Thebes, and Corinth, where Oedipus killed his father. Is there really anything like chance in such a coincidence? Lacan's phrase "*as if by chance*" dramatizes how in his thinking *tyche* becomes *moira*, chance becomes fate, the child is oedipalized, and a letter always arrives at its destination.

In Lacan's story of the child's accession to language, chance always becomes fate. This is an old story, at least as old as Oedipus, and it is an inescapable feature of any story: chance in narrative always and inevitably becomes fate. I want to turn now to a specific kind of narrative in order to consider the relevance and applicability of the Epicurean model of chance to the novel form.

The Novel

In this section I examine the particular relevance of chance experience to the rise of the novel, taking Daniel Defoe's *Robinson Crusoe* (1719–20) as an exemplary case. Drawing on the work of Michael McKeon and Ian Hacking, I relate the generic premises of the novel formulated in the early 1700s to two contemporary attempts to contend with a suddenly prominent interest in the randomness and contingency of life. The discovery of probability theory in the sciences and a theological movement that denied chance in the name of Providence are here aligned with the newly devised aesthetic practices of the novel, most notably its redefinition of existing theories of verisimilitude. I argue that the new genre we call the novel, probability theory, and the providential discourse that emerged in the late seventeenth and early eighteenth centuries are all attempts to recast literary, scientific, and religious ideas of certainty that had started to fracture under the pressures brought to bear on them by new forms of chance. Before examining the place and importance of chance in *Robinson Crusoe*, a brief discussion of the critical debates about the origins of the English novel, and the social and historical conditions of that time, is therefore in order.

In Ian Watt's *The Rise of the Novel*, the works of Daniel Defoe

---

political concerns, centered on Rome (as, among other things, the representative of Christian power), were displaced onto his/the father and expressed as oedipal patricidal urges.

occupy a crucial place in the history of the English novel. It is in part "the profound secularisation of his outlook" that makes Defoe, rather than Bunyan, "the first key figure in the rise of the novel."[41] The distinguishing feature of the novel for Watt is what he calls "formal realism,"* regarding which he states:

[I]t is certain that the novel's usual means—formal realism—tends to exclude whatever is not vouched for by the senses: the jury does not usually allow divine intervention as an explanation of human actions. It is therefore likely that a measure of secularisation was an indispensable condition for the rise of the new genre. (p. 84)

The Rise of the Novel in many ways articulates the sociohistorical dimension of Georg Lukács's famous philosophical claim that the novel is "the epic of a world that has been abandoned by God."[42] Watt's analysis of Defoe's *Robinson Crusoe* therefore considers the spiritual and providential reflections of the novel's hero as a gratuitous addition to the story, an addition indicative of Defoe's "merely formal adherence" (p. 81) to the tenets of Puritanism: "If . . . we turn to the actual effect of Crusoe's religion on his behaviour, we find that it has curiously little. Defoe often suggests that an incident is an act of Divine providence or retribution, but this interpretation is rarely supported by the facts of the story" (p. 80). According to Watt, the most important factors in the secularization process during Defoe's time were the consequences of economic and material progress:

It would seem, then, that Defoe's importance in the history of the novel is directly connected with the way his narrative structure embodied the struggle between Puritanism and the tendency to secularisation which was rooted in material progress. At the same time, it is also apparent that the secular and economic viewpoint is the dominant partner. (p. 83)

The main line of dissent to Watt's economic reading of *Robinson Crusoe* makes the religious theme "the dominant partner" in Defoe's uneasy marriage of spiritual and economic concerns.[43] The spiritual

---

*Here is Watt's definition: Formal realism, which depicts "a circumstantial view of life," is "the narrative embodiment of . . . the premise, or primary convention, that the novel is a full and authentic report of human experience, and is therefore under an obligation to satisfy its reader with such details of the story as the individuality of the actors concerned, the particulars of the times and places of their actions, details which are presented through a more largely referential use of language that is common in other literary forms" (p. 32).

reading finds beneath the surface realism of the story an underlying pattern of sin and regeneration that gives the narrative its true—that is, religious—significance.[44] According to this interpretation, *Robinson Crusoe* imitates a Puritan journal that records the details of everyday experience and, with retrospective reading, reveals providential patterns not immediately apparent.

In his book *The Origins of the English Novel, 1600–1740*, Michael McKeon goes a long way toward explaining the conflict between the mutually exclusive economic and the religious interpretations of *Robinson Crusoe*. McKeon's work presents a dialectical account of the rise of the novel, arguing that it emerged and diverged from the romance genre owing to the influence and prevalence of "naive empiricism" that applied strictly historicist criteria to justify the inclusion of narrative material. The attitude of "naive empiricism" was in turn invalidated by an attitude of "extreme skepticism" that rejected the details and minutiae characteristic of the historicist narrative as themselves depicting a kind of romance. The resulting invalidation of the empirical attitude, with its claim to historicity, both made possible and eventually gave way to "the autonomous realm of the aesthetic," where narrative authenticity is based not on historical veracity but on the idea of literary realism:

Doctrines of literary realism, which rise from the ruins of the claim to historicity, reformulate the problem of mediation for a world in which spirituality has ceased to represent another realm to which human materiality has only difficult and gratuitous access, and has become instead the capacity of human creativity itself. . . . The idea of realism exists to concede the accountability of art to a prior reality, without seeming to compromise the uniquely modern belief that such reality as it is answerable to already is internalized in art itself as a demystified species of spirituality.[45]

The codification of the principles of literary realism and the establishment of the autonomous aesthetic realm in many ways constituted a rediscovery of the Aristotelian idea of verisimilitude. In the *Poetics*, Aristotle distinguishes between history (which is factual and particular) and poetry (which is probable and universal), but this distinction, influential during the Renaissance, was for the most part eclipsed during the seventeenth century by the prevalence of empiricist thought which validated the evidence of the senses and equated history and truth. Verisimilitude provides a kind of narrative truth free of the historicist bias and aware of its own fictionality. "Of course," McKeon points out, "the claim to historicity is no less a rhetorical trope than verisimilitude; the difference is that it is not rationalized as such" (p. 53). Literary realism gained ascendancy in the eighteenth century by

gather[ing] up and sophisticat[ing] the scattered threads of verisimilitude and probability that Renaissance writers had teased out of the *Poetics*. It validates literary creativity for being not history but history-like, "true" to the only external reality that still makes a difference, but also sufficiently apart from it (hence "probable" and "universal") to be true to itself as well. (p. 120)

The autonomous aesthetic arose to mediate the aggravated conflict between the competing claims of materiality and spirituality; the seemingly irreconcilable contradictions between historical truth and divine justice in a secular age were eventually accommodated by the affirmation of *aesthetic* truth, with its verisimilar representation of *poetic* justice. The autonomous realm of the aesthetic, with its practice of literary realism, first finds a viable novelistic form in the works of Richardson and Fielding in the 1740s, and more or less dictates the subsequent formal properties of the novel. McKeon observes:

The implications of the formal breakthrough of the 1740s are pursued with such feverish intensity over the next two decades that after *Tristram Shandy*, it may be said, the young genre settles down to a more or less deliberate and studied recapitulation of the same ground, this time for the next two centuries. (p. 419)

Robinson Crusoe occupies a crucial place in the history of the novel because it in many ways initiated and anticipated a kind of fiction that eventually stabilized into the familiar aesthetic features we associate with the novel form. McKeon remarks:

[I]n writers of exceptional acuity, the autonomous aesthetic and the idea of realism can be seen to be lurking in the logic not only of extreme skepticism but even of naive empiricism. This can be said of the work of Daniel Defoe, who doggedly pursued the problem of the false claim to historicity for the better part of two decades. (p. 120)

Defoe wrote fictional narratives that insisted on their historical and factual accuracy and presented in a realistic mode the circumstances of daily life in all of their detail and contingency. Defoe remained faithful to the standards of historical truth from which his inventions derive and so never made the step from false claims about historicity to the assertion that the narrative fabrications tell the truth by being history-*like*. What Watt calls "formal realism" did not quite become "literary realism" with its rationale of verisimilitude. Instead, Defoe justified his fictions of historical truth by claiming that stories like *Robinson Crusoe* offer (in his words) "moral and religious Improvement."[46] The conflict between standards of empirical/historical veracity and the fictional enterprise is therefore resolved not in aesthetic terms but in religious ones, by affirming that the narrative conveys a transcendent religious truth.

If we return to the conflict between the economic and the spiritual interpretations of *Robinson Crusoe*, we can see how, in its own terms, the novel resolves this conflict by means of a utopian religious ideology. As many commentators have pointed out, the economic lesson that Robinson Crusoe learns in the solitude of his island habitation, a lesson he repeatedly rehearses, is the discovery of use value and the consequent depreciation of exchange value. Whereas before he valued things only through their commodification in the marketplace, on the island Crusoe learns that "all the good Things of this World, are no farther good to us, than they are for our Use."[47] He therefore famously (and temporarily) disdains the money he finds on the beached ship (p. 57). One of the things whose worth is altered for Crusoe from exchange value to use value is the Bible itself. Among the freight he rescues from the ship are "three very good Bibles which came to me in my Cargo from *England*" (p. 64). The Good Book eventually transforms Crusoe's use of the word "good" from meaning—as it does in this passage—an appreciation of undamaged merchandise (goods) to meaning an appreciation of the greatest good that comes with acknowledgment of and submission to God's will. He happens upon the Bibles while looking for some tobacco he wanted for medicinal purposes; but it is his discovery of the Holy Scriptures that cures his dis-ease. The Bible then ceases to be a commodity for Crusoe as it brings about his religious conversion. From that point on, Crusoe gradually learns how to interpret his experiences, actions, and impulses as manifestations of God's will: circumstance becomes Providence.

When Crusoe eventually returns to civilization, the transvaluation of his outlook has seemingly transformed the world. Not only is he capable of formulating providential explanations for his subsequent accumulation of wealth, but further all the capitalists he comes in contact with in the later sections of the novel are honorable and trustworthy. The Protestant ethic and the spirit of capitalism accomplish a quite effective and profitable merger. Of course, this vision of enlightened and benevolent commerce does not provide a "realistic" picture of capitalist activity; as Michael McKeon notes, Defoe is no doubt expressing "the tangible externalization of Robinson's now securely internalized utopia, in the representation of the psychological state of being a principled possessive individualist, fully reconciled to the naturalness and morality of the pursuit of self-interest" (p. 335). In McKeon's account of the novel, it is precisely "the notion of the human internalization of divinity" (p. 333) that qualifies the writer of *Robinson Crusoe* as (in Ian Watt's words) "the complacent apologist of nascent industrial capitalism."[48]

In his island solitude, Crusoe learns to reinterpret circumstance as Providence, which as it turns out serves his purposes quite well. Likewise in his capitalist enterprises after he leaves the island, he attributes his success in the business world to the benevolent grace of God. Robinson Crusoe first ventures himself, in his conversion on the island, and then his capital, in the marketplace, and in both cases he gets a handsome return on the investment. Concluding his narrative, he calls the sum of his experiences a "Life of Fortune and Adventure, a life of Providence's Chequerwork" (p. 304). By this he does not just mean that his life has been lucky and exciting. The various ventures of his adventure do indeed yield him a considerable fortune; and the word "Chequerwork," which he uses to characterize Providence, suggests not just a diversity of experience but also the term's etymological connection with the exchequer, the center of financial accountancy and authority.

What then does this summary of the origins of the English novel in relation to *Robinson Crusoe* have to do with chance? The most matter-of-fact answer to this question is, quite simply, that lots of things happen by chance in *Robinson Crusoe*—most obviously, the shipwreck that strands him on the deserted island, but also and insistently the haphazard encounters and casual collisions of his everyday life before, during, and after his island solitude. Again and again, it is chance that seems both to initiate and to direct the narrative action.

But Crusoe's education on the island consists partly in his learning how to transform what seems to happen by chance into Providence. Robinson thus eventually reevaluates the hazard of his shipwreck and his life "destitute of the Knowledge and Fear of God" before his conversion:

I had terrible Reflections upon my Mind for many Months . . . on the Account of my wicked and hardned Life past; and when I look'd about me and considered what particular Providences had attended me since my coming into this Place, and how God had dealt bountifully with me; . . . this gave me great hopes that my Repentance was accepted and that God had yet Mercy in store for me. (p. 132)

The most trivial of chance circumstances eventually becomes a sign of God's will for Crusoe. Describing how he discovered the opening of a cave, which became his shelter, he says: "The Mouth of this Hollow was at the Bottom of a great Rock, where by mere accident (I would say, if I did not see abundant Reason to ascribe all such things to Providence) I was cutting down some thick Branches of Trees to make Charcoal" (p. 176). The convergence of chance and Providence is perhaps most evident when the newly converted Crusoe practices bibliomancy, opening the Bible at random and interpreting the passage he happens upon as a direct message from God (pp. 94, 113).

The reinterpretation of (what seems to be) chance as Providence is of course a classical theological doctrine going back at least to Aquinas;* but the subject gained a new currency during the time Defoe was writing his narrative experiments. His contemporary John Tillotson, archbishop of Canterbury, sermonized:

[I]t must be acknowledged, that there is some other cause which mingles itself with human affairs, and governs all events; and which can, and does when it pleases, defeat the most likely, and bring to pass the most improbable designs: and what else can that be imagined to be, but the secret and overruling providence of Almighty God? When we can find no other, we are very unreasonable if we will not admit this to be the cause of such extraordinary events, but will obstinately impute that to blind necessity or chance, which hath such plain characters upon it of a Divine power and wisdom.†

*See Aquinas, *Summa Contra Gentiles*, bk. 3, especially chaps. 90–94. For an updated version of the same argument, which considers the element of chance in quantum physics, see Pollard, *Chance and Providence*.

†John Tillotson, "Success Not Always Answerable to the Probability of Second Causes," in his *Works*, vol. 3, p. 105. The sermon was preached before the House of Commons on April 16, 1690.

Tillotson attempts to refute both the Deist's idea of a detached and impersonal watchmaker God (causality as "blind necessity") and the belief that events are caused by mere chance. It was to answer this dual threat to orthodox Christian thought that a discourse of Providence arose in England during the late seventeenth and early eighteenth centuries.* This discourse usually made a distinction between general Providence (God's will expressed in and through natural causes) and special Providence (God's will expressed as miraculous intervention). In both forms of Providence, God's will is the final cause; in special Providence God operates by a special manipulation or violation of the laws of nature, while in general Providence the divine will manifests itself in and through so-called secondary causes, which obey natural laws.[49] The Providence that Tillotson invokes in his sermon as a form of causality is special Providence, "which can, and does when it pleases, defeat the most likely, and bring to pass the most improbable designs." The extraordinary and dramatic nature of special Providence was generally considered a more compelling indication of God's concern and control: "nothing can be a greater argument of providence," Tillotson says in the same sermon,

than that there is such an order of causes laid in nature, that in ordinary course every thing does usually attain its end; and yet that there is such a mixture of contingency, as that now and then, we cannot tell how nor why, the most likely causes do deceive us, and fail of producing their usual effects.

For . . . providence does suppose all things to have been at first wisely framed and with a fitness to attain their end; but yet it does also suppose that God hath reserved to himself a power and liberty to interpose, and to cross as he pleases, the usual course of things; to awaken men to the consideration of him, and a continual dependance upon him.[50]

Special Providence is thought to be a more compelling sign of God's will and agency because it defies the senses and controverts the usual workings of cause and effect. But it was general Providence that eventually became the focus of providential debates because it could mediate between an enduring belief in God's agency (through secondary causes) and the empiricist's faith in the evidence of the senses.

---

*J. Paul Hunter, citing a 1678 treatise by John Flavell as one of the early examples of the flourishing providential literature, observes, "For more than half a century thereafter, the concept of providence remained at the center of theological and philosophical controversy." Hunter, *Reluctant Pilgrim*, p. 56.

A shift from special to general Providence is enacted in a psychological mode in one of Crusoe's early island experiences; and with
that shift we can see Defoe's protagonist mediating his providentialist impulses and his empiricist commitment to the matter-of-fact
causality of natural laws. Before Robinson finds the Bibles, an incident occurs that for the first time encourages him to reinterpret a
chance event as a sign of Providence. He had at one point unthink-
ingly emptied out a bag of chicken feed, which had been marauded by
rats, near his fortification; but not all of the seeds were spoiled, and
Crusoe is amazed to discover some time later that stalks of English
barley and rice are sprouting in his front yard:

I had hitherto acted upon no religious Foundation at all, indeed I had very
few Notions of Religion in my Head, or had entertain'd any Sense of any
Thing that had befallen me, otherwise than as a Chance, or, as we lightly say,
what pleases God; without so much as enquiring into the end of Providence
in these Things, or his Order in governing Events in the World: But after I
saw Barley grow there . . . I began to suggest that God had miraculously
caus'd the Grain to grow without any Help of Seed sown, and that it was so
directed purely for my Sustenance, on that wild miserable Place. (p. 78)

When he later realizes how the grain came to grow there, he remarks: "[T]he Wonder began to cease; and I must confess my religious Thankfulness to God's Providence began to abate too upon the
Discovering that all this was nothing but what was common." This
confession of his lapsed faith in the face of a natural explanation for
what he thought was a supernatural phenomenon is immediately fol-
lowed by his retrospective reassessment of that occurrence; and here
we see Crusoe adjusting his faith to his circumstances. He simply
replaces the idea of special Providence with the idea of general Providence; and the latter proves to be quite amenable to the circumstantial
and metonymic nature of Defoe's formal realism. Crusoe continues:

[T]ho' I ought to have been as thankful for so strange and unforeseen Providence, as if it had been miraculous; for it was really the Work of Providence
as to me, that should order or appoint that 10 or 12 Grains of Corn should
remain unspoil'd, (when the Rats had destroyed all the rest,) as if it had been
dropt from Heaven; as also, that I should throw it out in that particular
Place, where it being in the Shade of a high Rock, it sprang up immediately;
whereas, if I had thrown it anywhere else at that Time, it had been burnt up
and destroy'd. (pp. 78–79)

That which seems to happen by chance becomes a sign of God's will: the effects of dissemination in this literal scattering of seeds are assimilated to providential design. The shift in emphasis from special to general Providence in theological debates and in Defoe's proto-novel consolidates a sense of religious faith in accord with the empirical world.

Despite his insistence on the influence of the guiding hand of God in his life, Robinson Crusoe's perceptions of both special Providence ("I began to *suggest* that God had miraculously caus'd this Grain to grow . . . purely for *my* Sustenance") and general Providence ("for it was really the Work of Providence *as to me*") sometimes seem self-serving. "I was sometimes led too far to invade the Soveraignty of *Providence*," Crusoe admits,

and, as it were, arraign the Justice of so arbitrary a Disposition of Things, that should hide the Light from some and reveal it to others, and yet expect a like Duty from both: But I shut it up, and check'd my Thoughts with this Conclusion, (1st.) That we did not know by what Light and Law these should be Condemn'd; . . . And (2d.), that still as we are all the Clay in the Hand of the Potter, no Vessel could say to him, Why hast thou form'd me thus? (p. 210)

The tension in Robinson Crusoe's religious codas, which makes his providential rationalizations seem at least ironic, if not hypocritical, derives from his seeming not so much "Clay in the Hands of the Potter" as, preeminently, the self-made man. What makes his story seem so strikingly a matter of self-fashioning is not his rebellious questioning of a divinity that metes out "so arbitrary a Disposition of Things" but his elastic ability to transform apparently arbitrary dispositions into occasions for his own advancement, justified as the will of God. As Michael McKeon points out, in *Robinson Crusoe* "Defoe gives to the notion of the true history of the individual so intimate and introspective a form" that "the metaphysical realm of the Spirit may be accommodated and rendered accessible as the psychological realm of Mind" (pp. 337, 336). The often-remarked aura of irony surrounding Defoe's narrative is the result not of authorial intention but of competing and contradictory discourses (economic and spiritual, individual and divine, psychological and metaphysical, etc.) in ironic relation to one another. And in the interstices opened up by this pervasive irony there emerges a kind of chance that is not necessarily effaced and erased by Crusoe's providential reading of events. The sense of things happening by chance in *Robinson Crusoe* emerges not out of its representation of events themselves but out of the persistent ironies adhering to the narrative machinery that normally and unobtrusively works to efface the aleatory elements of a story. The caustic nature of the discursive ironies permeating Crusoe's narrative leaves behind the traces of an indissoluble remainder, a kind of chance that is not altogether reclaimed or recuperated by the providentialist rhetoric.

It is this that makes the providential claims of *Robinson Crusoe*'s narrative problematic: there is no authoritative validation for such interpretations beyond Crusoe's own (self-)assertions. Providence in *Robinson Crusoe* has become an element *in* the plot but is no longer unquestionably identifiable *as* the plot. Peter Hulme explains: "Nothing defines Providence more clearly than its reliance on plot: Providence is history with a plot, authored by God."[51] But *Robinson Crusoe* is the history of an individual ostensibly authored by that individual ("Written by Himself," the title page proclaims). Crusoe himself is not always certain about his attribution of providential agency; and when he aggressively asserts its influence, one is hard-pressed to distinguish such claims from his ongoing self-aggrandizement. "When such delicate questions of interpretation are themselves turned into the very matter of fiction," Hulme notes, "Providence can in no way be said to provide a privileged master-plot to the narrative."[52] The element of chance that appears in and as the plotting of the novel then does not necessarily or completely yield to the interpretations of a providential master-plot.

Both the economic and the spiritual readings of *Robinson Crusoe* find the apparently random and contingent aspects of Defoe's historicist narrative unsettling and anachronistically apply the standards of an autonomous aesthetic in order to discount or dismiss such deficiencies. While granting that Defoe's novels "are the first considerable narratives which embody all the elements of formal realism" (p. 104), Ian Watt bestows the title "founder of the novel" not on Defoe but on Richardson: "Defoe is the master illusionist, and this almost makes him the founder of the new form. Almost, but not quite: the novel could be considered established only when realistic narrative was organized into a plot which, while retaining Defoe's lifelikeness, also had an intrinsic coherence" (p. 131). It is this notion of "intrinsic coherence" that characterizes the autonomous realm of the aesthetic: the work of art is both answerable to external reality and sufficiently removed from that reality to constitute its own idea of aesthetic integrity. Thus Watt asserts, "all Defoe's novels . . . make formal realism an end rather than a means" (p. 117); and implicit in this criticism is the belief that realism must maintain the semblance of literal authenticity as a means to an *aesthetic* end, "creating a literary structure in which narrative mode, plot, characters and moral theme [are] organised into a unified whole" (p. 208).

Watt faults Defoe's narratives for not employing the Aristotelian idea of verisimilitude, which conveys a sense of aesthetic truth different and removed from historical truth. After quoting the famous distinction in the *Poetics* between history, which is factual and particular, and poetry, which is probable and universal, Watt states: "Defoe's concentration on producing pseudo-history, although a crucial step in the development of the kind of plot suited to the novel's formal realism, was so exclusive that the other ends of fiction, the ends of poetry in Aristotle's sense, were inevitably crowded out of the picture" (p. 108). It is specifically the episodic nature of Defoe's plots—"a series of essentially casual encounters" (p. 111)—that Watt, invoking Aristotle, finds problematic. And for Aristotle, what makes the episodic the worst kind of plot is the fact that the events recounted seem to happen "of themselves or by mere chance."[53]

Reacting against Watt's implied criticisms, the spiritual reading of *Robinson Crusoe* actually adopts the same criteria to affirm the novel's ultimate literary and aesthetic value. This reading identifies the providential themes in *Crusoe* with the aesthetic ends that Watt finds lacking, an understandable (if unsuccessful) conflation since the aesthetic realm of transcendental value in many ways took over the functions of spirituality in an increasingly secularized world. The randomness and contingency of what seems to be an episodic plot are in the religious reading assimilated to a providential design; what seems like chance eventually, with careful rereading, reveals an underlying spiritual pattern that makes *Robinson Crusoe* a formally sophisticated and intrinsically coherent narrative. Describing the "thematic coherence" of spiritual autobiographies, which provide the model for Crusoe's religious development, G. A. Starr observes:

So long as the protagonist's inward vicissitudes obeyed the traditional pattern, either of growth or decay, and so long as individual episodes contributed to this pattern with some consistency, an autobiography might be regarded as structurally sound. Within such a convention, . . . a logic of spiritual change within the character took precedence over a logic of outward action; within such a convention, discrete, apparently random episodes might be held to possess a unity both sufficient and meaningful.[54]

By returning Defoe's historicist narrative to its historical context, *The Origins of the English Novel* allows us to understand the narrative operations of *Robinson Crusoe* without automatically and unconsciously applying the criteria and categories of the autonomous aesthetic that gained ascendancy and dictated the novel's form only after and, in part, as a result of Defoe's narrative innovations. What emerges in the generic interregnum exemplified by *Robinson Crusoe* is a kind of chance that is not altogether recuperated by a providential design nor altogether assimilated to the Aristotelian notion of probability that informs the realistic practices of the novel once the autonomous aesthetic realm is securely established.

The logic and practice of verisimilitude, which employs standards of probability to determine narrative veracity, work to expunge chance from the novel: where the providential narrative transforms random and casual experience into a sign of God's will in order to represent spiritual truth, the realistic and verisimilar narrative transforms chance into fate in order to represent aesthetic truth. The status of the narrative event as "probable" allows for its contingency while assimilating it to aesthetic conceptions of order and design where "what happens" was always already *meant* to happen.

In *The Emergence of Probability*, Ian Hacking analyzes why and how, in the same historical period as the origins of the English novel, the science of probability emerged in contradistinction to the standards of certain and demonstrable knowledge by the transformation of natural signs (which could be more or less reliable) into evidence.* McKeon speculates, but does not pursue the possibility, that "the ultimate triumph of scientific standards of probability over those of certainty may be related to the ultimate triumph of literary standards of verisimilitude over the claim to historicity" (p. 70). Hacking's analysis supports this idea by insisting that the emergence of proba-

---

*Hacking, *Emergence of Probability*. As Hacking points out, probability as we now conceive it first came into being around 1660 and was established as an independent discipline in its own right with the publication of Abraham de Moivre's *The Doctrine of Chances* in 1718.

bility theory had both an aleatory side, concerned with the stochastic laws of chance processes, and an epistemic side, concerned with degrees of belief. McKeon's analysis provides an exhaustive account of the way forms of belief undergo historical transformation, but he does not give sufficient credit or historical weight to the influence the experience of chance exerted on the novelistic experiments of the time. He observes that the Aristotelian idea of probability, which facilitated the redefinition of narrative truth in the novel, was simply rediscovered once the idea (or ideal) of historicist truth was discredited: it "lay like a time bomb in the cultural unconscious of the West" (p. 119). But I would argue that, like probability theory in the sciences, the probability informing literary verisimilitude had both an epistemic and an aleatory side, and that the latter side was also responding to specific historical imperatives. In both its literary and scientific forms, probability works to mediate conflicts at times of epistemic crisis; its implementation represents both an acknowledgement of, and an attempt to contain, the pressures brought to bear on notions of certainty by the eruption of chance phenomena.*

In genetics, quantum physics, and psychoanalysis, the three sciences examined in this chapter for which chance is a major factor, probability theory provides a technology designed to filter out as much as possible the element of chance in order to make calculated predictions about the outcome of events.† The importance of probability in the theory and practice of the novel in its early years helps to explain the relevance of the Epicurean *clinamen* to the history of the emerging genre. *Robinson Crusoe*, arguably the first English novel, introduces a kind of chance into narrative that eventually, with the implementation of novelistic verisimilitude based on notions of the probable, gives rise to a stable and ordered aesthetic form, the novel as we know it.

Robinson Crusoe tells us first thing that "mine was the middle

---

*For a thorough discussion of the uses of probability in eighteenth-century literary and scientific terms that takes exception to Hacking's analysis, see Patey, *Probability and Literary Form*. In *A Likely Story*, Robert Newsom considers the philosophical, scientific, and literary uses of probability in relation to the rise of the novel.

†This is clearest, of course, in quantum physics, which replaces the laws of causality with the laws of probability in calculating the behavior of subatomic phenomena. In genetics, probability theory is used to determine the frequency and likelihood of genetic mutations. I realize that the scientific status of psychoanalysis is questionable, but I consider Lacan's use of probability calculations in relation to *tyche* and *automaton* to be symptomatic of *his* claims for the scientific status of psychoanalysis.

State," referring to his socioeconomic standing; and it is the acuity with which Defoe's hero describes his place "in the Middle of the two Extremes" (p. 4) that makes this middling novel great. Of course it is too simple to say that before *Robinson Crusoe* chance in narrative was effaced to serve providential ends and after *Robinson Crusoe* chance in narrative is effaced to serve aesthetic ends. But the hybrid and transitional nature of Defoe's fiction clearly illustrates the generic premises for the problematic representation of chance in the novel.

Although I have emphasized and abstracted the differences between the providential and the aesthetic ends of narrative in relation to *Robinson Crusoe*, they are by no means mutually exclusive. The autonomous aesthetic of literary realism eventually takes over the functions of spirituality in an increasingly secularized world, but the two realms of transcendental value overlap and inform each other in novels that articulate a providential aesthetic well into the nineteenth century. The next chapter will examine the way the preeminent realist in English literature thematized chance in her fiction in order to purge the novel of its providential affiliations. But, as I will show, the closure that George Eliot brought to the providential epoch in the novel also brings with it some disconcerting disclosures about the aesthetic aspirations of late-Victorian novelists when the sense of chance that is repressed by the verisimilar practices of literary realism returns with a vengeance.

CHAPTER TWO

"A Practical Rebus": The Economy of Chance in *Middlemarch*

Charles Dickens had lunch with George Eliot and George Henry Lewes on March 6, 1870, during which he enthralled them with an anecdote. As George Eliot later reported, Dickens

> was telling us a story of President Lincoln having told the Council on the day he was shot, that something remarkable would happen, because he had just dreamt for the third time a dream which twice before had preceded events momentous to the nation. The dream was, that he was in a boat on a great river all alone—and he ended with the words "I drift—I drift—I drift."[1]

Dickens told the story "very finely," George Eliot remembered. The story and its telling, as dramatic as they undoubtedly were, became more poignant still when George Eliot later realized that the anecdote about a premonition of death was itself premonitory. Dickens's health at the time of this visit was shaky because of the strenuous public readings he had only recently given up on the advice of his doctor; George Eliot "thought him looking dreadfully shattered." Three months later he was dead.*

In *The Providential Aesthetic in Victorian Fiction,* Thomas Vargish considers coincidence in Dickens's novels in a way that would apply as well to the double coincidence of this anecdote (that Lincoln's recurrent dream portended his assassination, and that the telling of that story foretold Dickens's own death):

> A *coincidence* in its basic meaning is merely the concurrence or juxtaposition in time and space of two or more events or circumstances. . . . But coincidence in its common and most important literary use carries with it an

---

*Eliot, *Letters*, vol. 5, p. 102. The letter that recalls this visit was written shortly after Dickens's death. See also Haight, *George Eliot*, pp. 422–23.

element of surprise or astonishment that derives from the lack of apparent causal connection.

The meeting of Pip and Estella at the end of Dickens's *Great Expectations*, for instance, "is a *true* coincidence, one designed to push the reader toward a different level of causality . . . , an idea of causality perfectly real and comfortable to readers educated in the providential tradition."* For Vargish, the higher level causality of such a coincidence indicates that, though its existence or purpose might not be evident to us, there is a providential force that guides, controls, and orders lives and events.

"The business of art," Dickens wrote, "is only to *suggest*, until the fulfillment comes. These are the ways of Providence, of which all art is but a little imitation."[2] Inasmuch as Dickens's famous self-dramatization was an art, he was once again imitating—or arrogating to himself—"the ways of Providence" when he related the story of Lincoln's dream in a way that suggested his own death three months before it occurred.

"A Triply Coincidental and Melodramatic Plot"

At the time of this anecdotal luncheon George Eliot was working on her novel *Middlemarch* (1871–72), in which a character appears who is emphatically associated with coincidence—with several co-incidences, in fact, one of which (as I will show) is both typical of and a comment on Dickens's use of coincidence. But another of the coincidences associated with this character is something else again, marking as it does a qualitative change in the representation of chance in the English novel. In this chapter I will eventually be focusing on the character John Raffles, in *Middlemarch*, who, as his name suggests, embodies George Eliot's concern with chance. I trace two trajectories in the novel's treatment of Raffles that together convey Eliot's conflicted attitude toward chance in her fiction: the inclusion of Raffles in the plot of *Middlemarch* introduces a new sense of chance in the English novel that focalizes a corrosive critique of the genre's providential affiliations; and the eventual and violent expulsion of this character, who is morally debased and unworthy of sympathy,

---

*Vargish, *Providential Aesthetic*, pp. 7–8. Vargish is referring to the second ending of *Great Expectations*, which, in being more improbable, calls attention more insistently to the "different level of causality" at work.

works to purge the novel of chance in the name of a secular-humanist moral order founded on sympathy. Before considering Raffles and his chances though, I want to look more closely at George Eliot's relation to what Vargish calls "the providential tradition."

The Providential Aesthetic in Victorian Fiction argues in general that "the fictional representation of providence at work in the world is a major unifying thematic direction of the English novel before George Eliot."[3] A providential aesthetic shapes literary material in order to convey a sense of a Supreme Being who foresees and controls human events for some divine purpose. Providence means foresight, and refers both to the preparations one makes for the future and, more importantly, to God's benevolent supervision of his creatures, which assures that, though it might not be immediately apparent, there is order and design to their lives. George Eliot marks a certain closure of the providential epoch in the novel for Vargish because she "produced the first and greatest examples of the ways in which the aesthetic conventions and structural devices of the providential tradition can be turned to the service of what has become a generally secular art."[4] I am not altogether convinced that the providential tradition was as stable and pervasive as Vargish suggests or that novelistic ideas of order and design are necessarily and inextricably implicated in the theological frame of reference he describes. It is clear, however, that George Eliot was versed in this tradition and I agree with Vargish that her novels represent a real and explicit departure from the providential way of thinking. More often than not, Eliot's attacks on providentialism materialize in her novels in the form of chance events that have nothing to do with a benevolent divine will overseeing and directing human affairs.

The cultural context for George Eliot's adaptation of the providential aesthetic to secular imperatives, which Thomas Vargish does not consider in any detail, was an increasing interest in scientific and historical work that called into question scriptural accounts of the origin and purpose of life on earth. Probably the most formidable challenge to the providential worldview during the time George Eliot was writing was the concept of a "fortuitous evolutionary world" described by Darwin and other scientists of the period.* Darwin's theory of natural selection, which he proposed in *The Origin of Species* (1859),

---

*U. C. Knoepflmacher observes that George Eliot "could not place her faith in the fortuitous evolutionary world she regarded as real." *George Eliot's Early Novels*, p. 27.

contested the tenets of natural theology, which found proof for the existence of God in the design evident in natural phenomena.* Natural selection attributes the manifold diversity and adaptations of plant and animal life not to the benevolent design of a Christian God but to the preservation of certain variations in an organism that make it more or less fit for its environment and that it passes on to its offspring. In trying to account for these variations, Darwin was not quite comfortable referring their source to chance: "[C]hance . . . is a wholly incorrect expression, but it serves to acknowledge plainly our ignorance of the cause of each variation. . . . [W]e may be sure that there must be some cause for each deviation of structure, however slight."[5] Like Democritus, and Einstein in his objections to quantum theory, Darwin believed that phenomena that seem to be attributable to the workings of chance in nature are in fact the results of natural laws about which we are presently ignorant. Darwin's reluctance to accept chance as the source of variations in natural selection did not diminish the force of his attack on the teleological assumptions of natural theology. "I cannot look at the universe as the result of blind chance," he wrote, "yet I can see no evidence of beneficent design, or indeed of design of any kind, in the details." Darwin the naturalist had an eye for details, and he only grudgingly admitted: "[T]he details, whether good or bad, [are] left to the working out of what we may call chance. Not that this notion *at all* satisfies me."[6] The science of genetics eventually described the natural laws at work in the production of variations in nature; but far from eliminating chance, genetic research revealed that it is an essential element in the process of natural selection. Although not immediately acknowledged, even by Darwin himself, chance (in the form of minute random mutations) is the mechanism of evolutionary change that calls into question the order, design, and purposive power of Providence. As will become clear, George Eliot, like Darwin, found the idea of chance useful in refuting a providential understanding of the world she described; but she too had trouble finally endorsing chance as a satisfactory explanation for the way things happen in that world.†

---

*The most influential example of this position was William Paley's *Natural Theology: or, Evidences of the Existence and Attributes of the Deity, Collected from the Appearances of Nature* (orig. pub. 1802).

†The influence of evolutionary thought on George Eliot's work is discussed in Beer, *Darwin's Plots*; Shuttleworth, *George Eliot and Nineteenth Century Science*; and Levine, *Darwin and the Novelists*. Shuttleworth points out that for most of Darwin's contemporaries (including George Eliot) the importance of chance in evolutionary

The climate of increasingly secularized humanism prevalent during the formative years of George Eliot's intellectual development informed her attitude to established ideas of a providential force at work in the world. The positivism of Auguste Comte and the German Higher Criticism of the Bible were influential in Eliot's circle and reinterpreted religious belief in scientific, humanist, and historicist terms. The two German works Marian Evans translated into English before she became George Eliot the novelist—Strauss's *Das Leben Jesu* and then Feuerbach's *Das Wesen des Christentums*—both questioned the miraculous and divine aspects of the Bible. A passage from *The Essence of Christianity* (in Marian Evans's English translation of 1854) emphasizes the way chance problematizes an unquestioning faith in divine Providence:

> Religion denies, repudiates chance, making everything dependent on God, explaining everything by means of him; but the denial is only apparent; it merely gives chance the name of the divine sovereignty. For the divine will, which, on incomprehensible grounds, for incomprehensible reasons, that is, speaking plainly, out of groundless, absolute arbitrariness, out of divine caprice, as it were, determines or predestines some to evil and misery, others to good and happiness, has not a single positive characteristic to distinguish it from the power of chance.[7]

This passage from Feuerbach is pivotal because it symmetrically inverts the classical and hierarchical relation of chance to Providence that goes back at least to Aquinas: what *seems* like chance to us, theological doctrine claims, is only an aspect of divine Providence, which, because of our limited perspective and knowledge, we are unable to understand or appreciate.[8] Of course, as Thomas Vargish admits, not all Victorian novelists were concerned with the providential view of the world; George Eliot's position is exceptional and instructive, however, because she directly confronts and reworks the providential tradition—first in the works she chose to translate and introduce into English culture and later in the representation of chance in her novels.

The initiating crisis of *Silas Marner* (1861) demonstrates how, in

---

theory was only gradually acknowledged: "Few critics fully appreciated the potential implications of the actual mechanism of natural selection; the notion of chance, which threatened conceptions of ordered development, received little attention initially" (p. 15).

Feuerbach's words, "the divine will . . . has not a single positive characteristic to distinguish it from the power of chance," thereby problematizing an unquestioning faith in that will. Silas's life as an outcast begins after he is falsely accused of stealing money from the devout religious community in which he lives; when he denies the accusation, the members of the community draw lots to determine "by immediate divine interference" if he is the criminal.[9] The lottery declares that he is guilty, and he leaves the town disgraced. Silas's faith in divine Providence is shattered, but he acquires a new faith in the sense of community opened to him by his chance adoption of a daughter. At the end of the novel, which dramatizes Silas's reentry into society after having learned the principles of secular humanism, most of the things he had lost come back to him again; but his feeling of betrayal by God in the drawing of the lots is never adequately explained. The lottery as an emblem for George Eliot's interest in chance is picked up again in condensed form in *Middlemarch* with the name John *Raffles*.*

Raffles is connected to the various subplots in *Middlemarch* by three coincidences, which Jerome Beaty itemizes succinctly and censoriously in *"Middlemarch" from Notebook to Novel*:

We are ready not to disbelieve the coincidence of Mr. Bulstrode's old associate, Raffles, turning up as Joshua Rigg's stepfather. But to have Will Ladislaw, Casaubon's second cousin, the grandson of Bulstrode's first wife and the rightful heir, whom Raffles has helped Bulstrode keep from his inheritance, and to have them all in this same provincial town miles from where their former association found them, is perhaps too much for the most indulgent reader to tolerate. . . . That the two rather melodramatic plot complications had to be wound together into a triply coincidental and melodramatic plot is unfortunate.[10]

The sheer number of coincidences attached to Raffles is indeed striking, but I think Beaty's disapproval has partly to do with the nature of his critical project in *"Middlemarch" from Notebook to Novel*. He is more concerned with filling in the minute connections that constitute the background to the novel than he is with examining how and why they are deployed in the narrative. Raffles is coincidentally associated

*In George Eliot's later novels, the word "lot" is probably her favorite term for describing the conditions and course of her characters' lives, but its usage usually obscures the kind of arbitrary and aleatory experience Silas suffers in "the drawing o' the lots."

with Rigg, Bulstrode, and Will Ladislaw, but it is only his knowledge of Bulstrode's disreputable dealings that becomes essential to the plot of *Middlemarch* (Raffles brings about Bulstrode's disgrace, the scandal of which also destroys Lydgate's reputation). The third turn of the screw that so tests Beaty's tolerance as an indulgent reader—Raffles's knowledge of Will's antecedents—ends up having very little consequence in the resolution of the novel. And that is, I think, precisely the point.

The form of this coincidence—the discovery by a character with obscure origins of his or her parentage and relation to another character—is certainly a familiar one, especially in the work of Charles Dickens, where it provides the narrative framework for so many novels (*Oliver Twist, Nicholas Nickleby, Bleak House, Great Expectations*). But in *Middlemarch* this conventional and Dickensian coincidence is given an interesting twist. The revelation of Will's background comes at a crucial time: the codicil to Mr. Casaubon's will had cast aspersions on Will's character by suggesting with its explicit prohibition an improper intimacy between him and Mrs. Casaubon; Will hopes to overcome this impediment so he can be with Dorothea. But knowledge of his ancestry does not alleviate Will's predicament. Although he learns that his mother was honorable (she broke with her family when she discovered the criminal nature of the business Bulstrode eventually acquired by marriage), Will certainly does not find out that he is of noble birth—a frequent and convenient discovery in many stories, which allows two lovers separated by their stations in life to marry. Will's mother, it turns out, had run away and gone on the stage, a calling the Mrs. Cadwalladers of Middlemarch would hardly consider proper.

Besides the codicil's insinuations, there are serious financial difficulties separating Will and Dorothea. If she defies her husband's will and the provincial gossip by marrying Will Ladislaw, Dorothea will lose her first husband's considerable fortune. When Bulstrode learns of Will's connection to his past, he offers him a large sum of money as reparation for his past sins. The money Bulstrode offers Will would put an end to the financial difficulties preventing his marriage to Dorothea; but Ladislaw disdainfully and with moral repulsion refuses Bulstrode's offer. This scene of course provides a counterpoint to Lydgate's *acceptance* of Bulstrode's money, the last in a series of moral compromises that eventually results in the ambitious physician's demise. But in Will's refusal one can also sense George Eliot repudiating the kind of easy solution provided by a saving and implausible coincidence that, in a Dickens novel, would operate as a providential force, eventually making everything "turn out all right in the end."* To endorse such a resolution to Will and Dorothea's money problems would be to sanction a lack of initiative in the face of adversity, a lack chastened in the case of Fred Vincy's idle hopefulness that, somehow, his fortune would be made for him without effort or application. If Raffles's disclosure of Will's origins had become consequential, then I think Beaty's intolerance of the fact that Will's ancestry is one of the strands "wound into a triply coincidental and melodramatic plot" would be warranted. The Raffles-Ladislaw coincidence is a departure from the kind of realism summed up in George Eliot's description of her design for *Middlemarch*: "to show the gradual action of ordinary causes rather than exceptional, and to show this in some directions which have not been from time immemorial the beaten path."[11] But what is striking in George Eliot's treatment of such a "lapse" in realism is the way this coincidence itself departs from the conventions Dickens shamelessly exploited in his novels.

Peter K. Garrett observes in *The Victorian Multiplot Novel* that Raffles's association with Nicholas Bulstrode also echoes Dickens. He argues that the melodramatic aspects of the Raffles-Bulstrode subplot

should . . . be recognized as features of a mode which deliberately departs from the "natural" norms of domestic realism to pursue different purposes. As they do in Dickens, the contrivances of melodrama articulate the discontinuities and reversals of a life founded on the suppression of the past.

According to Garrett, Raffles is Bulstrode's "shabby double who parodies his rationalizing doctrines and revives his repressed guilt."[12] The return of Raffles to Stone Court, where he reacquaints himself

---

*The clearest example of providential coincidence in Dickens is certainly *Oliver Twist* (1837–39): it just so happens that all the people Oliver helps to rob (Mr. Brownlow early in the novel, the Maylies later on) turn out to be related to the orphan's mysterious origins (Mr. Brownlow was Oliver's father's best friend; Rose Maylie is his aunt). Oliver's compulsory criminal activities then providentially (and implausibly) make the cheery familial glow of the novel's happy ending possible. Although the later novels' use of coincidence is not so blatantly contrived, it frequently informs and helps to resolve their plots, as in the example from *Great Expectations* (1860–61) cited by Vargish.

with Bulstrode ("By Jove, Nick, it's you!" he exclaims all too famil-
iarly) is not explainable simply by the fact that Joshua Rigg, Raffles's
stepson, recently owned the estate. The reunion of the two men obeys
not just realistic but also psychological laws: the return of Raffles is
for Bulstrode the return of the repressed.

David Carroll first remarked the Dickensian quality of the bond
linking Raffles and Bulstrode in *"Middlemarch* and the Externality
of Fact," an insightful analysis of Raffles as a kind of doppelgänger
for Bulstrode. Carroll notes that their strange intimacy "brings us
close to the essential method of Dickens's later novels as two characters intimately tied together by exploitation seek their independence
through further exploitation." [13] I will eventually return to the uncanny doubleness that characterizes Raffles's relationship with Bulstrode. But first I hope to answer the question Alexander Welsh asks
but does not quite answer in *George Eliot and Blackmail* (which
provides the most detailed consideration of Raffles to date): "Who
or what does Raffles represent?" * For now, let it be noted that the
Raffles plot represents two major departures from George Eliot's
usual realistic mode, both of which have distinctive associations with
the work of Charles Dickens.† Moreover, one of these departures (the
inconsequential revelation of Will's antecedents) is notable for the
fact that it parodies Dickens's conventional use of coincidence as a
providential force that somewhat willfully makes everything turn out
all right in the end.‡

*Welsh, *George Eliot and Blackmail*, p. 245. This work examines Raffles's blackmail of Bulstrode in order to illuminate the growing Victorian "culture of information."

†Each of the critics discussed characterizes the exceptional mode of the Raffles-
Bulstrode story line differently: for Garrett (and Jerome Beaty) it is melodramatic,
for Carroll it is Gothic, and for Welsh it is sensational. Alexander Welsh remarks the
other critics' emphasis on the Dickensian tone of this part of the novel. As Audrey
Jaffe pointed out to me, even Raffles's *name* is Dickensian.

‡In fact, and contrary to Thomas Vargish's oversimplified account, Dickens—especially in the later novels—did not so completely endorse a providential outlook. As
Robert Newsom points out in *Dickens on the Romantic Side*, p. 20, for instance,
Bleak House (1852) highlights the element of chance in Chancery in a way that does
not so neatly conform to providential conventions. In "Chance and Design in *Bleak
House*," W. J. Harvey also makes some interesting points about chance and coincidence in that novel, though he does not actively distinguish them from the workings
of Providence. I nevertheless focus on George Eliot's treatment of chance because it
represents a more thorough and self-conscious break with the providential tradition
than anything that came before.

"A Bit of Ink and Paper"

George Eliot was invited to the centenary of Sir Walter Scott's birth, celebrated at Edinburgh on August 15, 1871. She originally accepted the invitation despite her aversion to such public appearances because she so venerated the novelist. "My worship for Scott is peculiar," she wrote to a Scottish admirer of her work; "I began to read him when I was seven years old, and afterwards when I was grown up and living alone with my father, I was able to make the evenings cheerful for him during the last five or six years of his life by reading aloud to him Scott's novels." [14] Marian Evans's relationship with her father during those last years of his life was often tense and confrontational—even for awhile what she called a "Holy War"—because she had come to reject the Evangelical religion in which she had been raised. When George Eliot was later asked what influence first unsettled her orthodox views, she replied, "Oh, Walter Scott's." * The rebellious daughter felt great satisfaction tending her father during his last days, finding a new peace in selflessly devoting herself to the ailing patriarch. But there might also have been some quiet aggression in her resignation, some self-assertion in her self-renunciation as she read aloud the novels that first prompted the reassessment of her religious faith to the father who condemned her apostasy. In his will Robert Evans left his set of Sir Walter Scott's novels, which Marian had read to him on his deathbed, not to her but to her half-sister. [15] Marian Evans eventually received a set of Scott's novels from the man she lived with for 24 years without benefit of marriage. On January 1, 1860, after the phenomenal success of *Adam Bede*, George Henry Lewes wrote on the flyleaf of the first of 48 volumes of Scott's novels: "To Marian Evans Lewes, The Best of Novelists, and Wives." [16] I mention this biographical incident in the first instance because it nicely illustrates how, by way of her engagement with literature, Marian Evans managed very shrewdly both to please and to defy patriarchal authority, and in the end get what she wanted. But further, I see the story of her father's will as informing the treatments of the two wills read in *Middlemarch*. At the end of this chapter I consider the effects

---

*Haight, *George Eliot*, p. 39. Haight speculates from her other recorded remarks about Scott that it was his sense of history in the novel that brought her to question her religious creed.

of these two wills as examples of the way chance can intervene and controvert the dictates of a patriarchal writing.

George Eliot did not attend the Scott centenary in Scotland after all. Shying away from the public festivities, she instead celebrated Scott's birthday by working quietly on *Middlemarch* and reading an article on the atomic theories of Epicurus and Lucretius.* George Eliot was at that time drafting Book IV of *Middlemarch*, in which the character John Raffles makes his first appearance in the novel.† I would therefore like to remark if not the historical then the allegorical significance of this moment in the evolution of English fiction: on the hundredth birthday of Sir Walter Scott, master of the historical novel, George Eliot read an article detailing the operations of the *clinamen*, the chance swerve in the Epicurean-Lucretian theory of atomic motion, at the time she was introducing a character into her own historical novel who represents a new understanding of chance and its effects in narrative. Raffles—the character, the name, the word—is the *clinamen* in George Eliot's most accomplished work of realism. The implications for the English novel of this coincidence of reading and writing on August 15, 1871, will be explored in the examination of Raffles that follows.

Mr. Borthrup Trumbull, the auctioneer of *Middlemarch*, knows very well how the power of speech can affect the value of things. "[K]eenly alive to his own jokes and sensible of his encyclopaedic knowledge," he distributes his articulate enthusiasm "on the equitable principle of praising those things most which were most in need of praise." [17] Mr. Trumbull employs rhetoric to increase the value of things; and his ability to assess things likewise increases the value of his rhetoric. Both personally and professionally, he enjoyed "estimating things at a high rate. He was an amateur of superior phrases, and never used poor language without immediately correcting him-

---

*Haight, *George Eliot*, p. 439. The article was probably Fleeming Jenkin's essay "The Atomic Theory of Lucretius," which appeared in *The North British Review* in June 1868. This article attempts to relate the classical atomists' theories to contemporary scientific discoveries (especially in chemistry) "now that men of science are beginning, after a long pause in the inquiry, once more eagerly to attempt some explanation of the ultimate constitution of matter" (p. 211).

†Jerome Beaty says the list of "private dates" in George Eliot's working notebook, which outlines among other plot developments the chronology of Raffles's appearance, "was probably drawn up in the spring or summer of 1871." See his *"Middlemarch" from Notebook to Novel*, p. 57.

self" (p. 303). Mr. Trumbull knows his own worth and takes delight in appreciating things: "[H]e was an admirer by nature, and would have liked to have the universe under his hammer, feeling that it would get a higher figure for his recommendation" (p. 591). There is a subtle pun on "figure" in this passage, a double meaning the auctioneer has already played on: a rhetorical question "is what we call a figure of speech—speech at a high figure as one may say" (p. 304). But it does not stop there; still another sense is added to the rhetorical and monetary senses of "figure." In the brief chapter where Trumbull presides over the auction of the Larcher estate, the word is used four times, three more or less in the double sense already mentioned and one in the description of the despicable John Raffles: "His large whiskers, imposing swagger, and swing of the leg, made him a striking figure" (p. 594).

The rhetorical, financial, and characterological cluster of meanings condensed in the word "figure" in Chapter 60 illuminates an earlier cryptic passage in which the narrator, not wanting to offend the reader, speaks of elevating a low subject: "[W]hatever has been or is to be narrated by me about low people, may be ennobled by being considered a parable" (p. 332). This follows "naturally" from the close of the preceding paragraph: "No soul was prophetic enough to have any foreboding as to what might appear on the trail of Joshua Rigg." Long before the actual appearance of Rigg's stepfather six chapters later, the narrator is here quite literally preoccupied with the figure of John Raffles. By invoking the rhetorical enhancement of a parable in anticipation of Raffles, the narrator engages in much the same kind of estimation and augmentation as does Trumbull when he "talks up" an item; and this increase in the figural worth of a figure in the novel is expressed in terms of an increased monetary value: "if any bad habits and ugly consequences are brought into view" in the novel's account of the low, base, and at this point still unnamed Raffles,

the reader may have the relief of regarding them as not more than figuratively ungenteel, and may feel himself virtually in company with persons of some style. Thus while I tell the truth about loobies, my reader's imagination need not be entirely excluded from an occupation with lords; and the petty sums which any bankrupt of high standing would be sorry to retire upon, may be lifted to the level of high commercial transactions by the inexpensive addition of proportional ciphers. (p. 332)

There is much going on here—a discreet author's apology (or parody thereof) to a sensitive Victorian audience for considering an unsavory character like Raffles, and the suggestion that Raffles might represent a political parable ("loobies," or clowns, can also refer to lords, and in the next paragraph the entire discussion is placed with great irony in the context of the first Reform Bill). The analogy suggests that Raffles's relative worth may be enhanced in the same way the numerical value of an integer may be increased by the arbitrary addition of so many zeroes. In the auction scene, rhetoric ("a figure of speech") and money (the "high figure" Trumbull achieves in a sale) are associated with the moral assessment of a character (the swaggering figure John Raffles). Likewise in the proleptic introduction to Raffles, the narrator's recourse to a rhetorical device (parable) elevates "petty sums . . . to the level of high commercial transactions" such that "low people" are "ennobled" and seem "of high moral rank" (p. 332); one need only add the requisite number of "proportional ciphers." But a cipher is not just a zero; it also suggests a puzzle or code, a way of transforming a text in order to conceal its meaning.

"Who shall tell what may be the effect of writing?" This question is posed immediately before Raffles is finally and actually introduced, by name, in Chapter 41 (p. 402). It is within the scope of this largely speculative question concerning "the effect of writing" that I will try to account for the narrator's apparent preoccupation with John Raffles. Deciphering the figure of Raffles will then help to clarify the value determinations governing the economy of chance in *Middlemarch*.

In the preamble to Raffles's first appearance in the novel, the narrator admits to being "uneasy" about this character. Just as the earlier ironic introduction to Raffles suggests that considering "low people" can be "ennobled by being considered a parable," so this introduction to Raffles opens with a "rather lofty comparison" that makes the narrator "less uneasy in calling attention to the existence of low people by whose interference, *however little we may like it*, the course of the world is very much determined" (p. 402, my emphasis). Both apologies for the narrative treatment of low people are witheringly ironic, but it is not at all clear at what or whom the irony is directed. Here is the "lofty comparison," quoted at length in order to remark the bizarre tone—an uneasy mixture of bombastic irony and scrupulous moral inquiry—which results when the narrator tries to inflate the value of a debased subject:

Who shall tell what may be the effect of writing? If it happens to have been cut in stone, though it lie face downmost for ages on a forsaken beach, or "rest quietly under the drums and tramplings of many conquests," it may end up by letting us into the secret of usurpations and other scandals gossiped about long empires ago:—this world being apparently a huge whispering-gallery. Such conditions are often minutely represented in our petty lifetimes. As the stone which has been kicked by generations of clowns may come by curious little links of effect under the eyes of a scholar, through whose labours it may at last fix the date of invasions and unlock religions, so a bit of ink and paper which has long been an innocent wrapping or stop-gap may at last be laid open under the one pair of eyes which have knowledge enough to turn it into the opening of a catastrophe. To Uriel watching the progress of planetary history from the Sun, the one result would be just as much of a coincidence as the other. (p. 402)

This is the narrator as auctioneer, working hard to attain a high figure for the worthless Raffles. The inflated rhetoric describing the broad sweep of historical forces "minutely represented in our petty life-times" is the verbal equivalent of the "proportional ciphers" that, when added to "petty sums," lift them to "the level of high commercial transactions" and make the Raffles narrative into a parable. Just what is the narrator trying to sell us with the figure of Raffles?

The "bit of ink and paper which has long been an innocent wrapping or stop-gap" refers to another and very different kind of chance attached to Raffles, one *essential* to the plotting of the novel: he happens to pick up a letter with Nicholas Bulstrode's signature on it while trying to wheedle money out of his stepson Joshua Rigg. The letter concerns Bulstrode's interest in buying the lands attached to Stone Court that Rigg recently inherited. It is only later that Raffles looks at the letter and realizes that his former associate is living a quite comfortable life in Middlemarch; he originally picks up the letter simply to stop a gap between his brandy bottle and leather flask.* In the narrator's lofty comparison, Raffles's eventual discovery of Bulstrode's letter is given the significance of the Rosetta Stone. In the most ex-

---

* Of course Raffles is eventually killed by brandy, administered by Bulstrode against doctor's orders. In a graduate seminar on George Eliot at U.C. Berkeley in the spring of 1983, Neil Hertz pointed out another moment in an Eliot story with this same peculiar proximity of writing and toxic intoxicants. In the "Janet's Repentance" story of *Scenes of Clerical Life* (1857), Janet is shakily practicing temperance when, looking for a letter in her husband's desk, she discovers instead a bottle of brandy in a hidden compartment. Hertz remarked, "She reaches for the letter and finds the spirits." And for Raffles the spirits killeth.

travagant conceit in *Middlemarch*, it is from Uriel's vantage point on the surface of the sun that this coincidence is seen as equivalent to a scholar's happening on a stone that deciphers history. The invocation of the all-seeing angel is the most extreme instance of the narrator's constant shift of attention and perspective in order to observe events adequately and objectively.* Not only is this petty coincidence expressed in the most elevated rhetorical terms, but Raffles's purloined letter gives rise to the most serious moral question for this earnest and conscientious writer: "Who shall tell what may be the effect of writing?"

It is a fluke, nothing more, that Raffles picks up the letter with Bulstrode's signature; but it has enormous consequences in the novel. Here then is an answer to Alexander Welsh's unanswered question, "Who or what does Raffles represent?" It is the throw of the dice, the impartial and casual coincidence that influences the course of events for good or ill, "however little we may like it," that the novel values with Raffles. His *name* is not a coincidence even if what he happens to represent is the principle of absolute chance. The Raffles figure denuded of all those proportional ciphers marks the "absolute zero" point (which, as in chemistry, is never reached) of narrative: Raffles is a parable for the unrestricted play of chance that is put to work as soon as it is named. He embodies and names the aleatory element in the plotting of a novel that becomes fateful the moment it is read.

At the auction of the Larcher estate, where Raffles enters the general society of Middlemarch, Mr. Trumbull puts up for bids "a collection of trifles" (p. 592). He offers for sale what he calls "an ingenious contrivance—a sort of practical rebus." Trumbull's attempt to achieve a high figure for this item again suggests the rhetorical enhancement the narrator of *Middlemarch* undertakes with respect to the enciphered figure John Raffles. Here is the auctioneer's description of this practical rebus: "[Y]ou see, it looks like an elegant heart-shaped box, portable—for the pocket"; a portable heart that is also a container. "[T]here again, it becomes like a splendid double flower—an ornament for the table"; not so practical now, "an orna-

---

*This recurring concern is illustrated for instance at the beginning of Chapter 40: "In watching effects, if only of an electric battery, it is often necessary to change our place and examine a particular mixture or group at some distance from the point where the movement we are interested in was set up. The group I am moving towards is at Caleb Garth's breakfast table" (p. 389).

ment," and not portable either, "for the table"—it now belongs in a domestic setting. " '[A]nd now'—Mr. Trumbull allowed the double flower to fall alarmingly into strings of heart-shaped leaves—'a book of riddles! No less than five hundred printed in a beautiful red' " (p. 592). From box to double flower to strings of riddles: from singularity to duplicity to multiplicity. "This ingenious article itself . . . ought alone to give a high price to the lot," Mr. Trumbull says appraisingly. The auctioneer's peculiar but practical rebus articulates a classical *mise en abyme* structure in and for *Middlemarch*. The realistic account of its display and sale itself describes the procedure, even provides a motto for George Eliot's metonymic realism: "rebus" is the ablative plural of the Latin word for "thing" (*res*); it means "by way of things." Trumbull's ingenious contrivance provides a model for the diacritical production of a realist text the results of which George Eliot understandably finds disturbing: this practical rebus exfoliates "alarmingly" into "a book of riddles!"

"A Providential Thing"

The enciphered figure named Raffles represents a parable for the impartial operations of chance in a realist text. Consider the other parable, the famous parable, of *Middlemarch*: place a candle in front of a pier glass, the narrator informs us, and the scratches on its surface "going everywhere impartially" will "seem to arrange themselves in a fine series of concentric circles round that little sun."

These things are a parable. The scratches are events, and the candle is the egoism of any person now absent—of Miss Vincy, for example. Rosamund had a Providence of her own who had kindly made her more charming than other girls, and who seemed to have arranged Fred's illness and Mr. Wrench's mistake in order to bring her and Lydgate within effective proximity. (p. 258)

This parable, which lifts "ugly furniture . . . into the serene light of science," injects a scathing irony into the traditional theological account of chance (it is only the sign of a Providence we cannot comprehend) by suggesting that it is merely egoism that transforms chance marks and events "going everywhere impartially" into a heliocentric Providence.

One would be hard-pressed to find a character in *Middlemarch* whose faith in Providence is untinged by the kind of self-interest illustrated in this parable. Mr. Farebrother is probably the least egoistical of the Middlemarchers, but the actions and preachings of the worldly vicar who plays cards for money betray no belief in a providential force in the world. When Mr. Casaubon considers Providence it is in complacent satisfaction of his fulfilled needs: "he was liable to think that others were providentially made for him" (p. 83); "Providence, in its kindness, had supplied him with the wife he needed" (p. 272). To find an unselfish and truly devout faith in Providence in a George Eliot novel one must go outside *Middlemarch*, either back to the followers of Savonarola in *Romola* (1863) or forward to Mordecai in *Daniel Deronda* (1874–76). "Back" and "forward" refer not simply to the chronology of George Eliot's works but to the temporal distance that seems to be necessary for the representation of a genuine providential faith in either the Renaissance past or the Zionist future.

Of course, the character in *Middlemarch* for whom self-interest and a faith in Providence are indistinguishable is Nicholas Bulstrode. For the money-and-power-hungry banker, the Protestant ethic and the spirit of capitalism coincide in the convenient conviction that he is chosen by God; his wealth and respectability are then simply the dispensations of a personal Providence.* Bulstrode is sincere in his belief, "[f]or the egoism which enters into our theories does not affect their sincerity; rather, the more our egoism is satisfied, the more robust is our belief" (p. 511). Bulstrode's faith in a self-serving Providence is mentioned several times immediately before his acquaintance with Raffles is renewed. Then his "old friend" throws the word back in his face: "I'm not so surprised at seeing you, old fellow," Raffles tells him, "because I picked up a letter—what you may call a providential thing" (pp. 512–13).† Raffles too is adept at turning chance scratches into Providence.

---

*The allusion to Max Weber is made by David Carroll in "*Middlemarch* and the Externality of Fact," p. 79, where he discusses how Bulstrode's capitalism intersects with his providentialism. An example: At the Larcher sale, where Trumbull auctions off the "practical rebus," Will Ladislaw bids on and buys a painting for Bulstrode. The painting, *Supper at Emmaus*, depicts a biblical scene in which the resurrected Christ appears to some disciples. As usual, Bulstrode is willing and anxious to *buy* revelation. The way the purchase of this painting comments on Bulstrode's acquisitive and proprietary religiosity is an instance of George Eliot's famous ability to use cultural references as condensed commentary on the actions of the story—narrative "by way of things."

†Peter K. Garrett also mentions the implicit rebuke in Raffles's remark in an illuminating discussion of Providence in the novel. See *Victorian Multiplot Novel*, pp. 160–61.

On the two occasions in *Middlemarch* that George Eliot becomes parabolic—a narrative device usually associated with religious teaching—she does so in order to expose the egoistic rationalizations of providential thinking. Her general critique of the providential frame of mind finds its most sustained and devastating expression in the confrontation of Bulstrode's hypocritical Evangelicalism with John Raffles, who, as I have suggested, works as a parable for the impartial operations of chance. Insofar as Bulstrode and Raffles "stand for" Providence and chance then, the dynamic between the two characters enacts the epistemic destabilization of Providence I am locating in the innovative representation of chance in *Middlemarch*. When Will Ladislaw first sees Raffles, he thinks he might be "one of those political parasitic insects of the bloated kind" (p. 595); Raffles himself, when asking his stepson to finance his tobacco business, says, "I should stick to it like a flea to a fleece" (p. 404). Raffles is indeed a parasite, and Bulstrode is his grudging host. Chance is always a parasite in relation to the operant frame of power-knowledge, both deriving its existence from and occupying a position of exteriority to the metaphysical system it is defined by and against.*

The agency of chance exposes the fact that providential thinking is imbued with egoism. It is this dynamic that I think explains the uncanny and corrosive bond linking the two characters: Raffles is the walking, talking—or more accurately, the swaggering, blustering— embodiment of Bulstrode's egoism writ large. At their first encounter, Bulstrode has come to Stone Court to look over the estate he has recently acquired from Joshua Rigg. The upwardly mobile banker is about to enter the ranks of the landed gentry. But there is an impediment partially occluding his proprietary gaze: to "Mr. Bulstrode's eyes" Raffles seems "an ugly black spot on the landscape at Stone Court" (p. 520). This image repeats an earlier visual metaphor attached to Mr. Casaubon: "Will not a tiny speck very close to our vision blot out the glory of the world, and leave only a margin by which we see the blot? I know of no speck so troublesome as self" (p. 409). In "Recognizing Casaubon," Neil Hertz examines the way "blot" and "margin" in this optic image for a kind of egoism con-

---

*For an interesting discussion of the parasite, see Michel Serres, *The Parasite*. Serres's exploration of the way the parasite forces a simple system to a higher level of complexity in order to absorb it is pertinent to my account of the way chance affects narrative forms.

jure up a secondary association with, respectively, ink and paper.[18]
The "bit of ink and paper" with Bulstrode's signature brings Raffles
back to Stone Court, where he becomes the objectified embodiment
of Bulstrode's egoism; Raffles is in Bulstrode's eyes a specular speck
and a very troublesome self.

Neil Hertz traces in his essay an interesting conjunction evident
in George Eliot's earliest letters: "Typically, apologies for what she
fears may seem like egotism are accompanied by apologies for her
handwriting."[19] Illegible scribbles are frequently linked with self-
centeredness in *Middlemarch*, most notably in reference to the handwriting of the prodigal and egocentric Fred Vincy. In Fred's script,
"the vowels were all alike and the consonants only distinguishable as
turning up or down, the strokes had a blotty solidity and the letters
disdained to keep the line" (p. 552).* The progress of Fred's moral
reformation can be charted by the way he and his handwriting are
brought into line. Under the tutelage of the Garth family he eventually
learns to resolve and apply himself: "He had been working heartily
for six months at all outdoor occupations under Mr. Garth, and by
dint of severe practice had nearly mastered the defects of his handwriting" (p. 659). When Caleb Garth first sees Fred's illegible scrawl
(thought to be the sign of a gentleman at the time, the narrator says),
he is appalled at Fred's willingness to obstruct "business" by "sending
puzzles over the country" (p. 553). There is an associative chain linking George Eliot's assured chastisements of characters' egoism with
her more anxious treatment of the "alarmingly" exfoliating practical rebus and her admitted uneasiness about John Raffles. Blotted
vision: blotted handwriting: illegible puzzles: a rebus of scripted
riddles: a ciphered figure. The apparent opacity and equivocality of
the elements in this series are in each case tokens of a condemnable
self-centeredness. Why and how the diacritical operations of a realist
text figured by the practical rebus might be imbued with egoism will
be examined shortly. There is, however, another anxiety attached to
handwriting, an anxiety implicit in the uses Raffles makes of his stop-
gap. If one's signature *is* legible, as Bulstrode's eventually is under
the eyes of Raffles, then one becomes available for appropriation in
some very disturbing ways.

---

*What this amorphous script apparently needs is differentiation—in the Dar-
winian, not the deconstructive, sense.

The Economy of Chance

There is both a centripetal and a centrifugal significance to John Raffles's presence in *Middlemarch*. The *inclusion* of a character whose name and effects suggest an aleatory agency aligns Raffles with George Eliot's realist project. Her dedication to realism in the novel included in its agenda the representation of the lower as well as the upper social classes and resolutely refrained from flattering and comforting the complacent novel reader with a depiction of reality that conformed to her or his (usually literary) expectations; Raffles is one of those "low people" who determine the course of the world "however little we may like it." The lapses in Eliot's usual realistic practice that I have already examined give the Raffles subplot a distinctively Dickensian tone. As early as her article "The Natural History of German Life," George Eliot articulated her realist aesthetic by both deferring to and differing with Charles Dickens.* George Levine argues in *The Realistic Imagination* that realism progresses by successive writers' incorporating and parodying a discredited literary mode; it is out of this ongoing recognition and rejection of novelistic conventions that a new sense of the real is imagined. As unrealistic as some aspects of Raffles's appearance in the novel may seem, the character provides a parodic critique of Dickens's conventional use of providential coincidence (in the story of Will's origins, which does not count as plot); and Raffles's appropriation of Bulstrode's letter represents an alternative, comparatively realistic kind of coincidence essential to the plotting of *Middlemarch* that is arbitrary, unmotivated, and simply a matter of chance.

The centrifugal importance of Raffles—his eventual and violent *expulsion* from the novel—indicates how uneasy George Eliot is with this character and what he represents. Raffles is poisoned (with Bulstrode's help) by his excessive taste for brandy; the "wild card" is tamed and discarded in the final deal. In "Recognizing Casaubon," Neil Hertz considers how Mr. Casaubon is "cast out" of the novel insofar as he is "a quasi-allegorical figure, the personification of the

---

*The article appeared in *Westminster Review* in July 1856; two months later she began her first work of fiction. In the article, she observes: "We have one great novelist who is gifted with the utmost power of rendering the external traits of our town population." She then goes on to criticize Dickens's lack of psychological penetration. In *Essays by George Eliot*, pp. 266–99; quotation from p. 271.

dead letter, the written word," and as well "the personification of the narcissistic imagination." [20] Along similar lines, I would now like to consider why and how Raffles is also cast out of the novel insofar as he is a parabolic personification of chance in *Middlemarch*.

In "Determinism and Responsibility in the Works of George Eliot," George Levine observes, "In *Daniel Deronda* and *Middlemarch* 'chance' becomes a dominant theme"; he mentions Gwendolen Harleth at the gambling table in *Deronda*'s opening scene and Lydgate's feverish gambling at billiards in *Middlemarch*.* "In less obvious ways [chance] appears in all her novels and is always associated with evil. 'Favourable Chance,' she says in *Silas Marner*, 'is the god of all men who follow their own devices instead of obeying a law they believe in.' " [21] Worshipping the god of Chance is just as reprehensible as invoking a self-serving view of Providence; George Eliot's use of Raffles as Bulstrode's double to make explicit the latter's egoism then is certainly not an example of the author's championing of Chance and its operations over and against the hypocritical Providence she criticizes. George Eliot's high-minded moral sensibility can find nothing good to say about Chance or about the debased John Raffles.

The two passages that anticipate and apologize for Raffles's appearance in the novel indicate that this character has something to do with the problematic status of history in *Middlemarch*. At the beginning of Chapter 41, the two discoveries (of the cryptic stone and of Bulstrode's letter) are coincidences of equal merit to Uriel in his impartial observation of "the progress of planetary history"; and at the end of Chapter 35, the justification by parable for introducing "a low subject," the narrator ironically observes: "As to any provincial history in which the agents are all of high moral rank, that must be of a date long posterior to the first Reform Bill" (p. 332). What part then does Raffles play in "the progress of planetary history" depicted in "the provincial history" that is *Middlemarch*?

In his essay "Narrative and History," J. Hillis Miller undertakes a deconstruction of Hegel's metaphysical notion of history as it operates in *Middlemarch*:

For those who have the eyes to see it, *Middlemarch* is an example of a work of fiction which not only exposes the metaphysical system of history but also

---

*Fred Vincy is also in the billiard room, which is a sign of his recidivism. In the original plan for the novel, Lydgate was to see Raffles there as well. See Beaty, *"Middlemarch" from Notebook to Novel*, p. 80.

proposes an alternative consonant with those of Nietzsche and Benjamin. . . . George Eliot . . . proposes a view of the writing of history as an act of repetition in which the present takes possession of the past and liberates it for a present purpose, thereby exploding the continuum.*

It is easy to see how Raffles operates by the principles of this "alternative" sense of history. Both in the way he makes use of documents (to fill the gap between his brandy bottle and flask) and the way he profits from his knowledge of the past (he extorts as much money and malicious pleasure out of Bulstrode as he can), Raffles is the negative image of a historical method that "takes possession of the past and liberates it for a present purpose." Raffles does not simply report the past and its arbitrary coincidences; he exploits them. The narrator therefore indicts Raffles's peevish self-interest: imagine what account of the spectacle of history would come from this character "who would aim at being noticeable even at a show of fireworks, regarding his own remarks on any other person's performance as likely to be more interesting than the performance itself" (p. 404). George Eliot criticizes through her characterization of Raffles an approach to history that Miller celebrates in his deconstructive reading; but the narrator remains uneasy about this character who raises questions about "the effect of writing" in a realistic narrative that purports to be history.

It is remarkable that there is no plea for sympathy or understanding for Raffles in this famously sympathetic novel, as there is for every other character (with the possible exception of the miser Peter Featherstone). For the narrator it is only in explicitly rhetorical terms—an enciphered parable—that Raffles acquires any substantial value. The economy at work in relation to Raffles is what Neil Hertz calls "an economy of anxiety," which shakily negotiates the commerce between a novelistic character understood as a moral agent, an ethically stable self, and "the somewhat less reassuring figure of a focus of semiotic energy."[22] A figure such as Raffles, a sign for the absolutely casual and purely accidental possibilities in a text, can-

---

*J. Hillis Miller, "Narrative and History," p. 471. Miller begins his essay by quoting an observation by Nietzsche about Hegel's understanding of history that is relevant to this discussion as well: "Hegel says: 'That at the bottom of history, and particularly of world history, there is a final aim, and that this has actually been realized in it and is being realized—the plan of Providence—that there is *reason* in history.'" From *Portable Nietzsche*, pp. 39–40; quoted by Miller in "Narrative and History," p. 455.

not be given free play in this most moral of novels when deciphering that figure reveals the arbitrary and self-interested nature of writing a history like *Middlemarch*. John Raffles is stigmatized and ejected from the novel not just because he is a nasty and self-indulgent scapegrace (though he is certainly that) but also because he is a scapegoat for the disconcerting aspects of chance that threaten to disrupt the moral economy of George Eliot's fiction. Raffles delights in irritating others, and his presence in the novel works like an irritant that cannot quite be dissolved by the narrator's caustic irony or assimilated to the stable, edifying, morally bracing system of values upholding Eliot's doctrine of sympathy. To extend sympathy to Raffles would reveal that he has his own narrative and his own history to tell, a story of intoxicating chances the sober novelist cannot endorse or altogether accommodate. Speaking rhetorically, Raffles may be elevated to the level of high commercial transactions; but on strictly moral grounds, he is devalued and condemned. Without sympathy.

Felix (Mea Culpa) Holt

The interest in chance that emerges in George Eliot's later fiction problematizes the idea of origins, which fascinated her Victorian contemporaries. Efforts to locate the source of the Nile, the etymologies of *The Oxford English Dictionary*, and so many novels (not all of them written by Dickens) that reveal the birth and background of an orphan with a mysterious past are all aspects of this Victorian preoccupation with the discovery of origins. As many commentators have pointed out, *Middlemarch* critiques a holistic and all-encompassing fantasy of origins in the researches of Casaubon and Lydgate. Casaubon's "Key to All Mythologies" and Lydgate's attempt to isolate "the primitive tissue" represent a deluded effort to find some originary substratum, a single source that unifies and integrates the manifold diversity of cultural or physiological phenomena. George Eliot's own treatment of the question of origins in her later work has strong affinities with Darwin's *The Origin of Species*, which, despite its title (and Darwin's own demurrals), is concerned less with the idea of primal origins than with the influence of chance variations on historical process.* In the narrator's orotund reflections about

---

*See Beer, *Darwin's Plots*, p. 194. Beer also mentions how prevalent the word "origin" and the idea of origins were in other areas of scientific inquiry at the time Eliot was writing.

Raffles's discovery of the letter in his brandy flask, the effects of this minute chance occurrence are placed in relation to the catastrophic convulsions of history (conquests, usurpations, invasions). Raffles is the character who knows all and tells more about Bulstrode's socio-economic and Will Ladislaw's familial origins. His acquisition of Bulstrode's letter is called "the opening of a catastrophe"; the novel's careful analysis of causal sequence traces the narrative origins of its major crisis to a first cause, the fortuitous and self-interested pilfering of someone else's writing.

In *Silas Marner*, the drawing of the lots that begins the story and so confounds its protagonist is never adequately explained. Near the end of the novel, Silas returns to Lantern Yard, his former home from which he was ostracized, hoping that the preacher there, "a man with a deal o' light," might clarify that mystery.[23] But coming full circle to supposed biographical (and novelistic) origins for final clarification yields no answers: Silas finds his way back to the right place but discovers that Lantern Yard has been replaced by a large factory; industrial progress has brought about the extinction of his former way of life. The "light" of Lantern Yard offers no illumination: "It's dark to me," Silas says about "the drawing o' the lots"; "I doubt it'll be dark to the last."[24] The origin has been effaced, and all that remains in its place are the tenebrous operations of the lottery.

The most pronounced and profound questioning of the idea of novelistic origins in Eliot's work is presented at the beginning of *Daniel Deronda*. The epigraph to the first chapter discusses "the make-believe of a beginning" (in science as much as in literature), concluding, "No retrospect will take us to the beginning." The novel proper then begins with—and never forgets—Daniel Deronda's first meeting with Gwendolen Harleth as she plays roulette at the gambling table. The self-consciously remarked arbitrariness of the novel's beginning depicts a chance encounter and takes place against the background of a game of chance. Gwendolen is excited by the play, betting extravagantly on the red and the black, the even and the odd, while Deronda's judgmental observation of her is bent on making *moral* differentiations. The first lines of the novel give us Deronda's view of Gwendolen: "Was she beautiful or not beautiful? and what was the secret of form or expression which gave the dynamic quality to her glance? Was the good or the evil genius dominant in those beams? Probably the evil; else why was the effect that of unrest rather than of undisturbed charm?"[25] The opening of *Daniel Deronda* dramatizes its own inescapably problematic and chance-laden (problematic *because* chance-laden) narrative origins; and with Deronda's efforts to distinguish between good and evil in Gwendolen's appearance, the process of moralizing the play of chance is under way. The gambler's economy of chance is condemned on moral grounds because, as Deronda says, "our gain is another's loss."[26] The novel is haunted by the possibility that the kind of moral distinctions it wants to make might be just as arbitrary as the distinction between the red and the black, the even and the odd of the roulette table. With Deronda's (and the novel's) persistent condemnation of all forms of gambling, George Eliot indicts the operations of chance that make the story possible in the first place.*

If, as George Levine claims, chance "is always associated with evil" in George Eliot's novels, it is a *necessary* evil in the narrative operations of those novels. A character's "lot" becomes "plot," and the various loci of chance (lotteries, billiard rooms, gaming tables) simply represent the fated machinations of narrative. Peter K. Garrett remarks about the parable of the pier glass in *Middlemarch*: "Certainly the model of the pier-glass is misleading in one respect, for while actual events, like the scratches, may be 'going everywhere impartially,' the events of a novel are always purposeful." In the plotting of the novel, Garrett observes, "George Eliot becomes the 'Providence' her irony attempts to dissolve."[27] Insofar as George Eliot is implicated in her own critique of Providence then, Raffles—as he is for Bulstrode—is a "black spot on the landscape" in the novelist's "panoramic view of provincial life."† The persistent parasite is a disturbing reminder of the self-interest informing the authorial dispensations of Providence.[28]

A typographical error in the Penguin edition of *Felix Holt* provides a revealing example of the way chance can intervene and call

---

*A thorough analysis that would do anything like justice to the many forms of chance in *Daniel Deronda* would lead me too far afield here. I should point out, however, that the novel's many coincidences (especially those linking Deronda with his Jewish ancestry and calling) that might seem to represent a regressive providential reclamation of chance are really doing something very different. The use Eliot makes of the Jewish plot is not exactly a reversion to a theological frame of reference; instead, it figures a relation to, and a vocation in, a transpersonal cultural tradition the transcendence of which is temporal—i.e., *the future*—rather than supernatural.

†George Eliot's description of the scope of *Middlemarch*, in Eliot, *Letters*, vol. 5, p. 241.

attention to the author's informing self-interest. In the correct version of this passage, the lawyer Matthew Jermyn is thinking with some trepidation of the possibility that Harold Transome might learn that Esther Lyon is the legal claimant to the family estate: "Not only would Harold Transome be no longer afraid of him [Jermyn], but also, by marrying Esther (and Jermyn at once felt sure of this issue), *he would be triumphantly freed from any unpleasant consequences*, and could pursue much at his ease the gratification of ruining Matthew Jermyn." [29] In the Penguin edition, the word "any" in the italicized phrase has been printed as "my"—an understandable confusion, especially if there were a speck in the printer's eye. [30] Imagine George Eliot saying that a character in her novel "would be triumphantly freed from *my* unpleasant consequences"! In a way different from Raffles's stop-gap, a letter has by chance gone astray in this typographical mistake, which for a moment exposes the author's active and self-interested involvement in the disposition of narrative events. Of course, a printer's error is simply a fluke and does not itself constitute an argument about how chance can affect our reading of a text. As George Eliot would say, this is a parable.

The disconcerting aspects of chance do not simply go away when we shift our attention from divine to authorial agency. Consider the passage from Feuerbach quoted earlier from this perspective: not the divine but the authorial will,

which, on incomprehensible grounds, for incomprehensible reasons, that is, speaking plainly, out of groundless, absolute arbitrariness, out of . . . [authorial] caprice, as it were, determines or predestines some to evil and misery, others to good and happiness, has not a single positive characteristic to distinguish it from the power of chance.

Middlemarch articulates a devastating critique of Providence; but the divine will, once it has been discredited, is not simply or necessarily supplanted by a more resilient and efficacious authorial will. There is more going on than the simple transfer of power and authority from God to novelist in *Middlemarch*'s thematization of chance. George Eliot is anxious about Raffles, but not just because this figure, as a narcissistic projection of her own narcissism, might show up her own "spots of commonness" (p. 147) in the form of a blinding egoism. Such egoism at least has a place and ethical value in a moral universe. But the agency that in George Eliot's novels "determines or predestines some to evil and misery, others to good and happiness," might just be the casual results of so many raffles; a deciphered Raffles then might really, simply, effectively represent *chance*, which is not so easily given a moral valence, and which has disturbing implications for the authorial as much as for the divine will.

Neil Hertz notes that George Eliot's anxiety about her narcissistic preoccupation with "self" in her writing both reveals and conceals a deeper anxiety about writing:

[T]he dislocation implicit in narcissism, the doubling of the self into an eye and an image, an eye and a blot, is a more manageable and comforting fiction than the more open and indeterminate self-dispersion associated with a plurality of signs or with the plurality of interpretations that writing can provoke.[31]

Just as writing discomposes the notion of a stable and integrated ethical self, so chance problematizes that self's ability to exercise a concerted will, however arbitrarily.

The disparity between the intentions and the outcomes of the two documentary wills read in *Middlemarch* demonstrates in general that when the will is expressed in and as writing it can generate unforeseeable effects. Peter Featherstone's will is designed to thwart the expectations of his relatives (including Fred Vincy), and Mr. Casaubon's will is designed to thwart his widow's desire to marry Will Ladislaw. But these vexing intentions are themselves thwarted. Joshua Rigg turns right around and sells Stone Court to Bulstrode rather than staying on as a living and illegitimate reminder of Featherstone's malice; then, in an effort to do a service for his wife's family after his disgrace, Bulstrode turns the management of the estate over to Fred. And rather than capitulate to the law of "the dead father" as it is laid down in Casaubon's will, Dorothea instead submits to another will and another kind of law, Will Ladislaw. Rather as Marian Evans's father was thwarted when she, in her errant way, managed to acquire a set of Sir Walter Scott's novels in spite of his spiteful will, the patriarchal authority transmitted by Featherstone's and Casaubon's wills is interrupted and thwarted by unexpected happenstance.

More specifically, and for George Eliot more disturbingly, the disconcerting way that chance can diffract a writer's will is figured in *Middlemarch* by Raffles's appropriation of Bulstrode's letter, which he puts to his own peculiar uses. Who shall tell what may be the effect of writing when chance can intervene and redirect its itinerary? Chance problematizes not just the origins of writing but also its destination. The purloined letter in *Middlemarch* indicates that writing, any writing, can be taken places and used for purposes over which the writer no longer has control.* Once chance is parasitically lodged in the notion of Providence, a text becomes legible in ways the authorial will could never predict or foresee.

Mr. Trumbull allowed the double flower "to fall alarmingly" into a string of five hundred scripted riddles. The lot containing this "ingenious contrivance" was finally knocked down at a guinea to "Mr. Spilkins," a young man of the neighborhood with a taste for riddles but no sense of economy; he "was reckless with his pocket money and felt his want of memory for riddles" (p. 593).† When all the bids are in, chances are that George Eliot's own estimation of this "practical rebus" is based on the singular fact that the plurality of riddles folds neatly back into its original form, a practical and portable heart-shaped box.

George Eliot's treatment of chance both constitutes a sustained critique of the providential tradition in the novel and represents a disturbing challenge to the operations of a realist aesthetic that purports to narrate history with scientific yet sympathetic detachment. Following Eliot's lead, most of the versions of realism, and especially naturalism, practiced in the latter part of the nineteenth century likewise rejected a providential order to the world, more often than not in the name of an applied Darwinism. Lillian R. Furst and Peter N. Skrine comment in *Naturalism*, a helpful overview of that literary movement, "In the development of Naturalism Darwin's theory is without doubt the most important single shaping factor." [32]

The naturalist novel is an important intermediary narrative form poised between George Eliot's and Joseph Conrad's treatments of chance.‡ I will not be examining specific works of naturalism in this study since my analysis of chance and the modern British novel has

---

*The debate between Jacques Lacan and Jacques Derrida about the effects of chance on the itinerary and destination of the letter in Edgar Allan Poe's "The Purloined Letter" will be considered in the next chapter.

†A wonderful name, "Spilkins"; one might almost say it is the name of dissemination.

‡For an abbreviated account of the role chance played in the transition from the Victorian to the modern novel, see the Appendix to this volume. The analyses of chance in the work of Thomas Hardy and Henry James consider more fully some of the changes in novelistic narrative that developed between Eliot and Conrad.

little to contribute to the lively critical discussions about that literary movement and the works it produced.[33] I only mean here briefly to position that movement and its general program for the novel in relation to the ongoing history of chance. George Eliot's later fiction affirms chance in contradistinction to the prevalent providentialist view, but finally denies chance in moral terms. In its adoption of Darwinian principles (the human has its basis in the animal world; existence is a constant struggle that only the fittest survive), naturalism not only rejected a providential worldview but also called into question the moralism of the Victorian novel. Ethical action and moral choice as George Eliot understood them are for the most part inconsequential in a world governed by impersonal and inexorable social, economic, and biological forces. Furst and Skrine observe:

[T]o the Naturalists man is an animal whose course is determined by his heredity, by the effects of his environment and by the pressures of the moment. This terribly depressing conception robs man of all free will, all responsibility for his actions, which are merely the inescapable result of forces and conditions totally beyond his control.[34]

There is no providential or moral order governing human action and experience, only the implacable workings of natural law. It is the naturalist novelist's duty to describe the workings of those laws impartially, observing and recording the determining effects of the initially random mixture of character and circumstance with scientific detachment and precision. The naturalist novel describes a world governed by scientific principles, adopts a scientific methodology in the novel's approach to its materials, and organizes narrative experience according to a scientific determinism that (but for the initial collocation of birth, temperament, and milieu) leaves no room for chance.

Reacting against the scientism of his time, especially as it materialized in the narrative practices of the naturalist novel, Joseph Conrad used the idea of chance in his novel of that name to challenge such a novelistic version of scientific determinism. In doing so, however, he found that his own writing was subject to a kind of *aesthetic* determinism to which it must inevitably capitulate. As I will show in relation to Conrad's novel, it is in the nature of any narrative finally to do away with chance. This is the case, and in a profoundly emblematic way, even when the narrative in question is explicitly about and literally called *Chance*.

CHAPTER THREE

Playing Old Maid:
Chance and the Proper Name

Just before Joseph Conrad signed on to the English ship the *Mavis*, the first step in his career as a sailor, he apparently reached a state of hopeless desperation. He was just twenty years old and deeply in debt. He tried to recoup his losses in one last gambling binge, but to no avail. Sometime in February 1878, Conrad attempted suicide, shooting himself in the chest. The bullet just missed his heart. Frederick R. Karl, in his biography *Joseph Conrad: The Three Lives*, offers some interesting speculations about this crucial incident in the writer's life:

In a larger sense, Conrad had "gambled" with his life, and his mounting debts were an outward sign of his failure; having tested out fate (his fate) and "lady luck," he had lost. The sole way to expiate his guilt was through the suicidal act. None of this, of course, can be definitive, nor is it intended to be, since we have such sketchy evidence. It is an attempt to find some consistency in an act of Conrad's early life which has no equal later, unless we choose to see his decision to write as itself an act of gambling and the endless sheets of white paper he faced each day as a quotidian equivalent of suicide.[1]

The gamble that finally paid off, relieving Conrad of the pressing and depressing financial instability that plagued him for most of his life, was the writing of a novel about a lucky survivor of suicidal urges whose life is transformed by going to sea, the phenomenally successful *Chance* (1913).

"The Sacrosanct Fetish of Today"

The experience of chance is necessarily dependent on the perspective of an observer, as George Eliot's treatment of Raffles's purloined letter makes clear. The narrative of *Middlemarch* goes to great lengths—to the surface of the sun, in fact, by invoking the angel Uriel—in order impartially to observe the effects of Raffles's aleatory appropriation of someone else's writing. George Eliot's recourse, albeit ironic, to a Miltonic perspective to depict this moment in "the progress of planetary history" registers the residual influence of the providential view of chance in the narrative practices of *Middlemarch*. The all-seeing, omniscient, omnipotent, and omnipresent narrator of the Victorian novel occupies a deistic position in relation to which narrative events never happen by chance. The etymological sense of "chance" and its cognates as a *falling* suggests in general the importance of the observer's perspective: the fall implies a position and a situation, a horizon of experience and a horizontality into which the vertical movement of the chance occurrence falls unexpectedly.[2] The abandonment of a god's-eye view of narrative events and the increasing concern with perspective in the post-Victorian novel therefore provides a helpful index to the influence of the concept of chance upon modernist narrative forms.

The theory and practice of novel writing developed by Henry James, for instance, programmatically defined a novelistic method structured by perspectival concerns.[*] The emphasis on characterological point of view in James's novels and their prefaces dispensed with the Victorian novel's panoramic and panoptic view of things; James's fiction instead presents narrative material for the most part shaped and limited by a particular character's psychological and perceptual frame of reference.[†] Of all Joseph Conrad's novels, *Chance* has prompted the most frequent comparisons with James's technique, starting with that of Henry James himself.[‡] He wrote of *Chance* that it is "a really supreme example of the part playable in a novel by the source of interest, the principle of provision attended to, for which we claim importance."[3] *Chance* thematizes (in a particularly vexed and intricate way) the importance of what James calls "the source of interest," the point of view that forms and informs narrative material.

The convoluted narrative structure of *Chance* (the difficulties of

[*]For a discussion of the role of chance in James's formal aesthetic, see the Appendix at the end of this volume.

[†]*Theory of Fiction: Henry James* provides a helpful compilation of James's reflections on the theory of the novel. On James's idea of characterological perspective, see chap. 12, "Point of View," pp. 234–56.

[‡]Elsa Nettels discusses *Chance*'s affinities with James's narrative method and mentions critics' tendency to connect them in *James and Conrad*, p. 21.

which James thought were "wantonly invoked")[4] both furthers and fragments the Jamesian obsession with perspective. The novel is a mosaic of reported observations, each from a limited perspective and colored by the observer's ignorance or preconceptions, which are pieced together and presented to an anonymous narrator by Marlow. Time and again, the reader is told that both the narrated events and the event of narration occurred *by chance*. The narrative form that accommodates such a representation of chance in the novel is marked by one of the most striking disjunctions between *fabula* and *sujet* in English fiction.* Like most of Conrad's novels, which are justly famous for their exploration of narrative technique, *Chance* is "about" narrative, and specifically about the problem of chance in narrative.

Chance is of course about chance; but a more obvious and emblematic example of the way chance affects Conradian narrative, with important consequences for what we have come to think of as modernist aesthetics, might better illustrate the broader context for the issues raised in and by this novel. In Conrad's *The Secret Agent* (1907), Stevie, an idiot boy, is for sinister political reasons and in complete ignorance sent to blow up Greenwich Royal Observatory (which marks the first meridian and supplies the standard for exact clock time and geographical space). Bombing the Royal Observatory is an act of political terrorism directed against what the terrorist mastermind calls "the sacrosanct fetish of today"[5]—*science*; and in the history of the novel, the cataclysmic explosion can be seen as an assault on the scientific grid of time and space that has tended to organize narrative experience since Aristotle. Stevie does not make it to the Observatory, though: chance intervenes. He trips *en route* and is blown to pieces.† The time frame of the novel then comes unstuck as the narrative jumps back and forth in time and, less obtrusively, from place to place. These disruptions in temporal and spatial continuity break the novel up into discrete fragments, the narrative correlative of Stevie's disintegrated body. The novel's formal innovations thus

---

*For a full discussion of these terms, which correspond roughly to the distinction between story and plot, see Genette, *Narrative Discourse*. In *Consciousness and Time*, pp. 172–73, Torsten Pettersson provides two tables that summarize the *fabula* and *sujet* of *Chance*.

†The police speculate that Stevie tripped over a tree root *en route* to the observatory; one might therefore say that the novel's treatment of this absurd assault on scientific notions of space and time is *radical*.

effect the familiar modernist shift from organicism to fragmentation, figured with and by the human body. Of course earlier novels organized experience differently from linear narrative with its implied causality, but *The Secret Agent* is instructive in its foregrounding of a chance-initiated narrative form against the background of scientific spatiotemporality.

Disruptions in the traditional conceptualization of scientific space and time were going on in other fields at the time Conrad was writing *The Secret Agent* and *Chance*. In what seems like a rediscovery of the Epicurean *clinamen*, quantum theory's formulation of subatomic processes introduced the question of chance into classical physics, thereby challenging the injunctions of what had previously seemed to be the necessary laws of causality.* The formulae and findings of quantum physics indicate that the description of subatomic processes in spatiotemporal terms and the principle of causality at the subatomic level "represent complementary and mutually exclusive aspects of atomic phenomena."† Another, related instance of such complementarity in quantum physics is the dual nature of electron description: depending on the circumstances and formulation of the experiment, electrons can be understood to behave either as waves or as particles. Wave theory and particle theory are both partial analogies for electron behavior that, like the laws of causality, break down at the subatomic level. The principle of complementarity in quantum theory indicates that scientific truth is always partial and plural inasmuch as it is a function of an informing narrative (e.g., electrons behave like particles/electrons behave like waves) and that the doctrine of causal necessity is riddled with chance.

In his "Introduction to the Structural Analysis of Narratives," Roland Barthes offers a pertinent account of the usual workings of causality in narrative:

*I admit to some anachronism here in reading findings of quantum theory that were not established until the 1930s back into the early years of the century. I do so because most of the later tenets were implicit in the initial theoretical formulations. Rather as the pivotal role of chance as the mechanism of natural selection in Darwin's theory only became manifest through later research in genetics, though it had been an element in that theory's conceptualization, so the full importance of chance for quantum theory only became clear sometime later (mainly in Heisenberg's work), when the technology became available to work out its implications.

†Heisenberg, *Physical Principles*, p. 3. See also Bohr, *Atomic Theory*, p. 77: "[I]n the interpretation of observation a fundamental renunciation regarding the spatiotemporal description is unavoidable." Both of these passages are quoted in Nagel, *Structure of Science*, p. 296 and p. 296n.

Everything suggests, indeed, that the mainspring of narrative is precisely the confusion of consecution and consequence, what comes *after* being read in narrative as what is *caused by*; in which case narrative would be a systematic application of the logical fallacy denounced by Scholasticism in the formula *post hoc, ergo propter hoc*—a good motto for Destiny, of which narrative all things considered is no more than the "language."[6]

To Barthes's fallacious motto for Destiny I would append my own equally dubious motto for Fate in and as narrative: "If it happens, it was *meant* to happen."

The implications of *Chance*'s narrative innovations for modernist aesthetics are not perhaps as blatant or explosive as those of *The Secret Agent*. *Chance* does not throw any bombs, but it is anarchic in its own quiet way, questioning as it does the logic of causal necessity that has traditionally determined the syntax of narrative. By insisting that there is an ineradicable element of chance influencing "what happens" in a story, Conrad problematizes the narrative machinery that inevitably concludes that "it was *meant* to happen," thereby generating a fateful reading of a text. At several critical moments in *Chance* Conrad's diction and imagery convey, within the constraints of what happens, a reverberation of what *could* have happened; in such instances, chance marks the place and the possibility that *it could have happened differently*. Such passages constitute a novelistic *clinamen* in the text, a narrative swerve that breaks with what Lucretius calls "the bonds of fate." *Chance*'s suggestion of narrative alternatives leaves the traces of a marked resistance to the kind of Destiny Barthes criticizes in the usual confusion of two different kinds of necessity, the *narrative* necessity of one-thing-following-another (consecution) and the *causal* necessity according to which a cause invariably produces its effect (consequence). "Tychology" (a neologism for the science or logic of chance) applied to narratology (the science or logic of narrative) indicates that neither chance nor narrative necessarily subscribes to a traditional scientific logic. By the time Conrad was writing, Providence was no longer a major concern for the writer of fiction, as it had been for the Victorians; chance for the modern novelist becomes a way of challenging a narrative of scientific determinism and its logic of causal necessity.

The species of novel that most clearly illustrates the tenets of scientific determinism, which *Chance* initially imitates but finally disclaims, is characterized by a kind of naturalism that depicts the usually miserable, if not altogether tragic, career of a protagonist as it is determined by inexorable natural laws. Naturalist narratives generally admit an element of chance in the original configuration of heredity and environment; but given this initially random mixture, the naturalist novel's plot obeys the rules of a causal logic dictated by impersonal and implacable social, economic, and biological forces. In making the heroine of *Chance*, Flora de Barral, of French extraction Conrad was probably thinking of the French school of naturalism— Zola in particular—in his depiction of her miserable and victimized existence. It seems that Flora, like most protagonists of naturalist works, is doomed from the start. The deck is stacked against her, and everyone who knows her, even her own father, assumes that the only way Flora will escape her life of passive and oppressive suffering is to kill herself. But then chance intervenes. The swerves of chance in Conrad's novel of that name break with the bonds of fate and redirect the itinerary of what seems like the most grimly deterministic of stories, sending Flora and the novel off in another direction entirely.

Reacting against the prevalent scientism of his time, Conrad uses chance in *Chance* to repudiate a narrative form based on scientific laws of causal necessity; but in doing so, he eventually yields to the coercions of an *aesthetic* determinism. *Chance* illustrates why and how chance is always and inevitably rendered as fate because the novel strenuously resists but ultimately capitulates to this narrative imperative.

At the same time that quantum theory was revolutionizing classical physics by insinuating the question of chance into scientific notions of causality, a new "science" was getting started that soon became the sacrosanct fetish of its day. Psychoanalysis—what one might call the science *of* the fetish—was launched with the publication of Sigmund Freud's *Interpretation of Dreams* in 1900, the same year that Max Planck published his watershed article on quantum theory. Freud's most extended consideration of chance, in *The Psychopathology of Everyday Life* (1901), first appeared in English in 1914, one year after the publication of Conrad's *Chance*. In distinguishing the psychoanalyst from the superstitious person in that work, Freud concludes:

I believe in external (real) chance, it is true, but not in internal (psychical) accidental events. With the superstitious person it is the other way round.

He knows nothing of the motivation of his chance actions and parapraxes and believes in psychical accidental events; and, on the other hand, he has a tendency to ascribe to external chance happenings a meaning which will become manifest in real events, and to regard such chance happenings as a means of expressing something that is hidden from him in the external world. The differences between myself and the superstitious person are two: first, he projects outward a motivation which I look for within; secondly, he interprets chance as due to an event, while I trace it back to a thought. But what is hidden from him corresponds to what is unconscious for me, and the compulsion not to let chance count as chance but to interpret it is common to both of us.[7]

Much of *The Psychopathology of Everyday Life* is concerned with establishing a causal explanation for seemingly arbitrary and inconsequential psychical phenomena that, even if they are overdetermined, are still *determined* by unconscious motives. Freud's efforts to dissociate himself from the superstitious frame of mind is of a piece with his affirmation of psychoanalysis's scientific status.

When he briefly mentioned chance in "Delusion and Dream in Jensen's *Gradiva*" (1907) a few years later, Freud continued to deny chance in psychic functions, suggesting that it might not exist in the external world either: "There is far less freedom and arbitrariness in mental life, however, than we are inclined to assume—there may be none at all. What we call chance in the world outside can, as is well known, be resolved into laws, which we are only now beginning dimly to suspect."[8] There is no such thing as chance, and little or no freedom, in mental life; like the "world outside," it obeys natural laws and conforms to a causal logic. Psychoanalysis is the science designed to explicate the workings of those laws. Like Democritus in his description of atomic motion, Einstein in his doubts about quantum theory, and Darwin in his thinking about natural selection, Freud believed that what seems like chance to us is actually the result of natural laws that we have not yet come to understand.

Freud's example of an external "(real)" chance event in "Determinism, Belief in Chance and Superstition—Some Points of View," the concluding chapter of *Psychopathology*, is a "small experience" that, he says, first started him thinking about such matters. Freud one day ordered a cabman to take him to the house of one of his patients, an elderly woman who he thought would probably die soon. The cab did not stop at the old woman's house but instead pulled up in front of a similar house with the same number in a parallel street nearby. "[I]f I were *superstitious*," Freud observes, "I should see an omen in the incident, the finger of fate announcing that this year would be the old lady's last. . . . *I* of course explain the occurrence as an accident without any further meaning."[9] Freud's prompt dismissal of this "accident" is curious since, after all, this event with no further meaning both initiated and came to exemplify his thoughts on the subject of chance versus superstition. Chance functions for Freud like the zero in arithmetic (a placeholder with no value), allowing him to distinguish between and evaluate two different compulsions to interpret chance: the *negative* tendencies of the superstitious mind and the *positive* (frequently positivistic) processes of the psychoanalytic mind. Imagining a scenario in which he made the journey to the old woman's house on foot and absentmindedly walked to the wrong house on the parallel street, Freud remarks, "This I should not explain as an accident but as an action that had an unconscious aim and required interpretation."[10]

Arriving at the proper address is an exemplary issue for another psychoanalyst's reflections about chance. In his "Seminar on 'The Purloined Letter,'" Jacques Lacan concludes that in the symbolic register of language "a letter always arrives at its destination."[11] The determinism that Freud's new science generally affirmed in psychical phenomena is located more rigorously by Lacan in what he calls the symbolic order. The discussion of Lacan's use of Aristotle's two kinds of chance (*tyche* and *automaton*) in Chapter One above considered why and how that which happens "as if by chance" in Lacan's thinking instantiates an altogether determined and formative psycholinguistic structure. In his version of chance, the child of *tyche* is always Oedipus. For Lacan, chance operates like a variable in an algebraic formula: it is a necessary element, but the specific content of the chance experience is irrelevant to the relational operations that always yield the same familiar results. Chance gets factored out of Lacan's psychoanalytic formulations; and, as Jacques Derrida argues in "The Purveyor of Truth" (the English translation of "Le facteur de la verité"), factoring out chance brings the analyst's self-addressed stamped envelope full circle, delivering to the proper mail slot the Truth of psychoanalysis.[12]

"A letter always arrives at its destination." There is clearly a sense of destiny in Lacan's determination of the letter's inevitable successful delivery. As Derrida points out, in the "Seminar" Lacan substitutes *destin* ("destiny") for the less determined *dessein* ("design") in the quotation from Crébillon at the end of Edgar Allan Poe's "The Purloined Letter." Lacan then somewhat willfully inscribes a sense of *destin* in the letter's destination.

It is the *atomistic* nature of the letter that guarantees such postal efficiency. Lacan's allusive and elusive way of making this point is typically linguistic: the word *lettre* in French does not take the partitive: the letter does not admit partition. The sense of an indivisible letter, Derrida claims, "sustains Lacan's entire interpretation of 'The Purloined Letter,' and particularly of its circular, ineluctable, and predetermined return to the point of departure despite all the apparently random incidents."[13] Derrida therefore counters Lacan's notion of the atomistic letter that always arrives at its destination with an Epicurean account of how the (divisible and differential) structure of the letter allows for a chance "swerve" that can redirect its itinerary.

In their discussions of Poe's story, both Lacan and Derrida pay attention to the structure and movement of the letter; but they do not explicitly thematize the importance of narrative in their analyses of chance in language and literature (except insofar as, for Lacan, the Oedipus story is the master-narrative determining specific linguistic and literary effects). In detailing the ways in which Conrad resisted as much as possible a kind of generic determinism in the novel with his exploration of the theme of chance, I will extend the Derridean analysis in this direction, focusing in particular on the operations and effects of chance in narrative. Guided by Derrida's critique of Lacan then, this reading of Conrad's *Chance* will be writing "against" the psychoanalytic version of chance by making the most explicit use of Epicurus's atomic theory.* The inscription of the possibility that things could have happened differently in *Chance*'s narrative replicates the structure of the *clinamen* in the atomistic letter, the literary atom. The linguistic entity that in the modern novel has an atomistic status in language (an elementary, fundamental, and indivisible unit of meaning) is the proper name. My analysis of *Chance* and the proper name in this chapter will consider why and how the atomistic

---

*Writing "against" psychoanalysis in the sense D. A. Miller employs in "Discipline in Different Voices," p. 99. In reference to deconstructive and Marxist criticism, Miller writes: "[I]t cannot exactly be a matter of repudiating these critical modes, but rather of writing against them, as against a background."

integrity, referential stability, and linguistic propriety of the proper name are affected by the operations of chance, with important consequences for the modern novel's narrative form.

In *The Politics of Reflexivity*, Robert Siegle quotes a passage from the serialized version of *Chance* (a passage deleted by Conrad before the text was published in novel form) that he analyzes in order to characterize the operations of chance in *Chance*. Conrad writes:

> For most people the pages of life are ruled like the pages of a copybook headed with some sound moral maxim at the top. They can turn them over with the certitude that the very catastrophes shall keep to the traced lines. And it is comforting, in a way, to one's friends and even to one's self to think that one's very misfortunes, if any, will be of the foreseen type.

Siegle's reading of this passage picks up Conrad's clever use of the typography and topography of the printed page to make the point that chance always occupies a marginal position. "A novel entitled *Chance*," he observes, "would seem to be about what intervenes from outside the cultural margins to upset the 'foreseen type.'"[14] Chance is by definition marginal in relation to the well-ruled pages of conventional narrative. But what happens when chance migrates from the margin to the magisterial title page, taking its place at the head of the text and organizing its narrative material under that rubric?

"The Wonderful Linking Up of Small Facts"

Chance events begin and end Joseph Conrad's novel *Chance*, the first germinal, launching the story with a coincidence that sends a young sailor to sea, and the last (in several senses of the word) quite effectively terminal. I will be looking at the last instance first since it nicely summarizes the narrative technique of the novel and offers a clear and literalized image of chance's effects in *Chance*. If much of what I have to say about *Chance* in this section is organized by a kind of "plot summary," it is because in this novel chance *becomes* plot in an unprecedented and illuminating way.

The unusual and strained marriage of Captain Roderick Anthony and his wife, Flora (*née* de Barral), forms the moral and psychological core of *Chance*. They met when Flora, desperate and alone, was about to kill herself. Though Anthony never knew of her suicidal intentions or fully understood the cause of her despair, he was moved by her abject helplessness and convinced her to run away with him. The first cause of Flora's troubles is her father, Mr. de Barral, an international financier imprisoned for fraud, the scandal of which has blighted Flora's upbringing. The first half of the novel documents Flora's miserable existence prior to her marriage and, but for the narrative experimentations, reads like a work of naturalism in its account of her victimization by or because of her criminal father. De Barral is released from prison the day after the couple's (unconsummated) marriage, and the ex-convict goes to sea (assuming the name "Smith") with the captain and his new bride on Anthony's ship, the *Ferndale*. The situation aboard ship is this: Anthony, uncertain whether his new wife loves him or simply needs a refuge for herself and her criminal father, agrees to take them on without pressing his conjugal claim. Although he desires her, he waits for her to say she loves him. Flora, however, is convinced that no one could love her and is moreover constrained by her father's will. De Barral wants his daughter to himself, hates being at sea, and despises Captain Anthony. It is "an uneasy atmosphere disturbed by passions, jealousies, loves, hates and the troubles of transcendental good intentions."[15] Metaphors of contamination and infection continually describe the effect of this false situation on the simple, honest, and pure life at sea: the "tension of falsehood, of desperate acting . . . tainted the pure sea-atmosphere" (p. 415). One sign of this corruption is the location of Anthony's sleeping quarters. Because he and Flora do not sleep together, he occupies, in violation of all nautical custom, a room on the port rather than the starboard side of the ship; this inversion of the normal order of things at sea almost leads to a catastrophe when, during an emergency, Anthony is summoned on the starboard side.

The topography of the ship below deck brings us to the major instance of chance in the novel. Both Mr. Anthony's and Mrs. Anthony's quarters are in the aft section, separated from the rest of the cabin (including de Barral's stateroom) by a heavy curtain, "making a privacy within a privacy, as though Captain Anthony could not place obstacles enough between his new happiness and the men who shared his life at sea" (p. 349). Powell, the ship's young second mate, notices by chance, while leaning over to pick up a coil of rope, that he can see through "the lighted skylight of the most private part of the saloon, consecrated to the exclusiveness of Captain Anthony's married life" (p. 410). One frame of the usually opaque skylight had been broken and replaced by clear glass that very day. This "wonderful linking up of small facts" (p. 411) gives Powell a privileged view into the inner sanctum of his captain's marital arrangement. And what "primal scene" does the young sailor observe?

He sees Captain Anthony with a book. He is sipping brandy and water. Marlow, to whom Powell relates his story, speculates that Anthony "used reading as an opiate against the pain of his magnanimity" (p. 416); Freud observes that brandy at bedtime is often a sign of sexual frustration.* But that is not all Powell sees: the captain leaves the framed field of vision, and a moment later "a short, puffy, old freckled hand" (p. 417) comes into view from behind the heavy curtain and drops a dose of poison into the captain's brandy glass. The primal scene stages not sex but death.

This chance moment in *Chance* provides a condensed image for the way chance is thematized in the novel. *Chance* depicts its characters as closed off, compartmentalized, confined—literally so in the case of de Barral's imprisonment (which he feels continues aboard the *Ferndale*) and figuratively so in Flora's sad history before Anthony rescues her (the loathsome, abusive cousin she was forced to live with after her father's arrest is a manufacturer of cardboard boxes, an apt image for her suffocating existence before she elopes with Anthony). Things are no less oppressive aboard the *Ferndale*, though. She felt "encaged" (p. 330) by the interlocking frustrations of her life at sea, and her husband likewise "was not the proud master but the chafing captive of his generosity" (p. 395). Powell's chance view into the doubly sealed "privacy within a privacy" is a rare glimpse into the inner workings of a veiled mystery the moral and psychological significance of which the observer himself cannot begin to comprehend. Powell has no idea why the captain needs to lull himself to sleep with brandy and a dull-looking history book; he is not aware that "Mr. Smith" is the once-great financier de Barral, nor does he have any inkling why Flora's father might want to poison Captain Anthony.

Powell is just one of the narrators in *Chance* who report actions and events they do not completely understand. The novel's intricate and

---

* "[Dora] understood very clearly what it was her father needed when he could not get to sleep without a drink of brandy." Freud, "Fragment of an Analysis," p. 118. In a felicitous coincidence, the English translator of Freud's explanatory footnote to this passage on the same page puns on Flora and Mr. de Barral's family name: "Her father could not sleep because he was *debarred* from sexual intercourse with the woman he loved." This coincidence in many ways anticipates the argument about chance and the proper name that is to follow.

convoluted narrative structure, which collects and transmits several narrators' limited observations, refracted through their own ignorance and preconceptions, has often (beginning with Henry James) been criticized as unnecessarily complicated. Powell's observation through the fragment of transparent glass clarifies the meaning of the elaborate narrative structure of the novel: it dramatizes how *partial* (in both senses of the word) our view of others' interiority is, and it thematizes how such moments of insight happen, if they happen at all, by chance.*

The naive and ingenuous Powell reports his story to Marlow, the main repository of the various narratives in the novel. Marlow knows Flora personally and has learned from various sources her entire history, including de Barral's rise and fall. Marlow relates all this to the anonymous "I," the all-encompassing narrator of the book, who observes and gives a somewhat distanced perspective on Marlow (for instance, the narrator occasionally challenges Marlow's severe remarks about women, which have been cited as evidence of Conrad's reputed misogyny). If we translate this series of narrators into the originally visual register of Powell's chance observations, then Marlow takes his position, as it were, looking over Powell's shoulder, where he can in principle take in more of the scene than Powell. "I let him go on in his way," Marlow says of Powell's narration, "feeling that no matter what strange facts he would disclose, I was certain to know much more of them than he ever did know or could possibly guess" (p. 311). The anonymous narrator then stands behind Marlow, with the reader the last in the series of "prying, spying, anyway looking" (p. 412) voyeurs. Powell himself felt "a sort of depraved excitement in watching an unconscious man—and such an attractive and mysterious man as Captain Anthony at that" (p. 416). The reader, too, if only by extension, is implicated in this chain of scopophilic fascination, where, like Lacan's rear-plucking ostriches, he feels secure only by virtue of the fact that there is not another observer behind him.†

---

*Marlow makes much the same observation in a figural description of his momentary intimacy with Flora: "Well, let us say that I had a look in. . . . A young girl, you know, is something like a temple. You pass by and wonder what mysterious rites are going on there, what prayers, what visions? The privileged man, the lover, the husband, who are given the key to the sanctuary do not always know how to use it. For myself, without claim, without merit, simply by chance I had been allowed to look through the half-open door" (p. 311).

†Lacan, "Seminar on 'The Purloined Letter,'" p. 44. I refer to the reader as "he" because the other observers (including almost certainly the anonymous narrator) with

But there *is* another observer watching Captain Anthony for much more sinister reasons, the evidence of which makes Powell forget his position as guilty voyeur and instead "rouse[s] his indignation" (p. 417). The residual shame and self-consciousness of Powell's (and perhaps the reader's) intrusive curiosity is defused by the outrage of de Barral's spying and subsequent poisoning attempt. This is just one of many ways de Barral bears the burden of some disturbing issues the novel raises but does not quite resolve, of which more shortly.

The serial narrators are brought into line by what Powell calls "the wonderful linking up of small facts" (the coil of rope, the newly re-paired skylight, the fortuitous timing), which occasions a revealing glimpse into the *folie à trois* of the novel's main characters. Marlow uses much the same words when describing the importance of nar-rative: "The purely human reality is capable of lyrism but not of abstraction. Nothing will serve for its understanding but the evidence of rational linking up of characters and facts" (p. 310). The impor-tance of the series of narrators, each with a limited perspective, is likewise thematized in the same discussion as an essential element of narrative (explicitly described in terms of chapters): "Yes, I know their joint stories which Mr. Powell did not know. The chapter in it he was opening to me, the sea-chapter, . . . however astounding to him in its detached condition was much more to me as a member of a series" (p. 309). The self-conscious reflections about the alignment of story elements and storytellers in a series makes explicit the way this chance moment in the novel provides a model in miniature for the narrative form of *Chance*.

To continue the story: Powell rushes into the cabin and informs Captain Anthony that his drink has been doctored. Flora emerges from her cabin at the sound of their voices, sensing that something is wrong. Without detailing the crisis, Captain Anthony informs her that her father has finally won, that he (Anthony) will surrender his claim on her. This precipitates *the* moment of moral choice in the novel: faced with the prospect of finally losing him, Flora lets out a cry, puts her arms around Anthony's neck, and says she does not want to be free of him.* The captain carries her to her cabin, and de Barral,

whom the reader is aligned are male. It is difficult to say how and where a female reader could sympathetically identify with the story of *Chance*; Flora de Barral is the focal character, but the narrative consists almost exclusively of male perceptions of her.

*That the most concerted moral choice for this woman who has heretofore been a victim of circumstances is to hang weakly on a man's neck argues strongly in favor

disgusted by the sight of his daughter yielding to the man he hates
and had tried to murder, promptly drinks the poisoned liquor and
just as promptly dies. Powell and the captain return the dead man to
his stateroom to be found in the morning, telling Flora nothing.

The entire tone of the novel changes with de Barral's death as the
narrative engines of recuperation turn this completely random and
haphazard instance of chance into fate, or—to use de Barral's word—
"luck." In a mere seven pages following de Barral's suicide, this bleak
and bitterly ironic story becomes a standardized romance.* We learn
that Mr. and Mrs. Anthony lived happily ever after (or at least for six
years, until Captain Anthony was lost at sea). The novel ends in the
most conventional way, with Powell and the widowed Flora about to
be married. This ending is all the more jarring since Marlow earlier
questioned Powell's naive equation of marriage and happiness:

> I suppose that to him life . . . was something still in the nature of a fairy-tale
> with a "they lived happily ever after" termination. We are the creatures of our
> light literature much more than is generally suspected in a world which prides
> itself on being scientific and practical, and in possession of incontrovertible
> theories. (p. 288)

Marlow's and the novel's last words are addressed to the anonymous
narrator (and perhaps as well to the ungenerous reader who chafes at
this pat ending with its "they lived happily ever after" termination):
"What on earth are you grinning at in this sarcastic manner? I am
not afraid of going to church with a friend. Hang it all, for all my
belief in Chance I am not exactly a pagan . . ." (p. 477; Conrad's
ellipsis). The well-trod path to the church this story retraces is here
set against the precepts of Chance elevated (with the capital letter)
for the first time into a principle to be believed in. The moment the
novel makes an explicit and conclusive claim for the power and efficacy of Chance occurs when the narrative is most generically and
conventionally determined—when, that is, nothing is left to Chance.

---

of those who find Conrad's view of women (especially in the later novels) a limited
one. It is true that the anonymous narrator takes exception to Marlow's criticisms of
women, but the plot turning on this conversion to abject dependency suggests that
Conrad participated in Marlow's tendency to make Flora the woman into Woman, a
feminine spirit whose dependent place and role are dictated by her essential nature.

*Fredric Jameson remarks a similar tonal shift from irony to romance in Conrad's
Lord Jim. See *The Political Unconscious*, pp. 206–80.

"Here's Luck"

The dénouement of *Chance* accomplishes a remarkable shift of tone. Attempting to account for the unexpected popularity of the novel, Frederick R. Karl observes that Conrad "certainly did cater to his audience" in using medieval chivalric figures for the two part-titles of the novel ("The Damsel," Flora, and "The Knight," Anthony), which "suggest a more romantic flavor than the novel actually has." [16] These titles operate for the most part ironically, as do most of the chapter titles, some of which ("The Governess," "The Tea Party") suggest a Henry James-ish drawing room atmosphere notably lacking in *Chance*. Suddenly though, in the concluding pages of the novel, the romantic implications and expectations of those division headings are realized.

This shift in tone from biting irony to insipid romanticism is signaled in the diction describing Flora's later married life with Captain Anthony. To understand how the passage marks this tonal shift you must first know that Mr. and Mrs. Fyne, who provided the outcast Flora with an insecure home-where-she-never-felt-at-home, are the targets for Conrad's most scathing irony. They operate in many ways as the negative doubles of Mr. and Mrs. Anthony, and their name, "Fyne," is obviously meant ironically. Mr. Fyne, a walking enthusiast, is often referred to as "the pedestrian Fyne," a labored pun that not only underlines his prosaic dullness but also opposes his way of life to the sailors' values espoused by Marlow and Anthony, who frequently express their disdain for "shore-people and their confounded half-and-half ways" (p. 372). Mr. Fyne is ridiculous and uxorious, dominated by his virulently feminist wife, who stridently affirms women's rights and the "theory and practice of feminine free morality" (pp. 65–66)—until a woman elopes with her own brother (Captain Anthony is her brother; he and Flora first met at the Fyne's house).* Ten years after the elopement and four years after Anthony's death, Flora tells Marlow that she once saw a letter from Mrs. Fyne addressed to Captain Anthony:

---

*Conrad is careful to provide what he and Ford Madox Ford called "justification" for Mrs. Fyne's rabid and unreflective feminism. She, like Flora, was raised by a domineering father and experienced a confined, almost carceral upbringing: "Her father had kept her strictly cloistered. Marriage with Fyne was certainly a change, but only to another kind of claustration" (p. 66). The castrating woman is then the claustrated woman. For Ford Madox Ford's account of character "justification," see his "Conrad on the Theory of Fiction."

"I found in it this sentence: 'For years I tried to make a friend of that girl, but I warn you once more that she has the nature of an adventuress. . . .' Adventuress!" repeated Flora slowly. "So be it. I have had a fine adventure."

"It was fine, then," [Marlow] said, interested.

"The finest in the world!" (p. 444, Conrad's ellipsis)

The Fyne "adventuress" has had "a fine adventure." The conversion is complete, the irony infusing the name "Fyne" has been defused, the word "fine" has been recuperated. The exact location in the text—the very word—where this pervasive tonal shift from irony to romance is effected will be pinpointed in a moment. For now, here is Flora's description of her happy ending:

"The finest in the world! Only think! I loved and was loved, untroubled, at peace, without remorse, without fear. All the world, all life was transformed for me. . . . The sea itself! . . . You are a sailor. You have lived your life on it. But do you know how beautiful it is, how strong, how charming, how friendly, how mighty?" (pp. 444–45; the second ellipsis is Conrad's)

It is not clear where Roderick Anthony is in this rapturous description of her married life unless he has merged in Flora's mind with her experience of the sea, which would explain the personified adjectives she uses to describe it. Her conversion then is from a shore person to a sea lover.

Conrad would have us believe that the shift in tone from trenchant irony to storybook romance in the resolution of the novel all follows naturally from Flora's change of heart when she detaches herself from her father's dominating will and transfers her attachment entirely to Captain Anthony. This shift has important consequences for the narrative form of the novel, which I will try to bring out by interpolating some pertinent questions into the interstices of Marlow's cant. Here is his commentary on Flora's conversion, which is after all nothing more than her final capitulation to a Marlovian categorical imperative:

Of all the forms offered to us by life [*does this include narrative forms?*] it is the one demanding a couple to realize it fully which is the most imperative. Pairing off is the fate of mankind [*so leaves no room for chance?*]. And if two beings thrown together, mutually attracted, resist the necessity, fail in understanding and voluntarily stop short of the—the embrace, in the noblest meaning of the word, then they are committing a sin against life, the call of which is simple [*as simple, perhaps, as the ending of Chance?*]. Perhaps

sacred [*hence necessitating a trip to church?*]. And the punishment of it is
[*and here the reader may hear the text describing the narrative form that it
has been practicing and that it is about to abjure:*] an invasion of complexity,
a tormenting, forcibly tortuous involution of feelings. (pp. 426–27)

Flora's eventually yielding to this "imperative" and accepting her
"fate"—the "necessity" of what Marlow delicately calls "the embrace"—would seem to account for the change in Mr. and Mrs.
Anthony's relationship, with the corresponding shift in tone, generic
standardization, and narrative simplification. But it is not quite that
simple.

When Powell peeks through the skylight into the hidden recesses
of the Anthonys' married life, he witnesses the insinuation of death
(by de Barral's hand) into that private place. De Barral's scheme then
recoils back on him and he dies of his own poison. This happens moments after Anthony, his "glance full of unwonted fire," "burdened
and exulting" (p. 431), carries Flora into her cabin—probably the
first time they have been alone together in that room. Powell witnesses de Barral's suicide and, horrified, approaches the stateroom
door to call the captain. As Thomas Moser no doubt correctly speculates, Mr. and Mrs. Anthony are probably at that moment finally
consummating their marriage; as Moser points out, "Conrad gives
us one brief hint of the meaning of Flora and Anthony's triumphant
embrace":[17] "It was very still in there," Powell reports; "still as death"
(p. 434). Approaching another "primal scene," young Powell again
senses not sex but death. Although Marlow's categorical imperative
asserts that the purpose of couples is to couple, the fatal stillness
Powell senses suggests that the ostensibly life-affirming sexual act
might actually be imbued with death.

To use the language of criticism when it considers contiguous and
possibly contingent circumstances, thus making a virtue of necessity, "it is no accident that" de Barral's suicide occurs at the moment
his daughter and son-in-law finally consummate their marriage. As
de Barral's toast when he downs the poison suggests, the coincidence of Flora's defloration and her father's death is *not* a function
of chance: "Here's luck" he says, knocking back the poisoned drink.
The bitter dose he swallows with this bitterly ironic remark is the
poison that cures: his toast is the last and most caustic instance of
irony in a novel that has to this point been characterized by pervasive

irony. De Barral's doctored drink effectively cures the narrative of its chronic ironic affliction, as we saw with the subsequent recovery of the word "fine." The word "luck" works like a knot in the story, with one line of narrative running into the word saturated with irony and with another narrative line extending out of that word having undergone a sea change: henceforth, the word "luck," and words in general, mean what they say.

The diction of the novel is in fact quite precise about the use of words like "luck," "chance," and "accident." The latter is usually associated with Mr. Fyne: Marlow came to know Flora by way of "an accident called Fyne" (p. 36). "Chance" is usually attached to Powell, starting with the first chapter, "Young Powell and His Chance." When "luck" enters the story, it is almost always to describe Flora's victimized career as "luckless," to the point that the word becomes her epithet (pp. 194, 309, 312, 370). Flora's luckless condition repeatedly brought her to the point of killing herself, but the chance interventions of Mr. Fyne, Marlow, and Captain Anthony on three separate occasions diverted her from her desperate course. And there is every indication that if things had continued as they were on the *Ferndale*, her suicidal urges would again have pushed her toward self-destruction. "I don't think you can stand it for long," her father observes blandly. "Some day you will jump overboard" (p. 394).

When de Barral toasts the Anthonys' new life with "Here's luck" and with his own death, he effectively ends Flora's luckless streak. As Thomas Moser notes, the circumstances of de Barral's death blur responsibility in *Chance*, which "prevents Anthony from having to face the real problems of his marriage."[18] The marital problems existed before de Barral came on the scene (on their wedding day, the day before the convict was released from prison, Mr. and Mrs. Anthony's honeymoon consisted of a walk in the park). Nevertheless, the responsibility for the Anthonys' marital failure seems to lie with de Barral, and their problems seem to die with him. It is as though when de Barral is buried at sea the *Ferndale* is finally cleansed of the falsehood and perversity infecting and contaminating its simple seafaring ways.

De Barral's poisoned corpse and the hint of death Powell senses outside the door during the consummation of the Anthonys' marriage have important formal consequences: the sunny sea-loving simplicity of the novel's dénouement, which unties the knot of de Barral's toast to "luck," spells the death of *Chance*'s hitherto complicated narrative form, which is literalized in Powell's chance view through the sky-light. Of course, the operations of closure are always violent and often deadly;[19] but what I am trying to bring out here is the way that violence is exerted in the novel to gather the thematics of chance and its vicissitudes under the rubric of "luck." The random and contingent aspects of the poisoning scene then take on an air of inevitability— *fate accompli.*

Powell calls the wonderful linking up of small facts leading to his revelatory eyeful "the precise workmanship of chance, fate, providence, call it what you will!" (p. 411). De Barral calls it "luck," but as is usually the case with de Barral's mordant remarks, it is not quite clear what he means. It is clear, however, that this chance event and its consequences exemplify the precise workmanship of *Chance*: the movement from Powell's fortuitous voyeurism to the generically and conventionally determined dénouement of the novel effectively illustrates how chance in narrative is systematically rendered as fate, a reading of events that were *meant* to happen. *Chance* assimilates the narrative imperative to render chance as fate to the sexual "imperative" to couple that Marlow affirms; but it does so at some cost. For all the hygienic romance of this sea story's happy-ever-after ending, de Barral's bitter toast to the newlyweds leaves a bitter taste in the mouth.

The story of de Barral's lucky demise would seem to support the psychoanalyst's account of chance as simply a variable in an algebraic formulation that always yields the same familiar results. As Jean Laplanche and J.-B. Pontalis observe of fantasies of origin like the primal scene, they constitute "a kind of language and a symbolic sequence, but loaded with elements of imagination; a structure, but activated by contingent elements."[20] For the psychoanalyst, the contingent aspects of a primal scene activate a structure that tells an old story. Powell's two primal scenes, one visual, one aural, facilitate and anticipate his oedipal ascendancy: his chance observations through the skylight allow him to expose and discredit the evil father, who is literally poisoned by his own poisonous will; and his eavesdropping attendance during the Anthonys' hymenal rites adumbrates his eventual replacement of the good father in Mrs. Anthony's bed.* But

---

*A psychologistic reading of the novel would also neatly illustrate Lacan's version of *tyche* and *automaton*, in which the traumatic, rupturing, and formative experience that happens "as if by chance" (*tyche*) continually materializes in displaced form

Powell experiences another kind of chance and witnesses yet another primal scene, neither of which conforms so neatly to the psychoanalytic schema. To uncover this other kind of chance and restage this other primal scene, one must travel upstream and against the current of the narrative to the novel's first chapter, "Young Powell and His Chance."

"The Capacity for Diversion"

The first instance of chance in *Chance* that launches the story on the current (Conrad's word) of Marlow's narration details how young Powell signed on to the *Ferndale* for that fateful voyage. Powell's story, which he relates to Marlow and the unnamed narrator, is briefly this: he had been looking for a berth on a ship for some time when he encountered an acquaintance who had just "got a ship" that morning. This friend urges him to speak to a Mr. Powell about a position: "Go to the private door of the Shipping Office and walk right up to him," he advises. The reader at this point does not know young Powell's name—he has been referred to only by pronouns—until he remarks of this Shipping Office functionary: " 'What was the most remarkable thing about Powell,' he enunciated dogmatically with his head in a cloud of smoke, 'is that he should have just that name. You see, my name happens to be Powell too' " (pp. 7–8). Powell-the-sailor plucks up his courage and finds his way (after some interesting wrong turns) to Powell-the-clerk's desk. At that moment, Captain Anthony bursts in saying he needs to replace his second officer (who has suffered an accident) before he sets sail the next morning. And before he knows it, Powell gets his first ship.

The interesting thing about Powell's "chance" is the double coincidence: not only was he in the right place at the right time, but further the Shipping Office clerk turned out, by chance, also to be named Powell. When the doubled name comes to the attention of others, it is interpreted not as a chance event but in terms of an easily recognizable design: Anthony assumes the two Powells are related; the Shipping Officer's motive for helping the second officer would then be simple

---

as a repetition compulsion (*automaton*). Flora's recurrent suicidal urges, which are thwarted by the chance interventions of solicitous men and eventually cured by her conversion to the life at sea, would then be the displaced repetition of Conrad's "lucky" survival when he shot himself at age twenty shortly before going to sea.

nepotism. It is only much later in the story that Powell disabuses Captain Anthony of this natural assumption. One obvious strategic effect of this early coincidence in the novel is to prepare the reader for further (and perhaps implausible) coincidences, as suggested in Powell's own reflections (reported by Marlow): "[T]he strangeness of being mixed up in what went on aboard ship simply because his name was also the name of a shipping master, kept him in a state of wonder which made other coincidences, however unlikely, not so very surprising after all" (p. 312).* But what other significance might the doubled name have in the novel, and what might the Powell/Powell connection have to do with chance?

Joseph Conrad knew all about doubles. His short novel *The Secret Sharer* (1910) is probably the definitive (indeed, textbook) example of the theme of the double in English literature. Except for the relatively minor way the Fynes operate as a negative version of the Anthonys, though, there are no clear cases of doubling in *Chance* (Powell, Marlow, and/or Anthony, because of their marine affinities, might be elected to play doubles, but this idea is never consistently developed in *Chance*).

The doubling theme, then, does not organize the characterological design of the novel. Conrad's retrospective "Author's Note" (1920), which introduces the novel, suggests, however, that there was once a double temptation in the plotting of *Chance*:

> Starting impetuously like a sanguine oarsman setting forth in the early morning I came very soon to a fork in the stream and found it necessary to pause and reflect seriously upon the direction I would take. Either presented to me equal fascinations, at least on the surface, and for that very reason my hesitation extended over many days. I floated in the calm water of pleasant speculation, between the diverging currents or conflicting impulses, with an agreeable but perfectly irrational conviction that neither of these currents would take me to destruction. My sympathies being equally divided and the two forces being equal it is perfectly obvious that nothing but mere chance influenced my decision in the end. It is a mighty force that of mere chance; absolutely irresistible yet manifesting itself often in delicate forms. (p. ix)

Of course, the choice of one rather than the other of two competing plot-lines, which seems relatively arbitrary at the time of writing,

---

*The climactic coincidence, Powell's voyeuristic peek through the skylight, is anticipated by the first line of the novel (spoken by the anonymous narrating "I"): "I believe he [Powell] had seen us out of the window" (p. 3).

must enter into much, if not all, experience of composition; but this experience leaves its mark on *Chance*. The doubleness of "the diverging currents or conflicting impulses" in the narrative stream, the course of which is directed by "mere chance," would make its impact felt in the story, if it does so at all, as the slightest reverberation. The traces of such contending plot-lines constitute a *clinamen* in Conrad's narrative: within the constraints of what happens, chance marks the place and the possibility that *it could have happened differently*.

In the first chapter, "chance" does indeed mark such a place and such a possibility. Powell arrives at the dock with his baggage late at night, ready to board the *Ferndale* for the first time. There are sinister figures lurking in the shadows, and two suspicious-looking fellows offer (or more accurately, demand) to carry his baggage to the ship for him. He soon meets the constable on duty, who informs the oblivious Powell of the risk he was running; and in the space of one page the word "chance" is repeated four times: "I tell you you've had a most extraordinary chance that there wasn't one of them regular boys [i.e., thieves] about tonight. . . . Well! You've had a chance to get in with a whole skin and with all your things" (pp. 27–28), says the constable; and Powell then himself uses the word twice. This striking proliferation of "chance"s marks a place in the text where one narrative line has been chosen over another, the novelist having rejected in this case the familiar *topos* of the hero who loses all material possessions before setting out on a journey to find himself (one has only to think of David Copperfield, who lost his box and money before setting out on the Dover Road to find his Aunt Betsey).* This plot-line is passed over I think to signal that Powell is *not* the hero of the novel; but the remarkable thing about the "chance" repetitions in this minor incident is the way they register, within the constraints of what happens, a reverberation of what *could* have happened.

A chance meeting at a crucial time in Flora's career diverts her from what seems to be her inevitable fate (suicide), and again, what does not happen in the story makes itself felt in the narrative as a suggestion of what could have happened. When Flora disappears from the Fyne house early in the novel, Marlow and Fyne go searching for her; and there is every indication in the diction and imagery of the scene that she is dead. The two searchers come across a freshly dug ditch

---

*F. R. Leavis remarks the generally Dickensian quality of *Chance*'s first chapter in *Great Tradition*, p. 224.

that smelled "like a *grave*"; Fyne "pushed his way into a *decaying* shed half-*buried* in dew-soaked vegetation." Marlow thinks of other, figurative suicides he has encountered: "I have come across . . .dead souls lying, so to speak, at the foot of high unscalable places." And a pun further underlines the expectation of finding a corpse: "Fyne fell suddenly into a strange cavity—probably a disguised kiln. His voice uplifted in *grave* distress"; and again, "The short flares illuminated his *grave* countenance" (pp. 52–54, my emphasis). Conrad had used a similar technique in *The Secret Agent* to suggest Winnie Verloc's eventual stabbing of her husband. The figural language becomes more literal (Mr. Verloc's appetite is "cut" by his wife's distress; he worries that his anarchist associates will "stab him in the back"; and in spying he ran the risk "of having a knife stuck into [him]") until Mrs. Verloc plunges a carving knife into his heart.[21] Mr. Verloc thus ends up so much meat, like the joint of cold beef he carves and eats throughout the scene. But in Flora's case the expectations conjured up by the descriptive, figural, and punning language are not realized: she does not end up in one of the many graves gaping open in this scene; she did not kill herself, it turns out, but instead eloped with Captain Anthony.

The residual traces of doubled and diverging narrative possibilities in *Chance* have not yet explained what the doubling of the name "Powell" means and what it has to do with chance in the novel. Powell offers a hint about the meaning of this coincidence when he recounts how the double name first came up between the sailor and the clerk. When the shipping master asked him his name he was embarrassed: "Somehow or other it didn't seem proper for me to fling his own name at him as it were. So I merely pulled my new certificate from my pocket and put it into his hand unfolded, so that he could read *Charles Powell* written very plain on the parchment" (p. 16). Powell's feeling that it is not proper to fling a name—"his own name" (in French, Conrad's second language after Polish, this would be "son nom propre")—suggests that the Powell/Powell coincidence has something to do with the questionable propriety of the proper name.

It is probably not a coincidence that in his essay on chance, Jacques Derrida discusses the status of the proper name at some length. His analysis will be outlined here in order to explicate the way the problematics of chance and the proper name are folded together in

Chance. What characterizes the letter and the proper name, Derrida claims, is their "insignificance in marking":

> That which I here call insignificance is the structure that establishes that a mark in itself is not necessarily linked, even in the form of the reference (*renvoi*), to a meaning or to a thing. Take, for example, the case of the proper name. It has no meaning in itself, at least insofar as it is a proper name. It does not refer (*renvoie*) to anyone; it designates someone only in a given context, for example (and for example only), because of an arbitrary convention. . . . No natural bond, to use Saussurian terminology, between the signified and the signifier.[22]

The insignificance of the mark is a result of its being, necessarily, re-markable:

> The ideal iterability that forms the structure of all marks is that which undoubtedly allows them to be released from any context, to be freed from all determined bonds to its origin, its meaning, or its referent, to emigrate in order to play elsewhere, in whole or in part, another role. . . . This iterability is thus that which allows a mark to be used more than once. It is more than one. It multiplies and divides itself internally. This imprints the capacity for diversion within its very movement. (p. 16)

This is no doubt familiar Derridean ground, which in its reiteration of "iterability" occasionally elicits some irritability. But this rehearsal of the repeatability and "divisibility or internal difference" (p. 10) of the insignificant mark takes an interesting turn when Derrida considers the "capacity for diversion" the mark enjoys. And it is here that the idea of the *clinamen,* the chance swerve that breaks with what Lucretius calls "the bonds of fate," becomes pertinent to an analysis of the proper name. The potential perturbation of the mark's itinerary has important consequences for the destiny and destination of a dispatch (*envoie*):

> [The mark] multiplies and divides itself internally. This imprints the capacity for diversion within its very movement. In the destination there is thus a principle of indetermination, chance, luck, or of destinerring. There is no assured destination precisely because of the mark and the proper name. (p. 16)

The word "destinerring," which Derrida discusses in *The Post Card,* registers the possibility of error or wandering (as in "knights errant") built into the seemingly predetermined idea of destiny. Derrida argues that the atomistic nature of the proper name is structured by a *clinamen* that can interrupt or divert the dispatch's circular route to its eventual and destined destination.

It is in fact just such an interruption or diversion that makes itself felt with the "chance" repetitions constellating around Powell's close brush with the dock thieves. "Chance" marks the place, and the Derridean mark places chance where things could happen differently, where for instance Powell might not realize his sailor's destiny and his baggage might not make it to its destination. Similarly, suicide seems the destiny and a grave the destination of Flora de Barral for most of *Chance*. But owing to a chance encounter, the open graves Fyne and Marlow happen upon do not become her final resting place; she discovers instead a new and romantic life at sea with Captain Anthony. Conrad's version of chance frees his heroine from the grim fate scripted for her by the deterministic plots of Naturalist fiction.

The place and the possibility of chance are opened up by the divisibility and repeatability of the proper name, which are literalized when Powell comes face to face with Powell. The sailor offers the clerk the unfolded (hence formerly folded) certificate "so that he could read *Charles Powell* written very plain on the parchment" as proof of his identity. But Powell's certificate also, necessarily, makes and marks a difference (and not just between the two men) that insinuates itself, as *self*-difference, into the structure of the proper name: the plicated parchment replicates the Powell/Powell interface by marking with the fold the irreducible duplicity of the proper name. The originary instance of chance in Conrad's novel, Powell's encounter with Powell that sends him off on his narrative adventures, illustrates the susceptibility of the atomistic letter and literary atom called the proper name to the chance operations of the *clinamen*: the differential structure of the proper name opens it to the play and the possibility of chance, which (at least potentially) diverts or deviates its plotted course to a destined destination.

"A Mausoleum of Proper Names"

As it happens, the character whose name comes up when the subject is the improper use of names and the questionable propriety of the proper name is Flora's father, Mr. de Barral. When Marlow learns that Flora is the daughter of the once-great financier, he at first has trouble recognizing the name:

But you know that my memory is merely a mausoleum of proper names. In de Barral's case, it got put away in my mausoleum in company with so many names of his own creation that really he had to throw off a monstrous heap of grisly bones before he stood before me. . . . The fellow had . . . a very pretty taste in names; and nothing else besides—absolutely nothing— no other merit. (p. 69)

The names de Barral fabricated, like "The Orb Bank" and "The Sceptre Trust," were of financial institutions that he started "simply, it seems, for advertising purposes. They were mere names" (p. 79). The greatest misnomer of all is the name of de Barral's parent company, the "Thrift and Independence Aid Association," which aided no one and had nothing to do with thrift (the money that people signed over was spent senselessly) or independence (Marlow is appalled that the public mindlessly turned their money over to de Barral). The financier merely exploited the word of the time—"Thrift." Like the names he created, he himself was (according to Marlow) a "mere sign, a portent. There was nothing in him" (p. 74).

An empty sign, a commercial man, a manufacturer of names.* Those "mere names" de Barral incorporated eventually collapsed; the "man who was raised to such a height by the credulity of the public" (p. 81) likewise took a fall. This declension is repeatedly enacted through the two epithets attached to the postlapsarian de Barral, the second one ("convict") always inevitably following the first ("financier"), as if by the logic of "every effect has its cause." Marlow suddenly remembers who de Barral is:

"The financier?" I suggested half incredulous.

"Yes," said Fyne; and in this instance his naive solemnity of tone seemed strangely appropriate. "The convict." (p. 69)

The insistence of the two epithets seems to divide de Barral into two different de Barrals, as in this chiasmus passing through his silk hat: "De Barral the convict took off the silk hat of the financier de Barral and deposited it on the front seat of the cab" (p. 362). When the two-

---

*De Barral's criminal financial ventures are insistently related to—almost equated with—his illegitimate linguistic practices. Despite the fact that the *Ferndale* is a commercial vessel, the sailing life is, in the novel's value system, always set in opposition to the world of finance. Wanting to escape their squalid surroundings tainted by the commercial transactions of London, Anthony for the first time takes Flora to "the uncontaminated, honest ship" (p. 334). He does not realize that, when he sets sail with Flora's father, the ex-financier, on board, he is taking the contamination with him.

faced de Barral is given another name, the word "avatar," used to describe his adoption of the alias "Mr. Smith" (pp. 377, 382), again suggests a fall or lapse. "Avatar," from the Sanskrit for "passing or crossing down," refers originally to a Hindu deity who descends to earth, usually in human form. The notion of "The Great De Barral" (one of the ironic chapter titles) as a god incarnated in the form of Mr. Smith is of course sarcastic. The doubleness of the proper name, enacted on the horizontal plane when Powell offers the folded name "Powell" to Powell, was certainly uncanny, but its treatment was not especially pejorative; with the theme of de Barral's fall, however, the duplicity of the proper name has been recast in the vertical register in a way that cannot but vilify. De Barral then ends up the "fall guy." *

There is some suggestion that de Barral's linguistic lapses constitute a *fortunate* fall. Marlow admits that, in all of de Barral's condemnable associations with illegitimate naming, there is one name attached to him that is fitting and proper: "The fellow had a pretty taste in names; and nothing else besides—absolutely nothing—no other merit. Well, yes. He had another name, but that's pure luck—his own name de Barral which he did not invent" (p. 69). The "pure luck" of de Barral's given name suggests that the appellation is somehow apt and fortunate. The narrator observes, "It's clearly a French name" (p. 70); I would like to assert that "de Barral" is a homonym for the French word "débarras" (as in "bon débarras!"—"good riddance!") since this reading supports the general thesis that the financier/convict serves as a scapegoat for the problematic attributes of chance

---

*The "double standard" a literary work applies to the doubling of the proper name (in this case, the unfolding of the Powell/Powell interface, on the one hand, and the declensions of de Barral's name on the other) is also a "double bind" because literature is initially empowered by the play of the proper name but is also entrusted with superintending its propriety. This is an old story: in Shakespeare's *Measure for Measure*, Angelo is another guy set up to take a fall, as his name ("Angel" + the "o" of desire) indicates. The sexual crimes of the fallen Angel-o allow the duke to purge Vienna of its unbridled licentiousness without putting the duke's own name or reputation at risk. Of course, the duke's vicarious crackdown on sexual excesses does not so much improve the civic morality as allow him to renegotiate and deploy his authority more effectively. As this necessarily abbreviated example illustrates, the part literature plays in monitoring and regulating the transgressions of the proper name is more often than not in the service of systems of power the jurisdiction of which by no means stops at the margins of a text.

For an account of the letter "O" as sign of desire in the Shakespearean name, see Fineman, "The Sound of O in *Othello*." This essay includes a helpful exposition of Lacan's analysis of the proper name and makes some provocative claims about the historical and literary importance of Shakespeare's use of names.

and the proper name. The margin of error is wide here, but I offer the suggestion because my argument is after all that there is always a margin of error encroaching on the legibility of the proper name.

De Barral certainly lives up to his name(s). "What frightened [Flora] most was the duplicity of her father" (p. 380), his ability to say cruel and vicious things while seeming to be the model father and father-in-law. He spoke his biting and cutting words with "invariable gentleness" (p. 357). And after the poisoning attempt, Powell is amazed at the old man's nonchalance. De Barral's actions and pronouncements are characterized by what Marlow calls a "sombre and venemous irony" (p. 435). I have already shown how the novel's irony seems to be cured by de Barral's lucky demise, as if the doubleness of language that characterizes the novel at least from the time Powell meets Powell could be purged with his death. If the narrative of *Chance* (unlike Mr. de Barral) survives the effects of such a drastic remedy (poisonous brandy, toxic intoxicants), it must be with quite a hangover.

Describing the way he pieced together Flora de Barral's story, Marlow refers to his deductive investigations as "the old-maiden-lady-like occupation of putting two and two together" (p. 326). If in his narrative desire to put two and two together Marlow is playing Old Maid (a game of chance, not skill), then perhaps we should review the rules.* One queen from the deck of cards is discarded; players then collect pairs, offering their hands of unmatched cards to the other players in rotation. The process continues until all the cards have been paired except for the odd queen, the holder of which is the "Old Maid." Discarding de Barral from the deck of the *Ferndale* allows the novel to put two and two together—first Flora and Anthony, then Flora and Powell—but this pairing is based on an original oddity ("odd man out"), and, in the last draw, when the happy coupling is over, there is an odd remainder. When the doubleness of language is co-opted by and naturalized as the coupling of man and woman—re-presenting the differential nature of language

---

*Although the card game Old Maid is probably not what Marlow's remark denotes, the game was certainly current at the time *Chance* was written. The rules presented here appear in the eleventh edition (1910–11) of *The Encyclopaedia Britannica*, vol. 20. I offer this "Old Maid" reading of *Chance* as a critical instance of the *clinamen* at work, introducing a chance swerve into the interpretive process that takes Conrad's words in a different direction.

in terms of the "natural" categories of sexual difference—there will always be an unaccountable and unmarriable remainder: an old maid. The "Old Maid" that gives the card game its name is the unmatched mate of that originally discarded queen. If in this game of *Chance* de Barral serves as the discarded oddity that allows the neat pairings to take place, who and/or where in the novel is his equally odd counterpart? That is to say, who is the Old Maid?

Fear of Flying

Chance is no doubt for the most part a romantic sea story and not (or not just) "writing about writing." But as the narrator continually points out (pp. 325, 327, 359), Marlow recounts his tale "in the shadow of the bookcase"; the sailor's sea-story is narrated in the shadow of writing. Consider for instance the other "primal scene" Powell witnesses, different from the two primal scenes that give him insights into the Anthonys' married life and "more" primal in its way (and not just because it comes first in the novel) than those not-sex-but-death scenarios. The passage will be quoted at length because its accumulation of dreary details helps explain the importance of the scene. Before finding his way to the shipping master's desk, young Powell wanders lost in the labyrinthine basement of St. Katherine's Dock House. Seeing a door he believes might lead to the Shipping Office, he opens it:

And lo! the place it opened into was hardly any bigger than a cupboard. Anyhow it wasn't more than ten feet by twelve; and as I in a way expected to see the big shadowy cellar-like extent of the Shipping Office where I had been once or twice before, I was extremely startled. A gas bracket hung from the middle of the ceiling over a dark, shabby writing desk covered with a litter of yellowish dusty documents. Under the flame of the single burner which made the place ablaze with light, a plump little man was writing hard, his nose very near the desk. His head was perfectly bald and about the same drab tint as the papers. He appeared pretty dusty too.

I didn't notice whether there were any cobwebs on him, but I shouldn't wonder if there were because he looked as though he had been imprisoned for years in that little hole. The way he dropped his pen and sat blinking my way upset me very much. And his dungeon was hot and musty; it smelt of gas and mushrooms, and seemed somewhere 120 feet below the ground.

Solid, heavy stacks of paper filled all the corners half-way up to the ceiling. (p. 11)*

The opened door reveals to Powell a scene of writing. This is a primal scene because Powell, a character in a novel, walks in on a figure for his author, the novelist hard at work. As Laplanche and Pontalis explain, "the primal scene pictures the origin of the individual."[23] But the origin of a novelistic character like Powell has nothing to do with relations between a man and a woman or the friction of sexual organs; Powell originates in the fictional activities of a writer at a desk, a pen on a piece of paper.†

A writer in the basement of St. Katherine's Dock House? Powell is amazed: "And when the thought flashed upon me that these were the premises of the Marine Board and that this fellow must be connected in some way with ships and sailors and the sea, my astonishment took my breath away" (p. 11). Powell is about to sign on for his first seagoing passage as second officer. As biographical critics have been quick to point out, Powell's experience in getting this position is similar to Conrad's description in his autobiography of how he became a second officer.[24] In this uncanny encounter, which out of context could easily pass for a scene in a Kafka story, the young Powell sees an older man writing, perhaps, about a young sailor about to get his start in life and begin his seafaring adventures. "For some reason or other," Powell comments, "I felt sorry and ashamed to have found him out in his wretched captivity" (p. 11).

Like Powell's other primal scenes, this scene of writing is imbued with death.‡ The generally moribund atmosphere of the closeted

---

*Not enough has been said here about the expressiveness of Conrad's prose, for instance the way this passage piles up dreary drab details like those stacks of faded papers, or the way the passage quoted from the "Author's Note" to *Chance* conveys the feeling of lackadaisical and ruminative drifting as Conrad pondered his narrative alternatives.

†There is a similar primal scene of writing in Virginia Woolf's *The Waves*, p. 13, when one of the children peeks over the wall into "Elvedon": "The lady sits between two long windows, writing. The gardeners sweep the lawn with giant brooms. We are the first to come here. We are the discoverers of an unknown land." Virginia Woolf's image of "the place of writing" is quite a bit more genteel than Conrad's.

‡When the instances multiply like this, it is perhaps inaccurate to speak of a "primal" scene. The constant associations with death and here with writing suggest that Powell's recurring primal scenes might be symptoms of a repetition compulsion. For

writing-scene (Powell in fact speaks of the room as "a gas-lighted grave") fits into the general image pattern of Powell's experience in the Dock House basement. The passages are like "catacombs"; it was "as still as a grave"; he passes through "a six-feet wide strip" into a "vaulted" room (pp. 10, 12). Powell, like Flora, manages to elude a sepulchral destiny by escaping to sea. He is in this scene about to book passage aboard the *Ferndale*; the imagery illuminates the terms of Powell's rite of passage—"passing through death into a new life"—which is signaled by the repeated pun referring to his position on the *Ferndale* as his "berth."

The accumulation of dreary details describing the writer's enclosure connects this figure in interesting ways, if we simply put two and two together, with de Barral. The "hot and musty room" "ablaze with light" which "smelt of gas and mushrooms" and seemed "somewhere 120 feet below the ground" suggests a living hell, and the stacks and stacks of paper a kind of clerical eternal torment.* Just before attempting to poison Captain Anthony, de Barral asks Flora "if she believed in—in hell. In eternal punishment?" (p. 394). The most salient feature of this passage's imagery, though, is the persistent suggestion of confinement and incarceration: "cupboard," "imprisoned," "that little hole," "dungeon," "captivity," and finally "gas-lighted grave." The connection with de Barral the convict, imprisoned for seven years, is clear.

The curious thing about de Barral's imprisonment is that it does not seem to end after he is released from prison. He thinks of himself as "locked up!" (p. 373) aboard ship; "[i]t's like being in jail," he says, referring to Captain Anthony as the "[h]ead jailer" (p. 381). Of course, imagery of confinement is often associated with other characters, Flora in particular. But in Flora's case, her love of the open and honest sea eventually (after her father's death) frees her.† Not so

---

an insightful discussion of how the fantasy of the primal scene becomes problematic in relation to writing and repetition, see Lukacher, *Primal Scenes*.

*The act of writing was often hellish for Conrad, who suffered mental and physical anguish whenever he was working intensely on a story. He suffered a nervous breakdown shortly after finishing *Under Western Eyes* (1911) and described his slow return to work on *Chance* as "like coming out of one little hell into another." He wrote to Ford Madox Ford about his progress on the novel, "I am writing, however, spasmodically, with long intervals of absolute dumbness. *Quel enfer!*" Quoted in Karl, *Joseph Conrad*, pp. 683, 699.

†Frees her, that is, to be dependent on her husband(s).

de Barral: when Flora first tells him of the plan to take him "away over the blue sea, the sure, the inaccessible, the uncontaminated and spacious refuge for wounded souls," he reacts like a trapped animal "scared by the first touch of a net falling on its back" (p. 365). De Barral is *always* behind bars; he is the unreformable, unregenerate prisoner who takes his prison with him wherever he goes—even to sea.

It is no doubt de Barral's own perversities that debar him from conversion to and liberation by the life at sea. There is, however, in the case of the landlocked Marlow, the slightest suggestion that he himself does not return to sea because he has (or "should" have) lost faith in its regenerative powers. The narrator observes: "The sea is the sailor's true element, and Marlow, lingering on shore, was to me an object of incredulous commiseration like a bird, which, secretly, should have lost its faith in the high virtue of flying" (p. 34). A strange use of the word "should" in this passage; does it mean the bird *has* lost faith in flying or that it *ought to* lose its faith?

There is in *Chance* a nostalgia for an Edenic sea life (signaled by the name of Captain Anthony's ship, the *Ferndale*), which is precisely paralleled by a nostalgia for Adamic naming. An unrealizable faith in the purity and propriety of the sea and the name cannot but lead to the inevitable fall. Perhaps then Marlow *should* have lost such faith. The fate of de Barral and of the name "de Barral" would restore these prelapsarian ideal states by cleansing them of the "contamination" they carry. De Barral is buried at sea having been poisoned by his own ironic toast to luck; and the name "de Barral," by means of its avatar into "Smith" and the conversion of Flora de Barral into Flora Anthony and then Flora Powell, disappears from the face of the earth.

De Barral never escapes his hellish prison; he takes it with him to sea and the sea becomes his grave, full fathom five. Powell wonders if the writer (who, no less than de Barral, fabricates names for money) fares any better: "I wonder sometimes whether he succeeded in writing himself into liberty and a pension at last, or had to go out of his gas-lighted grave straight into that other dark one where nobody would want to intrude" (p. 12). Joseph Conrad, the sailor turned writer, was working in his study, writing at his desk, the day he died.* We can only wonder with Powell if he ever wrote himself

---

*He was working on an article entitled "Legends." See Curle, *Last Twelve Years of Conrad*, pp. 202–12.

into liberty or whether his death was, like de Barral's, a passage from a gravelike prison to the eternal prison of the grave. "For some of us," Derrida states (joining company with Epicurus and Lucretius), "the principle of indeterminism is what makes the conscious freedom of man fathomable" (p. 8). Conrad's liberty from—and in—the infernal and funereal constraints of writing is a function of his endorsement of chance in *Chance* and his dissociation from the all-too-determined fate of de Barral.

There is something unmistakably uncanny going on when young Powell encounters the older writer and then comes face-to-face with Powell in *Chance*. In Freud's discussion of the experience of the uncanny, he concludes: "An uncanny experience occurs either when repressed infantile complexes have been revived by some impression, or when the primitive beliefs we have surmounted seem once more to be confirmed." But performing the psychoanalytic *unheimlich* maneuver on this scene from *Chance* does not explain its uncanniness. Freud acknowledges, "The uncanny as it is depicted in *literature*, in stories and imaginative productions, merits in truth a separate discussion." [25] Powell's chance encounters are uncanny because they demonstrate that, despite the scapegoating that goes on when de Barral is dispatched with such dispatch, those features Freud associates with the *unheimlich*—doubling, repetition, a relation to the death instinct—are intrinsic to writing. Powell's uncanny experiences in St. Katherine's Dock House stage a primal scene of writing that does not neatly conform to the psychoanalytic schema. The literary act of naming dramatized in Powell's encounter with Powell and that fictional character's encounter with his writer constitutes a fantasy of origins: the primal scene of literature is the proper name.*

---

*In his essay "Significance of Literature," Joel Fineman explains the connection between the proper name and literary language: "[T]he special propriety of a proper name with respect to common nouns corresponds precisely to the specialized charge of literature with respect to so-called ordinary language—"so-called" because there could no more be an ordinary language without its fictive complement than there could be a natural language bereft of its fantasy of the propriety of proper names" (p. 83). This essay also includes a helpful history of thinking about the proper name in linguistic philosophy (see especially ftn. 7).

When I say that the primal scene of literature is the proper name, it should be remembered that the applicability of such adjectives as "primal" and "proper," which register the element of fantasy in their makeup, is questionable in relation to an uncanny differential structure that necessarily entails repetition and duplicity.

The next chapter will examine the way the proper name works as the locus for James Joyce's treatment of chance; I will consider why and how the disconcerting aspects of chance and the proper name, which Conrad would expunge from his novel with the expulsion of de Barral ("Good riddance!"), find a place in and help to shape the narrative of *Ulysses*. Joyce's receptiveness to the operations of chance allows him to formulate a narrative mode that does not necessarily yield to an altogether fateful reading. *Ulysses* then marks a limit point in this study because it comes as close as any novel can to a representation of chance in narrative.

CHAPTER FOUR

Tittles and Asymptotes: The Hyperbolic Function of Chance in *Ulysses*

At a time when his failing vision prevented him from writing, James Joyce dictated some of *Finnegans Wake* (1939) to Samuel Beckett. Richard Ellmann recounts what happened on one of these occasions in his biography of Joyce:

[I]n the middle of one such session there was a knock at the door which Beckett didn't hear. Joyce said, "Come in," and Beckett wrote it down. Afterwards he read back what he had written and Joyce said, "What's that 'Come in'?" "Yes, you said that," said Beckett. Joyce thought for a moment, then said, "Let it stand." He was quite willing to accept coincidence as his collaborator.[1]

With the inclusion of the words "come in" in *Finnegans Wake*, Joyce blithely welcomed the dictates of chance into his text.

Chance is also made welcome in *Ulysses* (1922), though a critical tradition in Joyce studies has not been so hospitable. This chapter examines a theme *in* the novel (consubstantial becoming transubstantial paternity) and a critical approach *to* the novel (informed by that theme) that work to efface all traces of chance in *Ulysses*. After explaining the terms and conditions of the novel's transubstantial aesthetic, I consider the cluster of meanings attached to the word "throwaway" (which refers to both a racehorse and a piece of paper read and discarded by Leopold Bloom). The horse and the flier, which are emphatically associated with chance in *Ulysses*, together constitute a linguistic focus for the argument: the chance associations between the proper name "Throwaway" and the common noun "throwaway" graphically represent the aleatory aspects of language in Joyce's fiction. I then articulate an "aesthetic of the throwaway" that, in contrast to the transubstantial aesthetic, figures a way to think about chance in *Ulysses* that is not necessarily effaced by the novel's narrative operations. I argue that the transubstantial aesthetic characterizes not just the usual pattern of thinking about chance in *Ulysses*; it also represents the standard kind of thinking about chance in *any* novel. The deviations of the throwaway aesthetic in *Ulysses* then offer another way to think about chance in the novel (*any* novel) that does not necessarily yield to an altogether fateful reading.

Pater Semper Incertus Est

As is well known, *Ulysses* is structured by a relationship of father and son that answers in a different form Stephen Dedalus's appeal to his namesake-father at the end of *A Portrait of the Artist as a Young Man* (1916): "Old father, old artificer, stand me now and ever in good stead."[2] The father figure Stephen finds in *Ulysses*, who quite literally stands him upright (though none too steadily), is not an abstract symbol-name but a Good Samaritan named Leopold Bloom.* In Stephen's Shakespeare lecture he articulates—half-consciously ("What the hell are you driving at?/I know. Shut up. Blast you. I have reasons")—the paternal theme of the novel:

Fatherhood, in the sense of conscious begetting, is unknown to man. It is a mystical estate, an apostolic succession, from only begetter to only begotten. On that mystery and not on the madonna which the cunning Italian intellect flung to the mobs of Europe the church is founded, and founded irremov-

---

*"Mr. Bloom . . . bucked him up generally in orthodox Samaritan fashion which he very badly needed. His (Stephen's) mind was not exactly what you would call wandering but a bit unsteady." Stephen is drunk and has just been knocked down by a soldier's fist so probably more than his mind is a little unsteady. Joyce, *Ulysses: The Corrected Text*, chap. 16, ll. 1–5. Chapter and line numbers of quoted passages will henceforth appear in parentheses after the quotations. I choose to cite the Gabler edition although its authority is not final. Questions about what would constitute a finally authoritative edition of *Ulysses* are certainly part of the problematic considered here, though I do not pursue the argument into areas of editorial controversy. The recent debates about what should and should not be on the pages of *Ulysses* we read testify to the fact that, in an infinitely complex, matter-of-fact, and indelible way, chance has left its mark on the text of *Ulysses*.

ably because founded, like the world, macro and microcosm, upon the void. Upon incertitude, upon unlikelihood. *Amor matris*, subjective and objective genitive, may be the only true thing in life. Paternity may be a legal fiction. (9.837–44)

The terms of this well-known passage are echoed later, when Stephen describes his role as artist, in a passage that makes clear that the novel is elaborating aesthetic principles based on the thematics of paternal uncertainty: "He affirmed his significance as a conscious rational animal proceeding syllogistically from the known to the unknown and a conscious rational reagent between a micro and a macrocosm ineluctably constructed upon the incertitude of the void" (17. 1112–15). This reading of chance in *Ulysses* will begin by following Stephen's lead, "proceeding syllogistically from the known to the unknown" in order to determine why and how the narrative form of the novel is "ineluctably constructed upon the incertitude of the void." As I will show, the notion of chance encompassed by the idea of the uncertain void always leads to one certain place, a place that, finally, this reading will try to *a*void. I will therefore be going through the paces of this syllogistic logic only eventually to sidestep it and arrive at a more comprehensive understanding of chance as it informs the narrative structure of *Ulysses*.

In his Shakespeare theory Stephen elaborates a homology between the *dramatis personae* of *Hamlet* and the members of Shakespeare's own family in order to argue a correspondence between Shakespeare and (not Hamlet the melancholy prince but) the ghost of Hamlet senior, the cuckolded and murdered king. Stephen therefore concludes, "Hamlet, the black prince, is Hamnet Shakespeare" (9.883), William's dead son. A sketch of the homology (including presumptive adulteries) appears in Figures 1a and 1b. Stephen's homology collates nicely with the three-character structure of *Ulysses* adapted from the Homeric epic, all of which encourages the placement of Bloom and Stephen in the pre-coded relationship of father and son, as diagramed in Figures 2a and 2b. The problem with the configuration in Figure 2b, of course, is that the Blooms and Stephen simply are not related unless Leopold Bloom committed fruitful adultery with Stephen's far-from-promiscuous mother some 23 years previous to the day the novel takes place. This is not likely, nor is it the kind of unlikelihood structuring *Ulysses*'s paternal pattern. The actual family

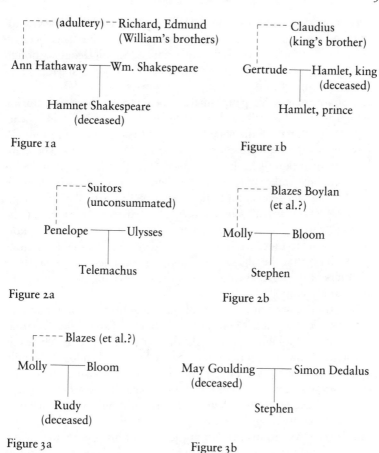

Figure 1a

Figure 1b

Figure 2a

Figure 2b

Figure 3a

Figure 3b

relationships of the three characters in the novel are sketched in Figures 3a and 3b.

As Bloom remarks, "Do anything you like with figures juggling. Always find out this equal to that" (11.833–34). In Buck Mulligan's parodic version of Stephen's theory, young Dedalus "proves by algebra that Hamlet's grandson is Shakespeare's grandfather and that he himself is the ghost of his own father" (1.555–57). Similarly, simple algebra transfigures the two distinct familial formulations (Figs. 3a, 3b) into an equation with the desired result (Fig. 2b), the symbolic structure that fits *Ulysses* to a T. All one has to do is factor out the three nonessential terms (Simon Dedalus; May Dedalus, *née* Gould-ing; and Rudy Bloom). These substitutions are all the easier because two of the supplanted relations are dead; and Simon Dedalus, though still alive, seems like a ghost haunting his own body, a spirit expired but still clinging to the site of its past glories. In the "Sirens" chap-ter, Simon makes his penultimate appearance in the novel, during which he sings Lionel's song from the opera *Martha* in Bloom's hear-ing; at the climax of the song Simon and Leopold merge in Lionel's lament in the one-word paragraph: "Siopold!" (11.752). The sym-bolic substitution of Molly for Stephen's mother is a bit more com-plicated, but it takes place when Stephen rejects his ghostly ghoulish mother and her sepulchral faith in favor of "[t]he intellectual imagi-nation!" (15.4227). Bloom's son, Rudy, and Stephen merge at the end of "Circe" (15.4956–67), when a vision of Rudy-if-he-had-not-died appears to Bloom as he stands guard over Stephen's unconscious body. With that the algebraic operation is complete; the final three chapters of the novel then work out the possible implications of this new family unit.

The transfiguration from consubstantial to transubstantial parent-hood works to efface the element of chance in the child's relation to his or her biological parents. In the most general sense, chance is insistent in the question at the core of what Freud called the family romance*—"Why was I born into *this* family?"—which raises the corollary question, "Why in the chromosomal shuffle of my concep-tion did I get dealt *these* genetic cards?" But an aspect of chance specific to consubstantial *paternity* informs *Ulysses*'s symbolic alge-bra. Joyce wrote to his brother at the birth of his son (in almost the same words Stephen uses in his discussion of Shakespeare): "I think a child should be allowed to take his father's or mother's name at will in coming of age. Paternity is a legal fiction."[3] The actual father of a child is and remains a mystery; there is then always an element of chance refracting the patrilineal link between father and son.

The "medium" that refracts the otherwise straight line of descent from father to son is of course the woman's body, which is specifi-cally a sexual body—the threat of adultery gives rise to the threat of filial illegitimacy. At the end of *Exiles* (1918), the play that Joyce

*Freud, "Family Romances." The realization that, as Freud puts it, *pater semper incertus est* while the mother is *certissima* is a constitutive factor in the specifically sexual stage of the family romance.

wrote between *A Portrait of the Artist as a Young Man* and *Ulysses*, the hero tells his wife (who may or may not have been unfaithful to him):

I have wounded my soul for you—a deep wound of doubt which can never be healed. I can never know, never in this world. I do not wish to know or to believe. I do not care. It is not in the darkness of belief I desire you. But in restless living wounding doubt. To hold you by no bonds, even of love, to be united with you in body and soul and in utter nakedness—for this I longed.[4]

In the "Notes" to the play Joyce remarked on the hero's desire to unite with his wife in this complete way: "He is jealous, wills and knows his own dishonour and the dishonour of her, to be united in every phase of whose being is love's end, as to achieve that union in the region of the difficult, the void and the impossible is its [that is, love's] necessary tendency."[5] Joyce's topographical phrasing—"the region of the difficult"—suggests one means of understanding the incertitude of what he calls here and in *Ulysses* "the void." The imagery of the hero's "deep wound of doubt which can never be healed" in *Exiles* comes from Wagner's *Parsifal*: Amfortas, king of the Grail, is bewitched by a beautiful woman and so loses to an evil sorcerer the Sacred Spear, which wounded Christ; he is himself wounded by the Spear, a wound that never ceases to bleed. The "wound" the hero receives (in *Parsifal*, in *Exiles*, and anticipatively in *Ulysses*) is not simply *inflicted* on the male body and the artist's sense of masculine integrity by female sexuality; the wound *is* female sexuality, and for Joyce this wound-womb is the dark, mysterious, and uncertain source of creativity.

The Past Repaired, the Future Provided

If paternity is a legal fiction, then perhaps fiction is the only way to ensure filial legitimacy. Late in the novel, when Bloom considers what for him "rendered problematic" any future contact with Stephen, two anecdotes indicate how chance permeates both the past and the future of paternity: a clown at a circus once accused Bloom of being his father (an example of "the irreparability of the past"); and a notched coin that Bloom circulated never returned to him (an example of "the imprevidibility of the future" [17.973–88]). Transubstantial paternity would repair the past, which is haunted by consub-

stantial paternal doubts—did Bloom father a clown? did someone
else father his son, Rudy, making Bloom a cuckolded clown?* It
would also provide for the future by prophylactically controlling the
disturbing consequences of dissemination (of the coin, without return; of the seed, without insemination). The accusing clown mocks
Bloom's progenitive past, and the unreturning coin figures the losses
of his filial future; the anxieties attached to the irreparable paternal
past and the imprevidible (unforeseeable) disseminal future, which
problematize Bloom's connection with Stephen, have their source in
the uncertainties of female sexuality.

Unlike Stephen, "conscious rational reagent between a micro and a
macrocosm ineluctably constructed upon the incertitude of the void,"
Bloom is described as "a conscious reactor *against* the void of incertitude" (17.2210–11, my emphasis). This we are told as Bloom
is affected by various "antagonistic sentiments" accompanying the
thought of Molly's sexual activities with Blazes Boylan. The "final
satisfaction" in which "these antagonistic sentiments and reflections,
reduced to their simplest forms, converge" is Molly's flesh, specifically her breasts and buttocks, the four car(di)nal points of Bloom's
world: "Satisfaction at the ubiquity in eastern and western terrestrial hemispheres . . . of adipose anterior and posterior female hemispheres, redolent of milk and honey and of excretory sanguine and
seminal warmth, . . . expressive of mute immutable mature animality"
(17.2227–36). In a famous letter to a friend about the "Penelope"
chapter, Joyce wrote: "It turns like the huge earth ball slowly surely
and evenly around and round spinning, its four cardinal points being
the female breasts, arse, womb, and cunt."[6] Bloom's omission of the
womb and cunt from his geography of the female body suggests that
Joyce had a more complete and sympathetic view of woman that included with equanimity the *topos* of female sexuality. Bloom is "a
conscious reactor against the void of incertitude," and the structure
of transubstantial paternity can easily be seen as a reaction-formation

---

*It is curious that, in a text and a husband haunted by the threat of adultery, the
question of who Rudy's father was never becomes a real issue. Bloom assumes his
paternity when he assumes the time and place of Rudy's conception (see 6.77–81).
The authoritative voice of the "Ithaca" chapter confirms Bloom's fathering of Milly
but only says that Bloom and Molly enjoyed sexual relations up until five weeks before
Rudy's birth; whether or not Bloom was there when "complete carnal intercourse,
with ejaculation of semen within the natural female organ" (17.78–79) resulted in
conception is an open question. The denizens of Kiernan's Pub have their doubts:
when someone mentions in Bloom's absence that his wife gave birth to two children,
the citizen sneers, "And who does he suspect?" (12.1657).

responding to that void, understood specifically as female sexuality: the transubstantial theme in *Ulysses* is one way to leave the womb and cunt out of account. I would nevertheless insist that the representation of the woman in *Ulysses* is a limited one—limited by Joyce's view of the female sex—and not simply a depiction of any one character's viewpoint. This is so because in Joyce's writing it is always a matter of representing—not *a* or *some* but—*the* woman.*

The shift from consubstantial to transubstantial paternity is a fantasy of parthenogenesis that would finesse the incertitude Joyce locates in the woman's body. The potential adulterations of consubstantial sexual relations are expurgated by the assured filiations of transubstantial fatherhood, which is modeled on Christological principles. In a revealing analysis of the culmination of the father-son theme in the "Eumaeus" chapter, Ralph W. Rader argues persuasively that Bloom and Stephen are united as Father and Son through a peculiar mediating Holy Ghost: Stephen, a stand-in for the young Joyce, unites with Bloom, the mature Joyce as he imagines himself in another; and the character in the novel who brings them together, a figure for Joyce the artist, is a rather unsavory sailor (repeatedly associated with Shakespeare) named D. B. Murphy.† The very different configuration of *trans*substantial paternity would then look like this: ‡

---

*It is perhaps a strange thing to say in criticism of Joyce today, but I find his treatment and representation of the woman *vulgar*. Not in the sense expressed by genteel readers (Virginia Woolf included) and Customs officials who criticized Joyce for his improprieties in representing the body and all of its functions; but vulgar in the sense that the woman's body is first made to be the carrier and transmitter of the thousand natural shocks that flesh is traditionally heir to (carnality, materiality, temporality, mortality, uncertainty, etc.) before it is exalted. As poetic as the description of Bloom's consolatory satisfactions in the face of his wife's adultery may be, the vulgar sense of the "adipose anterior and posterior female hemispheres" passage—from which I do not think it entirely dissociates itself—is "tits and ass." In order to resist such a vulgar rendering of the woman, this reading finally avoids the "void of incertitude" theme in *Ulysses* by considering chance not in gendered but in grammatological and mathematical terms, as indicated by the ti(t)tle of this chapter.

†Rader, "Exodus and Return." Before the corrected edition was published, it was thought that the sailor's name was W. B., not D. B., Murphy. The alacrity with which Rader adapted this new textual information to his theory testifies to the assimilative powers of what I call the transubstantial criticism of *Ulysses*. For such criticism, eucharistic wine (which Rader, following Ellmann, associates with Molly's menstrual blood) is a universal solvent. The response to the "D. B." emendation appears in Rader, "Logic of *Ulysses*," p. 571.

‡I include these diagrams of consubstantial and transubstantial family relations in order to emphasize the very different structures of these types of relations. The contrasting family configurations clearly highlight how the introduction of "middler the

Father:	Bloom	Mature Joyce
(Mary) [Holy Ghost]:	(Molly) [D. B. Murphy]	(Nora) [Artist Joyce]
Son:	Stephen	Young Joyce

This model of transubstantial fatherhood marginalizes the woman, thereby relieving the paternal doubts intrinsic to female sexuality. The (by definition) sexual woman in Joyce's father-son schema then acquires a different role: she is no longer the source of incertitude; she becomes instead the agent of destiny, opening "the portals of discovery" (9.229) to the artist. The woman initiates the young man sexually, inflicting a womb-wound that becomes a potential source of artistic creativity. In *A Portrait* Stephen explicitly linked artistic creativity with Christ's miraculous conception: "In the virgin womb of the imagination the word was made flesh," he says of the inspiration resulting in the composition of his villanelle.[7] The incarnation suggested by Stephen's Shakespeare theory has become overtly (not just metaphorically) sexual, a violent violation that the artist is both eager for and crippled by. Stephen says of Ann Hathaway's seduction of the young Shakespeare: "The tusk of the boar has wounded him there where love lies ableeding. . . . There is, I feel in the words, some goad of the flesh driving him into a new passion, a darker shadow of the first, darkening even his own understanding of himself" (9.459–64). Stephen is himself ripe for such a wound: after referring to the "bold-faced Stratford wench who tumbles in a cornfield a lover younger than herself" (that is, Shakespeare), his silent successive thought is, "And my turn? When? / Come!" (9.259–62).

Ralph Rader argues that *Ulysses* takes place on June 16, 1904, to commemorate the day when Joyce's future wife, Nora Barnacle, did to him what Ann Hathaway supposedly did to Shakespeare (and Stephen would like done unto him), that is, initiate him with a sexual experience from which he never completely recovered.[8] The biographical account of Joyce's initiation at the hands of Nora Barnacle as it is played out in *Ulysses* then replicates Stephen's biographical account of Shakespeare's relation with Ann Hathaway as it is played out in *Hamlet*:

Hamlet King	Mature Shakespeare
(Gertrude) [Hamlet Ghost]	(Ann Hathaway) [Artist Shakespeare]
Hamlet Prince	Young Shakespeare

Holy Ghost" (9.493) into the transubstantial schema mediates relations between men by marginalizing the threat of the sexual woman and the sense of chance she embodies.

Stephen does not say very much about Gertrude's possible influence on Prince Hamlet beyond her status as the sexual woman of the play; perhaps Joyce left the implications of a specifically sexual *amor matris* in *Hamlet* to "the new Viennese school" (9.780) Stephen mentions in his discussion of Shakespeare.

In the idiom of "mathematical catechism," as Joyce called the style of "Ithaca,"[9] what potential function might Molly perform in the incarnation of the son (Stephen) vis-à-vis the transubstantial father (Bloom)? The answer is appropriately mathematical. The rapport established between Stephen and Bloom in "Ithaca" is (as most commentators have observed) not altogether intimate or secure. The first of the chapter's clinical interrogatives sets the tone for the anticlimax of their halting and faltering rapprochement: "What parallel courses did Bloom and Stephen follow returning?" (17.1). "Parallel courses" does not suggest an emphatic coming together since, as we are soon reminded, "parallel lines meet . . . at infinity" (17.2086). On the next page following this Euclidean reminder we discover the reason for Bloom's worldly subjunctive smile on the subject of his wife's adultery:

If he had smiled why would he have smiled?

To reflect that each one who enters imagines himself to be the first to enter whereas he is always the last term of a preceding series even if the first term of a succeeding one, each imagining himself to be the first, last, only and alone whereas he is neither first nor last nor only nor alone in a series originating in and repeated to infinity. (17.2126–31)

If Bloom and Stephen follow parallel courses, then the infinity in which they meet might very well be Molly as the embodiment of female sexuality. "[P]roceeding syllogistically from the known to the unknown," like the letters S-M-P initiating the three sections of the novel (conventional signs for the three terms of a syllogism), has its logical conclusion (quite literally) *in* Molly.

The various homological versions of transubstantial paternity in *Ulysses* suggest that, along with the fatherly solicitude he receives from Bloom, Stephen may experience a sexual initiation with Molly similar to the one with Nora that Joyce apparently experienced and the one with Ann Hathaway that he claims Shakespeare underwent. And Molly would no doubt be glad to fill the bill: in "Penelope" she imagines a sexual relationship with Stephen, thinking simultaneously of her attraction for the statue of a young and wounded Narcis-

sus, which Bloom brought home one day (18.1349ff.); perhaps the
wound *she* would inflict on him would shatter the mirror of Stephen's
rarefied narcissism. Stephen is depicted throughout *Ulysses* as alien-
ated from his own "dogsbody"; the *nostos* he eventually experiences
might therefore be a homecoming to the flesh, a worldly incarnation
made possible by Molly's earthly and earthy teachings.

The *amor matris* Molly embodies is (it is suggested) that of "Gea-
Tellus" (17.2313), the Earth Mother. Her god is not the sepulchral
god of Stephen's consubstantial mother, "chewer of corpses" (1.278),
but a life-reveling creator: "God of heaven theres nothing like nature
the wild mountains then the sea and the waves rushing then the beautiful country . . . nature it is as for them saying theres no God I
wouldnt give a snap of my two fingers for all their learning why dont
they go and create something" (18.1558–65), which is (we are made
to think) what she and Bloom will enable the young Stephen to do.
In *Ulysses* the mature Joyce created an entire world, microcosm and
macrocosm; and like Shakespeare (who has created more than anyone except God [9.1028–29]), in the act of creation he became "not
the father of his own son merely, but, being no more a son, was and
felt himself to be the father of his own race" (9.867–69).

But hold your horses. This sanguine and eucharistic reading of the
novel, a reading that transubstantiates the familial relationships into
a trinitarian unity and mystery, would efface any trace of chance
in *Ulysses*. The theme of transubstantial paternity *in* the novel has
engendered a critical approach *to* the novel that transubstantiates
the aleatory features of *Ulysses* into "art"; according to this critical
school, chance becomes fate because "what happens" (the experience of the characters) is always already "*meant* to happen" (the
experience of the critically educated reader). The work of Ralph W.
Rader works out the logic and aesthetic principles of *Ulysses*'s transubstantial paternity theme, summarizing and synthesizing much of
what critics have said about the novel's artistic program. In Rader's
reading, which I consider the most insightful and persuasive articu-
lation of the transubstantial aesthetic in *Ulysses*, nothing is left to
chance. "As in the opening episodes we watch Stephen and his com-
panions move through their hours of contingency," he writes, "they
come to appear to us strangely uncontingent." This is because of
the Holy Ghost-like presence of Joyce's artistry, "the presence which
everywhere translates the random real to the order of art." [10] But this

Ghostly presence does not quite expunge all traces of contingency and randomness in *Ulysses*. There is a residue of intoxicating wine left unaltared in the chalice. After the artistic rites of transubstantiation have been performed there remains a ghost of a chance in *Ulysses*; that ghost is a horse named Throwaway.

A Ghost of a Chance

The terms and conditions of *Ulysses*'s transubstantial-paternity theme are explicated in three sections of the novel: most elaborately in Stephen's Shakespeare lecture in "Scylla and Charybdis"; in the "Eumaeus" chapter in relation to the character D. B. Murphy, who is repeatedly associated with Shakespeare; and in a pivotal scene of "Circe" (15.3821–3989)—a passage I will now consider in some detail—that also invokes Shakespeare. In the fantasmatic-dramatic style of the chapter, Bloom has just eagerly observed Molly and Blazes Boylan engaged in vigorous carnal intercourse when a character points to a mirror; the "stage directions" read: "(*Stephen and Bloom gaze in the mirror. The face of William Shakespeare, beardless, appears there, rigid in facial paralysis, crowned by the reflection of the reindeer antlered hatrack in the hall.*)" (15.3821–24). Stephen and Bloom unite under the cuckold's crown in and with the image of Shakespeare. Stephen then recalls fragments of the dream that had previously returned to him as he encountered Bloom at the end of "Scylla and Charybdis" (9.1207–8). In his dream Stephen flew, "[m]y foes beneath me. And ever shall be. World without end. (*he cries*) *Pater*! Free!" (15.3935–36). Stephen's dream is of Icarus-Dedalus in flight. But despite the repeated interjections of Bloom ("Look . . . ," "I say, look . . ."), Stephen thinks his father/son flight-dream refers to his *con*substantial father; Simon Dedalus therefore appears (for the last time in the novel) and the bird-men become two winged scavengers:

STEPHEN

Break my spirit will he? O *merde alors*! (*he cries, his vulture talons sharpened*) Hola! Hillyho!

(*Simon Dedalus' voice hilloes in answer, somewhat sleepy but ready*)

SIMON

That's all right. (*he swoops uncertainly through the air, wheeling, uttering cries of heartening, on strong ponderous buzzard wings*) Ho, boy! Are you going to win? Hoop! Pschatt! Stable with those halfcastes. Wouldn't let them within the bawl of an ass. Head up! Keep our flag flying! An eagle gules volant in a field argent displayed. (15.3940–49)

The stage directions then describe a fox hunt (*"A stout fox, drawn from covert, brush pointed, having buried his grandmother, runs swift for the open, brighteyed, seeking badger earth under the leaves"*), which segues (by way of the fox-hunting horses) into a ghostly horse-race: "(*A dark horse, riderless, bolts like a phantom past the winningpost, his mane moonfoaming, his eyeballs stars. The field follows, a bunch of bucking mounts. Skeleton horses, Sceptre, Maximum the Second, Zinfandel . . .*)" (15.3951–54, 3974–77).

The logical connections in the "Circe" chapter are specifically psychological; this scene dramatizes the motives of both Bloom and Stephen in their unspoken desire for filial and paternal connection. Bloom would have a son, the image of himself, whose legitimacy is not perforated by the impaling doubt accompanying the cuckold's horns; and Stephen would have a father to help him fly over and away from his squalid family and personal history and make good the family name. But Stephen is still not quite able to recognize or accept Bloom's fatherly concern; only when (nine pages later) he finally rejects the ghost of his consubstantial mother, also depicted as a scavenger ("The ghoul! Hyena!" Stephen screams at his mother's apparition [15.4200]) in the climactic chandelier-smashing scene, is he prepared to embrace the possibilities of transubstantial parenthood.

The indirect way into a reading of this scene, which links the transubstantial-paternity theme to a ghostly horse-race, begins with a consideration of riddles in *Ulysses*. Stephen tells the riddle of the fox burying his grandmother, which recurs in the "stage directions" describing the fox hunt, to his eager then frustrated students early in the novel (2.101–15). As Don Gifford and Robert J. Seidman point out, "Stephen's riddle is a joke at the expense of riddles since it is unanswerable unless the answer is already known."[11] This is true of several of the riddles in the novel, and I believe that, in a sense, these riddles all have the same answer. Gifford and Seidman go on in the same entry to give a source for Stephen's riddle: "See P. W. Joyce, *English as We Speak It in Ireland*, p. 187." I would submit that one— not the only, not even perhaps the most important, but certainly one—reason Joyce included this puzzling riddle was to suggest his own name by alluding to the name of the riddle's anthologizer, P. W.

Joyce (no relation).* Another explicit riddle in the novel, the identity of D. B. Murphy, is described first as a "rebus" (16.1234) and then as a mathematical puzzle: "[A]s to who he in reality was let x equal my right name and address, as Mr. Algebra remarks *passim*" (16.1635–37). And consider the most famous riddle of the novel, called "a selfinvolved enigma" for Bloom, which he asks himself before falling asleep: "Who was M'Intosh?" (17.2063–66), that is, the ghostly man in the macintosh who attends Paddy Dignam's funeral in the "Hades" chapter. All of these riddles are jokes at the expense of riddles because they are strictly speaking unanswerable unless the answer is already known; and the answer in each case is (or is it?) "Joyce." †

That the fox riddle suggests Joyce's name in this passage is further supported by the emblem on the flag that Simon Dedalus urges Stephen to keep flying ("An eagle gules volant in a field argent displayed"). Although it depicts a bird in flight, it is not the Dedalus flag; Gifford and Seidman point out that it is the coat of arms of the Joyces of County Galway.[12]

There is a crowd on hand for the horse race, playing various games of chance (*"dicers, crown and anchor players, thimbleriggers, broadsmen"*) while bookies clamor the odds they are offering on the horses. The race is a ghostly re-running of the Gold Cup at Ascot run

---

*James Joyce was certainly familiar with the work of P. W. Joyce, as we know since he included a reference to that author's *Irish Names of Places* in "Gas from a Burner," a poem that attacked the publisher and printer who refused to print *Dubliners*. The printer's name was Falconer, and in this passage Stephen and Simon Dedalus call and answer each other ("Hola! Hillyho!") with falconers' cries; the odds against *Dubliners*'s ever being published should then perhaps be kept in mind in the discussion of the horse race that follows. See Ellmann, *James Joyce*, pp. 335–36, for the text of "Gas from a Burner" and mention of P. W. Joyce's work.

†In "*Ulysses* as Ghoststory," Shari Benstock reviews other critical identifications of the man in the macintosh and goes on to suggest that he might be Joyce. Brook Thomas does likewise in *James Joyce's "Ulysses,"* pp. 67–74, and he makes some general observations about the way the name M'Intosh, given to the mystery man, reflects on the nominality of names (pp. 113–28). In *Joyce's Uncertainty Principle*, Phillip F. Herring concludes that the Macintosh riddle is not supposed to have an answer. (Judging from the title, it might seem that Herring's book would be relevant to this study of chance in Joyce's writing; in fact, though, *Joyce's Uncertainty Principle* has very little to say about Heisenberg's theories and even less to say about chance.)

Whether or not the man in the macintosh is "really" Joyce, he (M'Intosh) apparently agrees with him (Joyce) that "a child should be allowed to take his father's or mother's name at will in coming of age." When the man in the macintosh appears in "Circe," he says of Bloom: "Don't you believe a word he says. That man is Leopold M'Intosh, the notorious fireraiser. His real name is Higgins" (15.1561–62). "Higgins" was Bloom's mother's maiden name.

earlier that day, which was unexpectedly won by a dark horse named Throwaway who paid twenty to one. The winning horse is described with "mane moonfoaming, his eyeballs stars," which refers back to Stephen's image of Jonathan Swift, another beleaguered Irish writer, in a paragraph that begins considering the Dedalus family's decline ("Houses of decay, mine, his, and all" [3.105]). Simon Dedalus yells to his son, "Ho boy! Are you going to win?" and then—after two indirect references to the Joyce name—the race is run. Although the victorious phantom horse is "riderless," there is a lot riding on this ghostly race—no less than the family name, Dedalus *and* Joyce.

The phantom dark horse, like the ghostly manifestations of the man in the macintosh and D. B. Murphy, is an enigma that invites us (guided by Stephen's identification of Shakespeare with King Hamlet's ghost) to read into its opacity the ghostly presence of the author.[13] "What is a ghost?" Stephen asks, then answers: "One who has faded into impalpability through death, through absence, through change of manners" (9.147–49). By this account, a ghost signifies a haunting absence at least as much as it does a transcendental presence. Might there then be another way of determining the odds in this phantom horse-race, a way that is not dependent on the authorizing presence of a Joycean Holy Ghost? If the name "Joyce" is at stake in Throwaway's spectral re-running of the Gold Cup, then perhaps there is both something ghostly and something chancy about the name "Joyce"—and about names in general.* The "void of incertitude" theme defines one way to conceptualize chance in *Ulysses*. Throwaway—the horse, the name, the word—is the other major locus of chance in the novel.† Since there is a lot riding on this race, perhaps before we place our bets we should see Throwaway in action.

Both in *Ulysses* and in fact, "Throwaway" was the name of the horse that won the Gold Cup at Ascot Heath on June 16, 1904, a long shot paying twenty to one. Early in the day, Bloom is accosted

---

*In "Joyce the Verb," an extended meditation on the name "Joyce," Fritz Senn notes that, in reading Joyce, "we might learn about the chanciness of easy identification by nominal labels." Senn's work, which examines and exemplifies what it means for language to be "Joycean," frequently and insightfully demonstrates a receptiveness to the operations of chance. In *Joyce's Dislocutions*, pp. 79–80, he also remarks that variations on the words "throw away" form what he calls a "symbolic connection (by 'throwing together')." I am about to examine the convergence of the various "throw away"s in some detail; in my reading, their connection is not *sym*bolic but *hyper*bolic.

†The strands of chance coinciding in "Throwaway" are itemized in "Ithaca" (17.322–41).

by Bantam Lyons, who borrows his newspaper to consult the racing form. Bloom wants to shake free of the scrofulous Lyons so decides to give him the paper: "You can keep it," he says.

—I was just going to throw it away, Mr. Bloom said.
    Bantam Lyons raised his eyes suddenly and leered weakly.
—What's that? his sharp voice said.
—I say you can keep it, Mr. Bloom answered. I was going to throw it away that moment.
    Bantam Lyons doubted an instant, leering: then thrust the outspread sheets back on Mr. Bloom's arms.
—I'll risk it, he said. Here, thanks. (5.531–41)

Bloom unwittingly gives Lyons a hot racing tip about the dark horse Throwaway with his throwaway remark "I was just going to throw it away." This mis-taking of a proper name has dire consequences later in the novel, which I will consider here in preparation for a later demonstration of how chance informs the symbolic structure of *Ulysses*. The discussion that follows, a brief look at the "Cyclops" chapter, may seem for the moment to go off on a tangent, but it will curve back around to the issues accompanying the Throwaway theme in the subsequent geometry of the argument.

We find out in "Cyclops" that Bantam Lyons was dissuaded from betting on Throwaway; but everyone at Barney Kiernan's pub believes that Bloom has wagered and won a bundle. They attribute his closemouthed and tightfisted behavior to characteristic Jewish frugality and selfishness. The anonymous narrator sneers:

Mean bloody scut. Stand us a drink itself. Devil a sweet fear! There's a jew for you! All for number one. Cute as a shithouse rat. Hundred to five.
—Don't tell anyone, says the citizen. (12.1760–62)

And this leads to the attack on Bloom. There is no place in the citizen's ideal Irish republic for a Jew who refuses to buy a round of drinks for the local barflies. When Bloom retorts to his anti-Semitic jeers, "Your God was a jew. Christ was a jew like me," the citizen shows his true understanding of Christian piety by hurling a parody of the Host at the departing Bloom: "By Jesus, says he, I'll brain that bloody jewman for using the holy name. By Jesus, I'll crucify him so I will. Give us that biscuit box here" (12.1808–12).

The biscuit tin misses Bloom, but, the narrator observes, "if he got that lottery ticket on the side of his poll he'd remember the Gold Cup, he would so" (12.1897–99). The "lottery ticket" the narrator mentions refers to another incident in Bloom's past that has made the xenophobic Dublin citizens suspicious of the stranger in their midst. Bloom was apparently arrested in 1893 or 1894 for selling tickets to "The Royal and Privileged Hungarian Lottery." He has been stigmatized for this not just because the lottery was foreign but also because he somewhat mysteriously managed to escape prosecution through the intervention of fellow members of his Masonic Lodge (12.776–79). Instances of chance with high stakes—horse races, lotteries—seem to dramatize Bloom's position as an outsider and so the ease with which he is made a scapegoat. I have shown how in earlier novels less comfortable with chance and its vicissitudes the narrative works in a way similar to the sociology of Kiernan's Pub, stigmatizing, scapegoating, and ejecting characters associated with the disconcerting thematics of chance in order to purge the textual system of "impurities."

The atmosphere, characters, and subject matter of the "Cyclops" chapter make it the section of *Ulysses* closest to Joyce's *Dubliners* (1914). Barney Kiernan's pub, like the early collection of short stories, is populated by creatures trapped in meager, suffocating lives, constrained not simply by circumstances but by their own crippling prejudices and narrow-mindedness. But Bloom escapes this world. At the end of the chapter, Bloom's departure with Martin Cunningham in a carriage becomes Elijah's ascent into heaven, an escape from the world of *Dubliners* not entirely undercut by the inflated rhetoric or the colloquial tag at the end of the passage: "And they beheld Him even Him, ben Bloom Elijah, amid clouds of angels ascend to the glory of the brightness at an angle of forty-five degrees over Donahoe's in Little Green street like a shot off a shovel" (12.1915–18). The style of the "Cyclops" chapter—the "gigantism" of inflated rhetoric alternating with the deflating sneers of the anonymous narrator—parodies the puffed-up pride and blinkered chauvinism of the bullies and barflies inhabiting the pub. The interjected pastiches reveal and mock the rhetorical excesses (especially of Irish legends and heroes) informing their pretensions. When the Cycloptic style focuses on Bloom, though, it works differently: the hyperbole of the interjected parodies allows Bloom to convey humanistic sentiments without seeming altogether maudlin or ridiculous. Thus when Bloom remarks that what really matters in life is "Love," there follows a stream of sentimental adult child-talk (12.1493–1501). The mawkishness of this drivel does not completely undercut Bloom's sentiment, and, by comparison, it makes his offhand remark seem almost ascetic. Bloom/Elijah's biblical ascension likewise manages to convey the sense that Bloom really does transcend the world of the petty and peevish Dubliners in Kiernan's Pub without succumbing to the mental elephantiasis the chapter devastatingly satirizes. Just as the stylistic technique of "Nausicaa" allowed Joyce to rewrite as parody Stephen's Annunciatory encounter with the bird-girl in *A Portrait of the Artist as a Young Man*, so the treatment of ben Bloom Elijah's ascent into the heavens parodies the Dedalus flight theme in that earlier work. But the hyperbole of the styles attached to Bloom does not diminish the nobility of his quiet heroics in this scene. I will return to Joyce's use of hyperbolic rhetoric shortly. For now, let it be noted that the Greek "hyperbole," literally "throw beyond," has affinities with the word "throwaway."

For every Elijah ascending there is an equal and opposite Elijah descending. At the beginning of "Lestrygonians," a "sombre YMCA young man . . . placed a throwaway in the hand of Mr. Bloom" (8.5–6). This throwaway is almost again, like Bloom's inadvertent racing tip, the occasion for the mis-taking of a proper name. Bloom reads and thinks: "Bloo . . . Me? No. / Blood of the Lamb." The handout advertises an American evangelist: "Elijah is coming. Dr. John Alexander Dowie restorer of the church in Zion is coming" (8.13–14). Bloom crumples the throwaway and throws it away, tossing it into the Liffey from O'Connell Bridge. It falls at the standard rate of acceleration: "Elijah thirtytwo feet per sec is com" (8.57–58).

The time as Bloom lingers for a moment on O'Connell Bridge is just after 1:00 P.M.; high tide on June 16, 1904, was at 12:42 P.M. The current in the estuary of the Liffey ran west as high tide approached and then gradually shifted east as high tide receded.[14] In mapping the itinerary of this throwaway I would like to read into the geography of Dublin an allegory for the fate of chance in the British novel. West of the bridge about a mile is a residence called Moira House (mentioned at 10.786). If Bloom had discarded the flyer earlier in the day, this nexus of chance called a "throwaway" would have naturally drifted west toward the House of Fate. But the tide has turned: the throwaway instead floats east on the current and out to sea.*

The throwaway appears three times in the "Wandering Rocks" chapter (10.294–97, 752–54, 1096–99), each position a little farther eastward. The last mention reads: "Elijah, skiff, light crumpled throwaway, sailed eastward by flanks of ships and trawlers, amid an archipelago of corks, beyond new Wapping street past Benson's ferry, and by the threemasted schooner *Rosevean* from Bridgewater with bricks." "Beyond," "past," "by": the prepositions of extravagance are important here. In "Wandering Rocks" the throwaway symbolically corresponds to the pigeon released by Jason to test the passage between the cliffs that clashed together at the entrance to the Black Sea.[15] Joyce included this episode although it does not occur in Homer; in Book XII of *The Odyssey* Odysseus chooses to risk the passage between Scylla and Charybdis rather than attempt the Wandering Rocks (which only Jason's *Argo* had ever successfully navigated). The throwaway in "Wandering Rocks" therefore indicates, within the text of *Ulysses*, another route Ulysses could have taken, an aesthetic of the throwaway different from the aesthetic of transubstantiation laid out in "Scylla and Charybdis." My reading of chance in *Ulysses* will try to avoid both the Scylla of transubstantial paternity (because it effaces all traces of chance in the novel by imbuing random and contingent experience with the spirit of an authorial Holy Ghost) and the Charybdis of what Joyce calls "the void of incertitude" (because it represents the thematics of chance strictly in terms of what I consider a vulgar version of female sexuality). Rather than try to navigate or negotiate *between* these two alternatives then, this reading will *go another way*, following in the wake of the throwaway as it floats out to sea.†

---

*In *Rubbish Theory*, Michael Thompson considers why and how things and ideas that are considered rubbish (hence invisible or in the way) are occasionally transformed and transvalued, becoming in the process worthy of attention and interest. Using René Thom's catastrophe theory, Thompson elaborates a method for introducing an indeterministic component into closed and deterministic systems to account for such transformations. Thompson's analysis of rubbish and the transvaluation of values that it can sometimes undergo is in many respects applicable to chance as it is figured in and by Bloom's discarded piece of writing: with the narrative and linguistic returns of the throwaway, *Ulysses* reclaims and revalues chance. The extended play between "letter" and "litter" in the *Wake* continues Joyce's meditation on the idea and value of a disposable writing initiated by the throwaway.

†As will become clear, following in the wake of the throwaway as it drifts out to sea and defines an aesthetic in *Ulysses* leads into *Finnegans Wake* and its similar

In the transubstantial aesthetic articulated by Ralph W. Rader, the itinerary of Bloom's throwaway also figures prominently:

The identification [of Joyce with D. B. Murphy, who arrived in Dublin that morning on the *Rosevean*] is emphasized by the fact that during the day Bloom's throwaway religious circular with "Elijah is coming!" imprinted on it has floated out to sea and met the *Rosevean*, as the artist within the creation reaches out to make contact with himself coming in.[16]

But as I have already emphasized, the throwaway sails beyond, past, *by* the *Rosevean* as the *Argo* sails through and beyond the gnashing rocks that would violently close off its seaward passage. The aesthetic of the throwaway exceeds and is eccentric to the reading of *Ulysses* that comes full circle in Joyce's imaginative return to his homeland as an artistic Holy Ghost. In going beyond the completed circle of Father, Son, and Holy Ghost, the throwaway is a "throw beyond"— instead of a circle then, a hyperbola.*

The Aesthetic of the Throwaway

When Bloom throws the throwaway away, he tosses it from O'Connell Bridge to the hungry gulls circling over the river. But they do not fall for his ruse; they know instinctively that the crumpled paper is not bread. Then let them eat cake: the sympathetic Bloom buys two Banbury cakes, breaks them in his fingers, and throws the pieces to the greedy birds. The gulls know instinctively what it has taken us quite some time to learn: writing is not natural;† it is not bread

---

journey, in ALP's concluding monologue, through Dublin and out to sea. It is finally undecidable if the end of the *Wake* describes a process of dispersion and dissolution (as ALP merges and mingles with the sea in oceanic oblivion) or instead initiates a *ricorso*, a recycling back from the final "the" to the initial "riverrun." The terms of this open-ended ending are pertinent to the throwaway as well: Does it represent a *real* throwing away, of truly disposable writing? Or does it instead (with its recurrence in "Wandering Rocks") represent a kind of eternal return?

*The parameters of a hyperbola are defined in part by the circle (or circles—there can be two) to which it is eccentric. One sense of the "beyond" implicit in the term derives from the fact that the distance from the center to the focus of the hyperbola always exceeds the distance from the center to the vertex. The curve for which the two segments would be identical is a circle. See James and James, *Mathematics Dictionary*, p. 186.

†This is not to say that writing is necessarily *un*natural; I only mean that writing cannot be adequately understood or conceptualized from within a framework of "the natural." The attempt to contain and categorize writing under the rubric of "the

that can be infused with the animating spirit of the Creator; it is not Host but parasite. Bloom's gesture then is not quite a version of the biblical parable "Cast your bread upon the waters," which like the parable of the sower of the seeds describes a dispersal with an eventual high yield of return on the investment.* The arc and itinerary of the throwaway is not parabolic but hyperbolic.

I mention the parable of the sower of the seeds in contradistinction to the throwaway aesthetic of *Ulysses* because the latter describes a process of dispersion, a scattering of seeds that does not necessarily come full circle in a bountiful harvest of fruitful meaning—in other words, dissemination. Jacques Derrida distinguishes the dissemination of which he writes from an inevitable circular return: "[T]he truth that speaks (to) itself within the logocentric circle is the discourse of what *goes back to the father*."[17] Dissemination then is concerned with what does not return to the father. I will be relating the disseminating qualities of the throwaway aesthetic in *Ulysses* to the thematics of paternity in a moment; but first I want to consider a kind of writing that is associated in the novel both with chance and with a literal act of dissemination, Bloom's masturbation.

In the second half of "Nausicaa," which relates Bloom's state of mind after the voyeuristic and orgasmic enjoyment of Gerty Mac-Dowell's equally orgasmic exhibitionism, Bloom picks up a piece of paper lying on the strand and thinks: "Letter? No. Can't read. . . . Page of an old copybook. . . . Never know what you find. Bottle with story of a treasure in it, thrown from a wreck. Parcels post. Children always want to throw things in the sea. Trust? Bread cast on the waters. What's this? Bit of stick" (13.1247–52). The piece of illegible writing Bloom happens upon prompts him to think of other kinds of thrown away writing, sea-tossed missives launched by a childish trust and washed ashore, letters among the litter on the littoral that might just tell the story of a treasure. The page of faded script seems to urge Bloom to do his own writing since he picks up the "[b]it of stick" he notices and uses it to scrawl some literal letters in the sand: "I. AM. A." But there is no room to finish his message, so

---

natural"—like most uses of the term—is more often than not an ideological move. I will return to this point in a discussion of how the "Penelope" chapter is designed to naturalize chance and writing in *Ulysses*.

   * "Cast your bread upon the waters" appears in *Ecclesiastes* 11:1; for the parable of the sower of the seeds, see *Matthew* 13:3–23.

Mr. Bloom effaced the letters with his slow boot. Hopeless thing sand. Nothing grows in it. All fades. . . .

He flung his wooden pen away. The stick fell in silted sand, stuck. Now if you were trying to do that for a week on end you couldn't. Chance. We'll never meet again. But it was lovely. Goodbye, dear. Thanks. Made me feel so young. (13. 1266–73)

Bloom's letters, like his spilled seed, can find no fruitful hold in the barren sand; but the chance fall of his pen commemorates the chance encounter and rejuvenating splurge of pleasure with Gerty.

Bloom's experiences in this scene provide a counterpoint to Stephen's activities on the strand in "Proteus." On the same beach earlier in the day, Stephen successfully completes *his* act of writing—pencil on paper—after wedging his ashplant walking stick in a grike, a crevice in the rocks (3.285). The verses he writes about a vampire's kiss also commemorate an erotic encounter, albeit an imaginary one. And as David Hayman has persuasively argued, Stephen too probably masturbates on the beach, aroused by the sensuality of his compositional imaginings.[18] There is much to say about the way these scenes play off of each other—Stephen's abstracted and solitary auto-affection versus Bloom's comfortably carnal actions in a social and sexual world; Stephen's verses perhaps (though their derivative and overwrought imagery make it unlikely) leaving a mark in the sands of literary-historical time versus Bloom's effaced story and identity, which he cannot himself articulate.* I want to focus in particular on what a comparison of these scenes reveals about chance and writing in *Ulysses*. Chance is not an important factor in Stephen's experience on the strand or in his composition; nor is he comfortable acknowledging his own disseminating acts. If he consciously reflected on the onanism he apparently practices in this scene, he would no doubt consider the self-depletion of his passive lust an expense of spirit in a waste of shame. For the prodigal Stephen, his lust and his life *are* wasteful and shameful; and it seems the only way he can redeem his desires and salvage his life is to transubstantiate the bitter bread of his existence into "art."

Stephen's writing is associated with rock and Bloom's with sand. Stephen uses "a table of rock" (3.406) as his writing surface to record

---

*I am grateful to Katie Gunther Kodat for pointing out to me some of the correspondences between these two scenes, especially regarding Stephen's stick stuck in the "grike."

the vampire verses after willfully and securely wedging his stick in a rock crevice, as though to stake a claim or provide a landmark in a linguistic landscape where, as he observes, "[t]hese heavy sands are language tide and wind have silted here" (3.288–89). Bloom's stick, casually thrown away, by chance lands vertically in the sand after he uses it to write in that transitory medium an abandoned message that, he realizes, would soon be tramped on by some flatfoot or washed away by the tide. But the faded copybook page Bloom finds and the message he writes and then erases in the sand do not simply or necessarily represent the sterility of his self-expression or the inevitable erosions of time and nature to which such writing is susceptible. They also figure a kind of writing associated with chance and dissemination, a writing not written in stone but self-effacing and receptively open to other possibilities.* In the interstices of his own seemingly monolithic inscriptions, Joyce leaves some inviting blank spaces, which are not necessarily subject to the dictates of the novelist. The faded page of the copybook (Joyce's preferred writing medium) offers itself as a palimpsest, available for another layer of writing. And Bloom's incomplete message in the sand invites us to complete it, to speculate and to play with the possibilities of what might have, and what has not yet, been written. The stick that falls by chance upright in the sand stands ready for another writer to pick it up. This is the kind of writing associated with the disseminating qualities of the throwaway aesthetic.

In order to explicate how Bloom's discarded throwaway informs the aesthetic of *Ulysses* and figures a kind of dissemination, let me review the earlier discussion of female sexuality since, as I have tried to show, the predominant impulse of the novel is to locate chance, for better or for worse, exactly there. The sexual woman (a redundancy in Joyce) inflicts on the nascent artist a Parsifal-like womb-wound; it is out of this experience that the artist creates. "Out of this experience" in two senses: it is the source of creativity and, as Stephen

---

*Patrick McGee discusses the element of chance in Bloom's writing in a different and insightful way in *Paperspace*. He concludes his remarks on this scene by extending his analysis beyond specific comments on Bloom's legibility to a more general observation about chance that is relevant to the itinerary of the throwaway I am examining. Of Bloom's thrown stick and its chance landing, he writes (p. 90): "This is chance—the law which states that nothing returns without the possibility of its not returning, since everything returns with a difference."

says of Shakespeare, creation is also an attempt to get away from the wound and its consequences ("He goes back, weary of the creation he has piled up to hide himself from himself, an old dog licking an old sore" [9.474–76]). The womb-wound that for Joyce *is* female sexuality is characterized as "the void of incertitude," so-called because the woman-as-wife is always potentially adulterate and, consequently, the woman-as-mother always potentially gives birth to a bastard. The male artist's role in natural creation then is always subject to the incertitude of the cuckold. It is for the most part out of this experience (again in two senses) that Joyce writes of(f) chance: *Of*—in the way the novel celebrates the essence of woman in all her dubious carnality; *off*—in the way the theme of transubstantial paternity marginalizes the woman and certifies paternity, thereby leaving nothing to chance. The latter impulse provides a model for the male artist's creation free of the doubts accompanying natural creation, a legal fiction that, with the copyright, controls the reproduction and authorizes the legitimacy of the artist's seminal work.

Joyce wrote to a friend about the "Ithaca" chapter, which establishes the rapport (such as it is) between Bloom and Stephen as surrogate father and son, "[I]t is all geometry, algebra, and mathematics."[19] I have already shown how a kind of algebra commutes consubstantial to transubstantial parenthood by factoring out the nonessential terms; the geometry of Bloom and Stephen's relationship was suggested in discussion of their "parallel courses" in "Ithaca," which meet perhaps in a peculiar kind of infinity; I want now to continue the mathematical inquiry and chart the deviations of paternal certainty in the novel. A diagram of assured legitimacy appears in Figure 4. But the woman's sex is the locus of doubt, the void of incertitude, and as such her body is the "medium" that refracts the paternal line of descent from father to son. A diagram of the relations between consubstantial father and son, with the vertical axis indicating semination from the father and the horizontal axis representing certain legitimacy of the son, appears in Figure 5. The curve with this shape is called a hyperbola, each branch of which has an asymptotic relation to the axis; that is, the curve continually approaches the line as it gets farther from the origin but they meet only in infinity. The vertical branch of the hyperbola charts the irreparable paternal past and the horizontal branch the imprevidible disseminal future.

Transubstantial paternity—whether artistic or Christological—

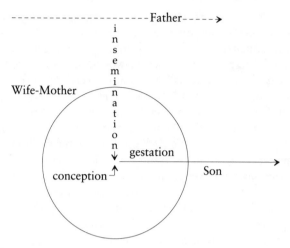

Figure 4

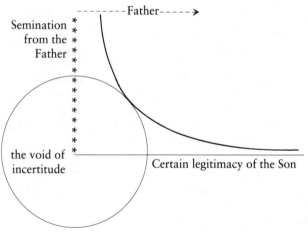

Figure 5

marginalizes the woman and claims the mysteries of fatherhood as its own property, "a mystical estate," as Stephen says. The medium and mediation joining Father and Son transubstantially is not the dubious woman but the transcendental Holy Ghost. The relation of Father and Son is then no longer a matter of chance: the three hypostases of

Figure 6

the Trinity are coequal, coeternal, and indivisible. The structure of transubstantial paternity is a closed and complete circle; this is the circle to which the route of the throwaway is eccentric (see Fig. 6). Some contact with the woman's body is still necessary in this transparent genealogy (whether as Virgin Birth or the infliction of a wound on the artist "there where love lies ableeding"); but the origin and destination of paternal and filial connection are assured—the past repaired, the future provided.

The hyperbolic curve that charts the uncertainty of consubstantial paternity also (I like to think) graphically and geographically plots the course of the throwaway as it drops from Bloom's hand, falls deflected by the wind ("Rough weather outside") to the water, and floats unimpeded on its way out to sea. The two loci of chance in *Ulysses*— "the void of incertitude" and "T/throwaway"—have a similar hyperbolic function in that they trace an eccentric curve with an asymptotic relation to the axes of certainty.* The curve of the hyperbola likewise describes the declension and deviation of the proper name "Throwaway" as it becomes the common noun "throwaway." In Chapter Three I argued, with Derrida, that within the structure of the proper name there always exists the possibility of a chance "swerve," or *clinamen*, which can deviate or divert the itinerary of the proper name on its way to its proper destination. The differential and reiterable structure of language is the "medium" in which the purity and

---

*The association of chance phenomena with an asymptotic curve has a history. In what Alan Young believes to be "one of the earliest theoretical considerations of aleatory principles in art by an English critic," Aldous Huxley writes of the sound of water dripping from a tap as a kind of music: "Perhaps for those who have ears to hear, this endless dribbling is as pregnant with thought and emotion, as significant as a piece of Bach. Drip-drop, di-drap, di-drep. So little would suffice to turn the incoherence into meaning. The music of the drops is a symbol and type of the whole universe; it is for ever, as it were, asymptotic to sense, infinitely close to significance but never touching it." Aldous Huxley ("Autolycus"), "Water Music," *The Athenaeum* 4712, Aug. 20, 1920, p. 243; quoted in Young, *Dada and After*, p. 60.

propriety of the proper name are exposed to the "contamination" of semiosis just as female sexuality threatens filial legitimacy with adulteration. The homonym calls into question the propriety of the proper name, and the always possible bastard problematizes assured paternity.* With mention of the throwaway, "Throwaway" no longer simply or necessarily refers to a singular and self-identical entity; the certainty of the referent opens asymptotically on other possibilities.†

Of course there is something vaguely disreputable about the "proper" names of racehorses from the word go, if only because they frequently derive in the first place from a common noun elevated to an appellation. But the Throwaway/throwaway split dramatizes a potential swerve that is built into the seemingly monolithic structure of any proper name. Consider for instance the name "Elijah" as it both ascends and descends in its association with the two T/throwaways. As we have seen, in "Cyclops" Bloom is violently expelled from Barney Kiernan's pub because the regulars—especially the citizen—think he has won big with his bet on Throwaway and refuses to share the wealth. In this chapter, Throwaway is called "a rank outsider" (12.1219), and Bloom the outsider is himself called "a bloody dark horse" (12.1558). Bloom's equine exit is then described as though it were Elijah's ascent unto heaven. As has already been observed, this is hyperbole, which *The Oxford English Dictionary* defines thus: "A figure of speech consisting in exaggerated or extravagant statement, used to express strong feeling or produce a strong impression, and not intended to be taken literally."[20] I would like to suggest that the entire symbolic apparatus of *Ulysses* oper-

---

*Onomastics and questions of paternity are logically and legally connected by what Stephen and Joyce call "a legal fiction," the attribution of the patronymic: the propriety and the property of the family name are enjoyed by the son only if he is legally considered the true and legitimate child of the father.

†We see this process in reverse in relation to the naming of the mystery man at Dignam's funeral, which is still another mis-taking of a proper name. That which cloaks the identity of the stranger (a macintosh) by synecdoche *becomes* his identity (he is listed by name in the newspaper account of the funeral: "M'Intosh" [16.1261]).

More comprehensively, the M'Intosh misnomer is not simply a reversal of Joyce's usual and insistent deflation of proper names to common nouns but a completed linguistic circuit since the word "macintosh" derives in the first place from the proper name of the overcoat's inventor, George Macintosh. I take the "full circle" of this completed circuit as an allegory for Joyce's treatment of the proper name: the name "M'Intosh" returns "macintosh" to the realm of the proper, but it is not quite a return of/to the same; it is now haunted by the ghostly qualities of its bearer and orthographically transformed by the chance mis-taking of a proper name.

ates in exactly this way. For instance, the informing proposition of the novel's Homeric correspondences—a middle-aged, middle-class Jewish ad canvasser in Dublin named Leopold Bloom is a modern-day Ulysses—is nothing if not hyperbolic. It does indeed produce a strong impression as we read the heroic accretions of an entire culture into Bloom's quotidian experience; but it is also not to be taken literally.

The name "Elijah" as it descends ("Elijah thirtytwo feet per sec") and floats out to sea operates differently.* The name is associated with the floating flyer ("Elijah, skiff, light crumpled throwaway") in a way that has nothing to do with the metaphorical sense of the name; the original metaphor (Alexander J. Dowie, the American evangelist, is the second Elijah) has been metonymically deflected. The "Elijah" throwaway is literally a floating signifier, and its seaward passage exemplifies the metonymic drift of language in *Ulysses*. We can then map the hyperbolic arc of the names "Throwaway" and "Elijah" onto what Roman Jakobson calls "the metaphoric and metonymic poles" of language[21] (see Fig. 7).

The hyperbolic function of the names "Throwaway" and "Elijah" graphically represents, with linguistic specificity, the often-remarked double impetus of *Ulysses* as symbolic and realistic novel; it illustrates the peculiar way both poles make claims on the proper name, allowing metaphoric symbolism and metonymic realism to coexist and interact without foreclosing each other. Thus *chance*, which operates and exists in and as the metonymic realism of "what happens" in *Ulysses*, does not (or at least it does not have to) get altogether effaced or sublated or transubstantiated into *fate* by the symbolic and metaphorical associations suggesting that "it was *meant* to happen." In a real sense, and despite volumes of criticism explaining and extrapolating their symbolic destinies, Bloom and Stephen meet each other on June 16, 1904, by chance.†

---

*Jacques Derrida, in a way different from but congenial to the argument of this chapter, discusses two Elijahs in *Ulysses*—the Elijah of total mastery, head of what he calls "the megaprogramotelephonic network," and the Elijah of the Passover service, who represents "the unforeseeable Other for whom a place must be kept." As Derrida makes clear, reserving a place for the latter Elijah means (among other things) maintaining an openness to the operations of chance. "Ulysses Gramophone," p. 59.

†The biographical germ for Joyce's novel seems to have been a fortuitous encounter with a (so rumor had it) cuckolded Jewish Dubliner named Alfred A. Hunter, who helped him up and took him home after a street brawl. A chance meeting then was apparently an essential feature of the novel's composition from its very beginnings. The

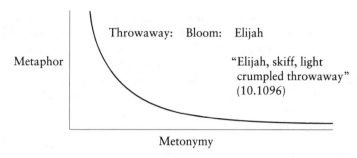

Figure 7

What has here been called the transubstantial reading of *Ulysses* tends to emphasize the metaphoric operations of language. Accompanying this emphasis is the frequent nonrecognition of what Joyce's stylized use of hyperbole ought to clarify—namely, that since a metaphor always operates with a certain difference, the metaphorical association should not be taken literally; the hyperbolic curve, even when ascending, touches the asymptote only in infinity. An emphasis on metaphor also tends to slight Joyce's metonymic use of language, which includes homonyms, puns, anagrams, displacements—linguistic associations that gave Joyce a great deal of pleasure.

An example of a pun metonymically generating Joycean discourse occurs for instance in the first chapter of *A Portrait of the Artist as a Young Man*. At one point Stephen thinks of what his father had let slip about their family friend Mrs. Dante Riordan: "But he had heard his father say that she was a spoiled nun and that she had come out of the convent in the Alleghenies when her brother had got the money from the savages for the trinkets and the chainies."[22] One of the purposes of this obscure passage is to bring two proper names together in the same linguistic field, where they form a wonderfully improper pun worthy of *Finnegans Wake*: Dante Allegheny.*

---

chance aspects of the proper name, which I have analyzed in textual terms, also have a biographical dimension: two of the Dubliners who served as models for Leopold and Molly Bloom were a Mr. and Mrs. Chance. See Ellmann, *James Joyce*, pp. 161–62 (about Hunter) and p. 375 (about the Chances).

*"Dante Allegheny—get it? It's a pun on Dante Alighieri!" Such elbow-in-the-rib explanations are always awkward and obtuse; a certain offhandedness seems to be a necessary feature of the linguistic play I am examining here. In some sense then the hyperbolic graphs are charting what the comedian calls "a throwaway line."

The itinerary of the "Elijah, skiff" throwaway is I believe plotted by a Dantean metonymic association. In Canto XXVI of the *Inferno*, Dante approaches the tongues of flame in one of which perpetually burns the false counselor Ulysses; these flames are compared to "the chariot of Elijah at his departure when the horses reared and rose to heaven," which burned so brightly that Elisha "could not follow it with his eyes so as to see anything but the flame alone like a little cloud mounting up." * When Dante has later himself ascended to *Paradiso*, he looks down on "the mad track of Ulysses" as he (Ulysses) penetrates beyond the bounds of the known world. In discussion of the throwaway in "Wandering Rocks" it was suggested that its course marks another route Ulysses could have taken; it could also be said that the throwaway marks the route another Ulysses has already taken. By means of a displaced metaphor, the throwaway on its way from the middle of Dublin out to the wide open sea proceeds "syllogistically from the known to the unknown." The logic of the syllogism is this: the flame containing Dante's Ulysses burned as brightly as Elijah's ascending chariot; Dante's Ulysses sailed past the bounds of the known world; therefore, "Elijah, skiff" sails past the bounds of the known world. This is a strange logic, but it leads to interesting places. The proximity and contiguity of Elijah and the extravagant Ulysses in Dante's text lead to a strange linguistic fusion altogether different from the metaphorical fusion of father and son transubstantially. Such a linguistic entity might be considered a bastard— even a monstrous deformity—in its combining of two metaphorical strains in an adulterated form; it might, but for the fact that it figures a kind of creation that can no longer be understood in terms of the metaphorics of natural creation.

It's Only Natural

The logic of the transubstantial reading of *Ulysses* leads to one predictable place, although the way there turns out to be something of

---

*Dante, *Inferno*, canto 26, ll. 35–39 (pp. 322–23). Elijah the faithful counselor provides an obvious contrast to Ulysses the false counselor as the fiery ascension of the prophet's chariot contrasts with the eventual sinking of treacherous Ulysses's ship. Dante's Ulysses says, "[W]e made of the oars wings for the mad flight" (l. 125), which associates his proud excesses with the hubristic flight and fall of other seekers of experience, including Icarus, Dedalus's son (see *Inferno* 17:109–11). The lines from the *Paradiso* referring to Ulysses are 27:82–83 (p. 391).

a surprise. In "The Logic of *Ulysses*; or, Why Molly Had to Live in Gibraltar," Ralph W. Rader argues that "after fusion" with his creation, by means of the Holy Ghost D. B. Murphy, Joyce "separates himself from his characters, rising high above them in Ithacan intellectual autonomy, before his great descent, as, yielding up the intellect's claim to primacy, he immerges and immolates himself and the reader in the imagined flesh of Molly's body."[23] This leads to a brilliant reading of the transition from "Ithaca" to "Penelope" suggesting that the authorial consciousness enters the bodily consciousness of Molly through the anus, which is figured in the novel by the black dot at the end of the "Ithaca" chapter. Rader argues that Molly's association with Gibraltar indicates the role her body plays in marking the limits of the known world, as the two rocks of the strait of Gibraltar, the Pillars of Hercules, mark the limits of the known world beyond which Dante's Ulysses ventures.

The logic and the aesthetic of the throwaway provide an understanding of chance in narrative that does not necessarily lead to or derive from Joyce's peculiar understanding of female sexuality. To celebrate the essence of woman (as Joyce certainly does) is still to essentialize *the* woman, though it is no doubt preferable to the denigration that usually accompanies that process. In "Penelope," to represent the essence of the woman is to make her the embodiment of nature. For Molly nature is supreme: "nature it is as for them saying theres no God I wouldnt give a snap of my two fingers for all their learning why dont they go create something" (18.1563–65). Creation for, in, and as Molly is always natural. Rather than designating as alien and then deporting chance and writing (as we have seen earlier novels do), *Ulysses* for the most part *naturalizes* them, finding a place for what might otherwise be considered alien within the borders drawn by its map of the woman's body. But the diversions and deviations of the throwaway aesthetic do not obey natural laws, nor does its geography conform to Joyce's map of the woman's body.

The *nostos* of *Ulysses* is a homecoming to the flesh, a return to the body, an inhabitation of the specifically female, thus necessarily sexual, body. And what could be more natural? Recent critical interest in the body has been questioning this presumptive "it goes without saying" attribution of naturalness to the body, arguing and demonstrating instead that ideas and representations of the body are in fact historically constructed and constituted, and that, moreover, the assumption and assertion of the body's natural status more often than not facilitates specific deployments of power over the corporeal subject.[24] The body is the master-trope for an ideology of "the natural."

Molly's body is the mediating center of the "Penelope" chapter from and through which all meaning and experience radiate. The return to the flesh in the form of the woman's body then parts company with the impulses of the transubstantial paternity theme, which would marginalize the woman and her sexuality; parts company, that is—and here we see the implementation of a value system based on criteria of "natural"ness—with an erotics that has traditionally been characterized as the defining case of "the unnatural." The three sections of *Ulysses* that articulate the terms and conditions of the novel's transubstantial-paternity theme all disparagingly suggest a homosexual element in the attraction of Bloom the father for his surrogate son, Stephen. At the end of "Scylla and Charybdis," after Stephen's Shakespeare lecture, Buck Mulligan mockingly says to Stephen after Bloom passes between them: "Did you see his eye? He looked upon you to lust after you. I fear thee, ancient mariner. O, Kinch, thou art in peril. Get thee a breechpad" (9.1209–11). In "Circe," Mulligan the mocker likewise testifies in Bloom's mock trial as a doctor and sex specialist, stating, "Dr. Bloom is bisexually abnormal" (15.1775–76); the implications of this charge are then played out at length in the antic dramatics of "Circe" before Bloom and Stephen unite with and in Shakespeare's hornmad visage in the mirror. The theme of transubstantial paternity seems finally to be consummated when in "Eumaeus" Bloom and Stephen unite in the person of D. B. Murphy, the unsavory sailor repeatedly associated with Shakespeare. Tattooed on Murphy's chest are "the figure 16 and a young man's sideface" (16.675–76). Murphy pointedly ignores the question when someone in the cabman's shelter asks him the meaning of the number, but Gifford and Seidman are more forthcoming: "[I]n European slang and numerology the number sixteen meant homosexuality."[25] The tattooer of and model for the young man's profile was a fellow now dead and sorely missed by Murphy, named Antonio. Antonio, Murphy tells us more than once, was a Greek. The sharp-sighted, sharp-witted, sharp-tongued Mulligan earlier commented on Bloom's classical inclinations in that direction: "O, I fear me, he is Greeker than the Greeks," he says of Bloom's inspection of the goddess statue in the National Museum; "[h]is pale Galilean eyes were upon her mesial groove" (9.614–15). It is Bloom's interest in the "posterior rectal orifice" (17.2077) that Molly's value system condemns; of his "rere regardant" goodnight kiss she says, "hed kiss anything unnatural" (18.1402–3). The name of D. B. Murphy's young Greek companion suggests the homoerotic and anal interests of another merchant marine named Antonio, Shakespeare's merchant of Venice, as well as the sailor Antonio of *Twelfth Night*, who loves Sebastian so faithfully. Bloom mentally reviews some of the anomalies attached to Murphy, following a natural (if desultory) progression of thought toward conclusions about unnatural behavior:

Briefly, putting two and two together, six sixteen which he pointedly turned a deaf ear to, Antonio and so forth, jockeys and esthetes and the tattoo which was all the go in the seventies or thereabouts even in the house of lords because early in life the occupancy of the throne, then heir apparent, the other members of the upper ten and other high personages simply following in the footsteps of the head of the state, he reflected about the errors of notorieties and crowned heads running counter to morality such as the Cornwall case a number of years before under their veneer in a way scarcely intended by nature. (16.1195–1203)

As Bloom and Stephen go off "arm in arm across Beresford place," they pass the sleeping sentry, whose somnolent state is described as "in the arms of Murphy" (16.1734, 1727). The song "The Low-Backed Car," one line of which closes the chapter, describes two lovers riding off together in the low-backed car "To be married by Father Maher." *

The persistent association of the transubstantial paternity theme with homosexuality—specifically the older man's sexual interest in the young man—admits the possibility of homoerotic desire in such intense male bonding. Though the potential volatility of same-sex desire in the Bloom-Stephen rapport is partially defused by the nastiness of Mulligan's insinuations and the proximity of the disreputable Murphy, its suggestion testifies to Joyce's shrewd acknowledg-

---

* For the lyrics to the song, see Gifford and Seidman, *"Ulysses" Annotated*, pp. 562–63. Ralph W. Rader points out the arm-in-arm connection of Stephen and Bloom by way of Murphy/Shakespeare/Joyce ("Exodus and Return," pp. 164–65), but he does not mention the homoerotic implications of their union. In *The Book as World*, pp. 214–16, Marilyn French does discuss the homosexual connotations in this scene, but she does not consider how they fit into a larger pattern of sexual ideology in the novel.

ment that in such transactions of power and intimacy between men there is certainly a homosocial and possibly a homoerotic connection that cannot be altogether written out of the story.[26] And, as I have already suggested, the repeated invocation "CONTRA NATURAM" (as Joyce's frequently fascist friend Ezra Pound sententiously says)[27] in the Bloom-Stephen relationship encourages a rebounding and redounding "pro natura," which effects and endorses the naturalizing process in "Penelope."

Richard Ellmann in his biography of Joyce relates a curious anecdote:

> Sometimes Joyce entertained [his male friends] by producing a miniature pair of drawers (he never accepted the word 'panties'), which appeared to exert the same fascination upon him that they do upon Bloom. He scandalized a homosexual poet (Siegfried Lang), to his friends' entertainment, by placing two fingers inside the drawers and walking them towards the unhappy poet.[28]

I wonder what it is that scandalized the unhappy but gay poet in this curious scene. Is it the threat of a strangely embodied female sexuality approaching the phobic homosexual? Or is it the way Joyce's manipulations figure and parody Lang's own desire to be "like a woman"? Or might it be the vulgar way Joyce fetishizes the woman's body? In any case, one thing is certain about this scandalous case of transvestism: Joyce's hand, his writing hand, dressed in bloomers finger-walking toward a homosexual writer—there is nothing natural about it.

Sartor Resartus

The thematization of chance by the two T/throwaways, along with the chance associations between the proper name and the common noun, suggests an alternative to the transubstantial reading of *Ulysses*, a logic and an aesthetic that are directed by displaced metaphor and that displace metaphor in another direction. Not only that: words like "directed" and "displace" suggest some apparent agency at work, but the very notion of a controlling and intentional authorial subject is called into question when the linguistic associations at play are so insistently a function of chance. If "Joyce"—that seemingly monumental proper name—is the ghost in the machine that is *Ulysses*, the novel's thematization of chance seems to include instructions for its own exorcism. *Ulysses* is a remarkable textual machine, which, in the blithe spirit of its creator, teaches us to rejoice in things that happen by chance.

As the earlier chapters of this study have demonstrated, the transubstantial reading that transforms the random and contingent elements of a narrative into "art" characterizes not just the usual reading of *Ulysses* but also the standard treatment of chance in the British novel. The deviations of the T/throwaway theme in Joyce's novel then do not just provide an alternative understanding of chance in *Ulysses*; they also provide a model for reading any novel with a sensitized appreciation of how chance can enter into that reading experience. For reasons I spell out more clearly in the Conclusion, *Ulysses* marks a limit to the representation of chance in narrative; from the vantage of this limit point it becomes possible to read other novelistic narratives in terms of a logic and an aesthetic informed by a receptiveness to the operations of chance.

It was earlier suggested that the symbolic structure of transubstantial parenthood fits *Ulysses* "to a T." But does it? Or does it have to? Might there not be another way of cutting *Ulysses*'s paternity suit, one tailored to the problematics of chance, which also in its way fits *Ulysses* to a T? The expression "to a T" means "exactly, properly, to a nicety," and probably derives from the earlier expression "to a tittle."[29] "Tittle" means a dot or jot such as a diacritical mark or the dot of an "i," and so refers as well to a pip on dice. To fit *Ulysses* "to a T" might suggest an endorsement of an aesthetic based on the T-shaped genealogy in which Bloom and Molly realize Stephen's transubstantial family romance and help him to create, naturally. It might also suggest an endorsement of a logic "proceeding syllogistically from the known to the unknown," which always has its logical conclusion (signified by the dot, or tittle, at the end of "Ithaca") *in* the woman's body. But I would like to offer another application of the expression, which suggests an alternative logic and aesthetic, one more conversant with diacritical marks and the throw of the dice for which the tittle is a necessary feature. The T to which I would fit *Ulysses* marks the chance associations between a racehorse and a discarded piece of writing. It's a long shot, but my money's on T/throwaway.

Conclusion:
Chance and the Modern Novel

Before commenting on the importance of *Ulysses*'s T/throwaway theme to the subject of chance and the modern novel, I would like to consider for a moment two quotations, which predate and postdate the historical period that this study has been examining. These two examples of chance's producing a legible text will allow us to measure some of the changes in the thinking about chance that developed during the interval they delimit. The first quotation is from a 1664 sermon by John Tillotson, archbishop of Canterbury:

I appeal to any man of reason whether any thing can be more unreasonable, than obstinately to impute an effect to chance which carries, in the very face of it, all the arguments and characters of design and contrivance? Was ever any considerable work, in which there was required a great variety of parts, and a regular and orderly disposition of those parts done by chance? Will chance fit means to ends, and that in a thousand instances, and not fail in any one? How often ought a man, after he had jumbled a set of letters in a bag, fling them out upon the ground before they would fall into an exact poem; yea, or so much as a good discourse in prose? And may not a little book be as easily made by chance, as this great volume of the world? [1]

The second quotation is from Tom Stoppard's play *Travesties* (1975):

(TZARA *comes forward with rare diffidence, holding a hat like a brimming bowl. It transpires that he has written down a Shakespeare sonnet and cut it into single words which he has placed in the hat.*)

TZARA: All poetry is a reshuffling of a pack of picture cards, and all poets are cheats. I offer you a Shakespeare sonnet, but it is no longer his. It

comes from the wellspring where my atoms are uniquely organised, and
my signature is written in the hand of chance.

GWEN: Which sonnet—was it?

TZARA: The eighteenth.

GWEN (*sadly*): "Shall I compare thee to a summer's day . . ."

　　　　　　　　　　　. . .

(GWEN *hesitates but then takes the first slip of paper out of the hat.*)

GWEN: "Darling".

(*She now continues, holding on to all the pieces of paper she takes out.*)

　　　　shake thou thy gold buds
　　　　the untrimm'd but short fair shade
　　　　shines—
　　　　see, this lovely hot possession growest
　　　　so long
　　　　by nature's course—
　　　　so . . . long—heaven!

(*She gives a little shriek, using "heaven," and turns her back on the hat,
taking a few steps away from* TZARA, *who takes out the next few words,
lowering the temperature . . .*)

TZARA: and declines,
　　　　summer changing, more temperate complexion . . .[2]

　　　Tillotson's sermon was delivered to edify his presumably devout
congregation, and Stoppard's scene is performed to charm and amuse
a bourgeois theater audience. The first presents a rational argument
for God's providential agency in the world, and the second parodies
the modernist avant-garde's polemical pretensions. The archbishop's
argument against chance is meant to repudiate what he calls "the Epicurean account of the original of the world"; his negative example—
the unlikelihood of someone's composing a poem or prose discourse
by casting letters onto the ground like a handful of seeds—is realized
in the playwright's staging of Tristan Tzara's chance composition.
Writing during the time the novel was emerging as a distinct genre,
Tillotson offered the classical theological account of chance: it is unreasonable even to consider chance at work in a world so clearly the
result of God's benevolent design; the Author of the world and the
author of a poem or prose discourse are both evident in the "regular
and orderly disposition" of their literal and legible creations. In Stoppard's farce, the founder of Dada is confounded when the fragmented
body of the literary tradition re-forms to betray his own body's in-

cipient desire. Tzara's poem drawn from a hat signifies not just his erotic arousal, due to Gwendolyn's proximity, but as well the desire for chance to tell a story. Despite the apparent differences between the two textual lotteries, they both demonstrate that there is in fact no such thing as chance.

Stoppard's *Travesties* qualifies as a postmodern work by almost anyone's definition, and not just because it takes as its parodic subject matter the artistic and political controversies of the modern period. The play at least flirts with the ideas of immanence and indeterminism (Hassan's definition); it consists almost entirely of nostalgic pastiches (Jameson's); and it self-consciously invokes a delegitimized master-narrative (Lyotard's).[3] The theatrical master-narrative that structures the series of competing narratives in Stoppard's play is Oscar Wilde's *The Importance of Being Earnest*, which with perfected artifice tells and mocks the age-old story of boy meets girl, boy loses girl, boy gets girl, played out against the itinerant deviations of the proper name.[4] *Travesties* begins with Tzara pulling words out of a hat in a random fashion to make what seems to be a genuinely aleatory poem ("I'll raced alas whispers kill later nut east"). But, as the scene quoted demonstrates, in this postmodern text chance inevitably yields to narrative desire.

Of course other artists and writers of the postmodern period have been interested in the idea and operations of chance, and have given the subject more than just the clever and superficial attention it receives in *Travesties*. John Cage's aleatory musical compositions and, in the novel, William Burroughs's cutups, the multiple plottings of Julio Cortázar's *Hopscotch* (1966), and Chance the gardener in Jerzy Kosinski's *Being There* (1970) all indicate that, if anything, interest in chance has intensified in the postmodern period. I would nevertheless argue that Joyce's treatment of the subject in *Ulysses* marks a limit to the representation of chance in narrative which subsequent efforts do not—indeed, probably cannot—move beyond.* In Stoppard's artistic and historical farce, it turns out that the hat into which Tristan

---

*This is not to say that the introduction of chance into the composition process in Cage's scores and Burroughs's cutups is not a new and interesting development in the history of chance. Incorporating chance elements into the creative activity certainly problematizes the agency and intentionality of the creator; it does so, however, by the imposition of another kind of narrative, the story of the work as process. The music or the text that is composed on aleatory principles does not any more represent chance simply because it is the result of chance.

Tzara puts the fragmented body of a Shakespeare sonnet and out of which his lady love pulls piecemeal a poem about erotic bodies belongs to James Joyce. During the debate that follows between Tzara the iconoclast and Joyce the spokesman for "art for art's sake," the actor playing Joyce returns the pieces of paper to his hat and, invoking the "magic" and "genius" proper to the true artist, proceeds to pull a rabbit out of his hat. Stoppard's Tzara claims about his poem, "[m]y signature is written in the hand of chance"; but the reason Joyce's treatment of chance in *Ulysses* defines the limitations of its representation is that, by ingenious sleight of hand, chance in *Ulysses* is indelibly marked with the signature of James Joyce.

It is not Joyce's name "itself" that marks the limit of chance's representation in narrative but his explicit, rigorous, and relentlessly playful subjection of the proper name to antonomasia (a rhetorical figure for the deflation of proper names into common nouns).[5] The proper name is the locus of chance in *Ulysses* (Throwaway/throwaway, Elijah/Elijah); and the name "Joyce" resists such aleatory semiotic solicitations only by occupying a position transcendent to the text it signs.

As became clear in the reading of *Ulysses* above (Chapter 4), the family name—"Joyce" as much as "Dedalus"—is at stake and riding on the success of the dark horse Throwaway. Of course, the insinuations of the proper name "Joyce" that appear in conjunction with the phantom horse-race won by Throwaway in "Circe" are just a local and more literal manifestation of a pattern informing all of Joyce's later writings. Specific reference to the author's name is certainly not necessary for a piece of writing to be distinctively "Joycean," and this is not simply a matter of a recognizable style. Beginning with *Ulysses*, and increasingly legible with its various and intensified experiments with style, Joyce's prose generates a "signature effect," which marks the writing with the unmistakable name of its author. "Joyce's writing is Joycean": what makes this banal observation not altogether tautological is the fact that it replicates the circularity, reflexivity, and emptiness of the proper name itself. The signature effect endows the contingency of a writer's given name with a necessity and inevitability that is self-validating and self-fulfilling.

The Joycean signature effect is most clearly evident in *Finnegans Wake*, which, in being capaciously *sui generis*, is also and emphatically inscribed *ego scriptor*. In *Writing Through Finnegans Wake*,

John Cage composes a series of what he calls "mesostics (not acrostics: row down the middle, not down the edge)," which provide an emblematic literalization (in the literal—that is, lettered—sense of the word) of what I am calling the Joycean signature-effect. "What makes a mesostic as far as I am concerned," Cage writes, "is that the first letter of a word or name is on the first line and following it on the first line the second letter of the word or name is *not* to be found. (The second letter is on the second line.)"[6] Cage composed his first mesostic after opening *Finnegans Wake* at random, and eventually (with some omissions) he worked through the entire text. An early example from the end of the *Wake*:

> my lips went livid for from the Joy
> of feAr
> like alMost now. how? how you said
> how you'd givE me
> the keyS of me heart.
>
> Just a whisk brisk sly spry spink
> spank sprint Of a thing
> i pitY your oldself i was used to,
> a Cloud.
> in pEace

In the mesostics that constitute the text of *Writing Through Finnegans Wake* Cage removed the punctuation from the *Wake* passages: "[T]he omitted marks were kept, not in the mesostics but on the pages where they originally appeared, the marks disposed in the space and those other than periods given an orientation by means of *I Ching* chance operations." The resulting mesostics carry no punctuation, but their margins are peppered with arbitrarily placed semicolons, parentheses, exclamation points, and so on. Cage explains:

[M]y work was merely to show, by giving it a five-line structure, the relation of Joyce's text to his name, a relationship that was surely in these instances not in his mind, though at many points, as Adaline Glasheen cheerfully lists, his name was on his mind, alone or in combination with another name.[7]

These mesostics are emblematic for the Joycean signature effect not just because they literalize how Joyce's prose is everywhere inscribed with the magisterial (if not always majuscular) mark of his/the proper name. They also indicate how the signature effect marginalizes and

minimizes chance effects: the punctuation marks, which signal relations of logic and meaning in normal prose, are given free play in
their chance disposition, but they are also completely incidental in
relation to the formidable logic and meaning of the signature effect,
which organizes and articulates along the metaphorical spine of the
name "James Joyce" textual material that is not explicitly and inten-
tionally connected to that name ("a relationship that was surely in
these instances not in his mind").

The signature effect in Joyce's writing inscribes seemingly random
and contingent textual material and narrative events with the authorizing name of the creator. It is therefore questionable whether
there is really anything like chance informing the linguistic associations and narrative operations of the Throwaway/throwaway, Elijah/
Elijah passages in *Ulysses*. After all, *Joyce* makes those associations
and *Joyce* directs those operations: their casual nature itself testifies
to the author's agency, control, and intentionality, even if those active
and directed intentions are about the subject of chance.

The signature effect vis-à-vis chance recapitulates the providential
denial of chance in a purely nominal form: every element of the text
bears the unmistakable mark of its author, just as the world carries (in
Tillotson's words) "all the arguments and characters of wise design
and contrivance." The transcendent nature of Joyce's signature aligns
the author of the Joycean text and the Author of the world: as Stephen
Dedalus says in *A Portrait of the Artist as a Young Man*, "The artist,
like the God of the creation, remains within or behind or beyond
or above his handiwork, invisible, refined out of existence, indifferent, paring his fingernails." [8] And there is no place for chance in such
"handiwork" when it is indelibly inscribed with the author's name. In
a remarkable recuperative move, the providential argument against
chance claims that those events that seem to have no clear purpose
or design all the more surely indicate God's transcendent power; it is
precisely the (seeming) arbitrariness of God's dispensations that testifies to the omnipotence of His will. The ghostly omnipresence of the
name "Joyce" in *Ulysses* likewise becomes increasingly legible precisely when the linguistic operations that proliferate under its aegis
seem arbitrary.*

---

*The other British novel that most clearly exemplifies the playful arbitrariness
of its author, along with a receptiveness to the operations of chance, is Laurence
Sterne's *Tristram Shandy* (1759–67). When he was writing as a clergyman, at least,
Sterne endorsed the conventional providential view of chance. In the sermon on "Time

Perhaps the best way to describe the linguistic associations and narrative functions attached to the T/throwaway theme in *Ulysses* is to say that they are arbitrary. This suggests that they are the result of a mere whim or impulse that transgresses the law but also and at the same time describes the exercise of a powerful will not limited by the law (as in a tyrant's arbitrary dispensations). The logic and the aesthetic of the T/throwaway describe the operations and effects of a certain *pleasure*, the expression of a capricious whim, a vagary that is erratic and unmotivated (a signature written in the hand of chance); and they describe as well the operations and effects of a certain *will*fulness, a testament to the authorial agency directing and intending the representation of chance in the novel (a text everywhere inscribed with the signature of James Joyce). The hyperbolic function of chance in *Ulysses* marks a limit to the novelistic representation of chance because it is finally undecidable whether such a "throw beyond" is the function of a pleasure that transgresses the authorial will or the function of a will that legislates its own pleasures. This is why *Ulysses* marks the limit to the representation of chance in narrative: it either rejoices in things that happen by chance or it re-Joyces in things that happen by chance.*

---

and Chance," in *Sermons of Mr. Yorick*, he writes: "[F]or though at sundry times—sundry events fall out—which we, who look no farther than the events themselves, call Chance, because they fall out quite contrary both to our intentions and our hopes,—yet at the same time, in respect of God's providence overruling in these events, it were profane to call them chance, for they are pure designation, and though invisible, are still the regular dispensations of the superintending power of the Almighty Being, from whom all the laws and powers of nature are derived, who, as he has appointed,—so holds them as instruments in his hands." Writing as a novelist, however, Sterne does not exactly practice what he preaches. His characterization of the many digressions initiated by chance associations in *Tristram Shandy* as "deviations from a straight line" connects his novel way of telling a story to the Epicurean-Lucretian *clinamen*. Like other constituent features of the novel, *Tristram Shandy*'s treatment of chance anticipates early in the genre's development the insights that would emerge in later novels that self-consciously reflect with a sense of history on the possibilities and limitations of the form. Much of what I go on to say about the undecidability of pleasure and will in Joyce's work would apply as well to Sterne's novel. The quoted passage from his sermon appears in Sterne, *Works*, vol. 6, p. 97, where he also refers to the Tillotson sermon on the subject of chance, which repudiates "the Epicurean account of the original of the world." The reference to "deviations from a straight line" in relation to his narrative technique appears in chapter 14 of the first volume of *Tristram Shandy*, in *Works*, vol. 1, p. 39.

*As Joel Fineman has argued, and as Stephen Dedalus intimates in his Shakespeare lecture (9.921–28), the writer in the English tradition who definitively thematized his/the proper name in relation to a distinctively literary use of language was William Shakespeare. Thus it is a Shakespeare sonnet that is fragmented when Tzara's signa-

As it happens, the undecidability of pleasure and will evident in *Ulysses*'s treatment of chance is inscribed in the history of chance from its very beginnings. At the place in *De Rerum Natura* where Lucretius is explaining how the *clinamen* frees us from the bonds of fate, there is a famous textual crux that has occupied classicists for centuries: it is not clear if the crucial word is *voluptas* (pleasure) or *voluntas* (will). The English translation favoring *voluptas* reads:

Again, if all movement is always interconnected, the new arising from the old in a determinate order—if the atoms never swerve so as to originate some new movement that will snap the bonds of fate, the everlasting sequence of cause and effect—what is the source of the free will possessed by living things throughout the earth? What, I repeat, is the source of that will-power snatched from the fates, *whereby we follow the path along which we are severally led by pleasure*, swerving from our course at no set time or place but at the bidding of our own hearts? *

---

ture is written in the hand of chance in Stoppard's *Travesties*; and it becomes legible in a new form when pulled out of James Joyce's hat. The undecidability of will/pleasure inscribed in the structure of the signature effect defines a literary tradition marked at its beginnings by the willfulness of Will and at its closure (not to say the end) by the rejoicings of Joyce. For a thorough discussion of Shakespeare and the proper name in relation to the invention of "the literary," see Fineman, *Shakespeare's Perjured Eye*. The Epilogue of this work discusses the possibility of an "extraliterary" literature that might succeed the literary tradition defined by what Fineman calls "the Shakespearean."

*Here is the original passage in Latin, *De Rerum Natura*, bk. 2, ll. 251–60 (vol. 1, p. 87):

> Denique si semper motus conectitur omnis
> et vetere exoritur semper novus ordine certo
> nec declinando faciunt primordia motus
> principium quoddam quod fati foedera rumpat,
> ex infinito ne causam causa sequatur,
> libera per terras unde haec animantibus exstat
> unde est haec, inquam, fatis avolsa volu[p/n]tas
> per quam progredimur quo ducit quemque volu[p/n]tas
> declinamus item motus nec tempore certo
> nec regione loci certa, sed ubi ipsa tulit mens?

A version of the manuscript has *voluptas* in line 257 and *voluntas* in 258. Most editors transpose them (it is on this reading that the English translation quoted is based). Another editor reads *voluptas* in both places. The translation that favors "will" purges the passage of all pleasure by reading *voluntas* in 258 and, quite willfully, substituting *potestas* (power) for the questionable word in line 257. See Lucretius, *De Rerum Natura*, vol. 1, p. 87, for the textual variants. The English version of this passage is from *Nature of the Universe*, p. 67.

The translation which favors *voluntas* translates the italicized passage as "by which we go forward whither the will leads each."[9] *Voluptas/voluntas*: a letter has by chance gone astray at the moment the Lucretian text is explicating the operations of chance. The definition of the *clinamen* itself constitutes a *clinamen* in the Lucretian text.* This *clinamen* articulates the standard deviations of chance in narrative.

The novel has always been of (at least) two minds, evidencing in its realist mandate a fidelity to experience in all of its contingency and, at the same time, obeying a generic imperative to structure its material in an aesthetically autonomous and unified representation. A novelistic concern with chance is then always engaged in a simultaneous affirmation and denial of its existence, the affirmation eliciting a new appreciation of the casual contingency of life while the denial helps to define a new sense of narrative coherence and design. The novelistic affirmations of chance considered in this study materialize in relation and response to an already established system, an order of power-knowledge with a corresponding narrative order. The instance of chance serves a critical function in relation to that system, exposing its limitations by occupying a position of exteriority and opacity that can no longer be adequately contained or explained by the operant frame of power-knowledge. The history of chance and the novel I have outlined here considers exemplary works, poised at moments of epistemic (and so generic) instability, that reformulate the role chance plays in narrative experience.

Briefly put, that history proceeds as follows. In *Robinson Crusoe*, Defoe affirms chance in the quotidian experience and capitalistic

---

*Derrida makes this point in "My Chances/*Mes Chances*": "The mere difference of a letter introduces a *clinamen* precisely when Lucretius is at the point of explaining the extent to which the *clinamen* is the condition of freedom and will or voluptuous pleasure that has been wrested from destiny" (pp. 7–8). He then continues: "But in all cases the context leaves no doubt as to the link between *clinamen*, freedom, and pleasure. The *clinamen* of the elementary principle—notably the atom, the law of the atom—would be the pleasure principle." Inasmuch as the hyperbolic function of chance in *Ulysses* has to do with the atomistic status of the proper name then, the "throw beyond" of the T/throwaway theme in *Ulysses* outlines one sense of the beyond of the pleasure principle. But, as Freud's grandson demonstrated with his *fort/da* game in *Beyond the Pleasure Principle*, there may be some strings attached: the pleasure and the willfulness involved in the gesture of throwing away or throwing beyond may also entail a movement of return that consolidates a sense of power, control, and mastery.

enterprise of his protagonist but denies it in providential terms. In *Middlemarch*, George Eliot affirms chance in order to repudiate a providential view of the world but denies chance in moral terms. The naturalist novelists affirm chance in the initial and ultimately determining configuration of heredity and environment in order to disclaim both a providential and a secular humanist moral order, but they deny chance in scientific terms. In *Chance*, Joseph Conrad affirms chance in order to challenge such a novelistic version of scientific determinism but ends up denying chance in the fated machinations of narrative. And in *Ulysses*—which offers the most successful treatment of chance in British fiction—Joyce affirms chance in order to problematize the aesthetic determinism of narrative, but his treatment of the subject goes as far as any novel can, marking and defining a limit to the representation of chance in narrative. From the vantage of this limit point, it becomes possible to read other novelistic narratives with a sensitized appreciation of the ways chance can enter into that reading experience.

In analyzing and resisting the narrative imperative to conflate chance and fate, this study began by considering the phrase "Chance is the fool's name for fate." As the argument proceeded, the point of emphasis in the middle term poised between "chance" and "fate" shifted from "the *fool's* name" (fools are characters who operate as scapegoats for the problematic aspects of chance) to "the fool's *name*" (proper names, being atomistic in nature, are structured by the chance operations of the *clinamen*). In the three novels that have been examined in some detail, incidental pieces of paper with names written on them become interestingly coincidental in the narrative. The letter with Nicholas Bulstrode's signature, purloined by Raffles in *Middlemarch*, becomes the occasion for George Eliot's *parabolic* treatment of chance; the folded paper with "Charles Powell" written on it, which Powell hands to Powell, offers a *symbolic* representation of how chance structures the duplicitous differentiations of the proper name in Conrad's *Chance*; and a newspaper with the name "Throwaway" and a throwaway with the name "Elijah" together delineate the *hyperbolic* function of chance in James Joyce's *Ulysses*. Parabolic—thrown side by side; symbolic—thrown together; hyperbolic—thrown beyond: these three throws of the dice tell the story of chance and the modern British novel.

Appendix

Appendix:
Chance in Hardy and James

I consider here in general terms the place and importance of chance in the work of Thomas Hardy (by my account the last Victorian novelist) and Henry James (the first modern novelist), paying particular attention to the way their narrative practices exemplify a movement from providence to perspective in the novel at the turn of the century. This material is meant to illustrate chance's role in the development of narrative forms during the transitional period from the Victorian to the modern novel. Hardy's fiction, as I will show, repudiates the residual providentialism inherent in the formal properties of the Victorian novel, while James's fiction opens up new novelistic ground with his notion of organic form organized and informed by characterological perspective. The first section examines chance in Hardy's fiction, which brought the narrative forms of the nineteenth-century novel he inherited and subverted to a dead end, where he abandoned them; and the second section considers chance in the aesthetic program of Henry James, whose narrative innovations paved the way for the modern novel of the twentieth century.

Chance in Hardy

The novels of Thomas Hardy adopt, but are not completely comfortable with, the forms and conventions of the Victorian novel. As Irving Howe notes, Thomas Hardy

came at a difficult moment in the history of English fiction: he could neither fully accept nor quite break away from the conventions of his Victorian predecessors. He felt obliged to use a variant of the overelaborate and synthetic plot that had become fixed in the Victorian novel, the kind of superstructure that, becoming an end in itself, could smother seriousness of thought. . . . [H]e wanted plot to serve as a sign of philosophic intent and this seduced him into relying too heavily upon mechanical devices. . . . Hardy supposed that the motions of fate—which he declared to be ethically indifferent while often writing as if they were ethically malicious—could be revealed through the manipulation of plot. . . . The result was that he often seems to be coercing his plots, jostling them away from their own inner logic. And sometimes in his passion to bend plot to purpose, he seems to be plotting against his own characters.

The result is, according to Howe, "coincidences which cannot be justified even in terms of his darkening view of life."[1]

Hardy writes in a traditional narrative mode the formal properties of which derive for the most part from a providential aesthetic; but in his own thinking he emphatically denied the existence, or at least the benevolence, of an all-seeing deity. He therefore manipulates his plots, arranging sometimes implausible coincidences, in order to illustrate his belief that there is *not* a supreme being who foresees and controls human events for some divine and ultimately benevolent purpose. As a result, chance in Hardy's novels usually signifies an *inverted* Providence, which is indifferent or malevolent in relation to what is called in *Tess of the D'Urbervilles* (1891) "the harrowing contingencies of human experience."[2] Like flies to wanton boys are Tess and Jude to Providence—they seem to suffer only for the sake of suffering. Hardy is no doubt referring to Gloucester's famously caustic observation in *King Lear* that the gods "kill us for their sport" when he concludes *Tess* with the remark "the President of the Immortals . . . had ended his sport with Tess" (p. 489).*

Hardy usually insisted that he was demonstrating not the malevolence but merely the indifference of the higher powers who oversee the situation and sufferings of his maladapted heroes and heroines. He wrote in his journal: "The world does not despise us; it only neglects us."[3] But time and again, Hardy's novelistic rendering of such "neglect" confuses or conflates a malicious and an indifferent attitude to human misery. For instance, when Tess finally relates her past life to her new husband, thereby shattering any hope of happiness

---

*A reviewer strenuously objected to this concluding remark in *Tess*, saying, "If there be a God, who can seriously think of him as a malicious fiend?" This prompted Hardy to quote Gloucester's lines from *King Lear* as an early example of someone who "exclaim[s] illogically against the gods." In the "Preface to the Fifth and Later Editions," July 1892; included in Hardy, *Personal Writings*, p. 28.

for her and Angel Clare, the change in their relationship seems to be reflected in their surroundings:

But the complexion even of external things seemed to suffer transmutation as her announcement progressed. The fire in the grate looked impish—demoniacally funny, as if it did not care about her strait. The fender grinned idly, as if it too did not care. The light from the water-bottle was merely engaged in a chromatic problem. All material objects around announced their irresponsibility with terrible iteration. (p. 291)

This passage unevenly blends several idioms to remark how, personally and psychologically, the lovers' world is undergoing an apocalyptic alteration. It is not at all an impersonal and detached account of the scene even though it eventually modulates into the language of scientific objectivity ("merely engaged in a chromatic problem"); the "material objects" are imbued with the pervasive animism of the entire passage, even if it is repeatedly to deny their implication in the scene they witness. The fire and the fender are anthropomorphized in an almost totemic way, all of which is supposed to register their indifference, at this calamitous moment, to the tragic events transpiring before them—it was as if they simply "did not care." But what they *show*, in their animistic response to the annihilation of Tess and Angel's love, is not indifference but a malicious delight in the lovers' desolation: grinning impishly, seeming "demoniacally funny," is not at all the same thing as not caring.

At the crucial moment in *Tess* that begins the heroine's career of misery—her sexual violation by Alec d'Urberville—Hardy stops to ask: "[W]here was the providence of her simple faith? Perhaps, like that other god of whom the ironical Tishbite spoke, he was talking, or he was pursuing, or he was in a journey, or he was sleeping and not to be awaked" (p. 91). Hardy's allusion is to *I Kings* (18:27), where Elijah the Tishbite mocks the prophets of Baal by saying, "Cry aloud: for he is a god; either he is talking, or he is pursuing, or he is in a journey, or peradventure he sleepeth, and must be awaked." Hardy turns Elijah's mockery back on the Christian God, who abandons Tess to her fate.

At the next moment of crisis in Tess's life, when she is about to marry Angel Clare, chance intervenes and a letter goes astray: the note explaining her sexual past to her future husband, which she slips under his door, slides under the carpet and is never read. She realizes too late that Angel has not seen the letter, and marries him, with disastrous results.* Tess's undelivered letter, or the horrific consequences of Father Time's accidental misunderstanding about Sue and Jude being troubled by too many children in *Jude the Obscure* (1896), shows how Hardy exerts an authorial will in order to deny the existence of a divine will ordering narrative events. Rather than indicating a causality directed by a benevolent God, Hardy's frequent and obtrusive use of chance and coincidence demonstrates that, in Angel Clare's words, "God's *not* in his heaven: all's *wrong* with the world!" (p. 324). This negation of Browning's pat optimism in *Pippa Passes*, like the use of scripture to characterize the negligent God supervising Tess's violation, illustrates how Hardy's resistance to Providence takes its bearings from traditional theological doctrine and consists in an inversion or negation of it. Just as he uses religion against religion, Hardy uses the conventions of Victorian plotting—coincidence in particular—to resist and repudiate the providential affiliations of that narrative form.

"What has Providence done to Mr. Hardy," Edmund Gosse asked in a review of *Jude the Obscure*, "that he should rise up in the arable land of Wessex and shake his fist at his Creator?"[4] The virulent backlash that greeted the publication of *Jude the Obscure* eventually brought Mr. Hardy to abandon the novel form. And as Hardy observed in his journal, it was in part his stubbornly defiant attitude toward Providence that eventually made poetry rather than the novel his preferred mode of expression:

---

*Coincidences abound in *Tess of the D'Urbervilles*: Tess repeatedly tries to flee her past but runs into the same man who knows of her shame on three separate occasions; and she encounters Alec D'Urberville again and again after her blighted marriage to Angel Clare, when she is most vulnerable to his renewed solicitations. These are the kinds of coincidences that Bert G. Hornback considers in *The Metaphor of Chance*. According to Hornback, coincidence in Hardy is a means of expressing "the intensity of experience" by bringing two different time frames together in "the metaphorical juxtaposition of past and present." This seems to me an accurate but limited way of understanding the Aristotelian coincidence of causal series in Hardy's plots. Hornback helpfully distinguishes between coincidence and chance in Hardy's novels; despite its title, and as Hornback himself admits, *The Metaphor of Chance* is more concerned with the former than the latter. About matters and metaphors of chance like the letter accident in *Tess*, which are not so easily explained by Hardy's treatment of temporal disjunctions, Hornback has very little to say. He remarks of this incident, "[T]he fates haven't willed this, Hardy has," but he does not explore the implications of this authorial complicity. Quotations appear on pp. 4, 42, and 6.

Perhaps I can express myself more fully in verse ideas and emotions which run counter to the inert crystallized opinion—hard as rock—which the vast body of men have vested interests in supporting. To cry out in a passionate poem that (for instance) the Supreme Mover or Movers, the Prime Force or Forces, must be either limited in power, unknowing, or cruel—which is obvious enough, and has been for centuries—will cause them merely a shake of the head; but to put it in argumentative prose will make them sneer, or foam, and set all the literary contortionists jumping upon me, a harmless agnostic, as if I were a clamorous atheist, which in their crass illiteracy they seem to think is the same thing.[5]

Hardy did indeed find verse a less restrictive form of expression; he later remarked about his poetry, "I would say that, unlike some of the fiction, nothing interfered with the writer's freedom in respect of its form and content."[6] The decision to devote his literary energies to poetry allowed him not only to air his allegedly agnostic views in a less controversial way, but also to express himself more fully on the subject of chance by abjuring narrative. He wrote in his Preface to *Poems of the Past and the Present* in 1902, "Unadjusted impressions have their value, and the road to a true philosophy of life seems to lie in humbly recording diverse readings of its phenomena as they are forced upon us by chance and change."[7] Hardy's lyric treatment of chance does not simply constitute (as it does in the novels) a negation or inversion of a Providence that is in every respect found lacking.

In the later poetry, Hardy uses coincidences for the most part to signify the operations of what he called "the Immanent Will," a blind force at work in the universe inevitably and irresistibly determining the course of circumstances. The Will Hardy sees at work in the world is immanent, not transcendent; it is a force of nature, not the manifestation of divine agency. As J. Hillis Miller explains:

It is a version of the inherent energy of the physical world as seen by nineteenth century science: an unconscious power working by regular laws of matter in motion. Though what happens is ordained by no divine lawgiver, the state of the universe at any one moment leads inevitably to its state at the next moment. Existence is made up of an enormous number of simultaneous energies each doing its bit to make the whole mechanism move. If a man had enough knowledge he could predict exactly what will be the state of the universe ten years from now or ten thousand. All things have been fated from all time.[8]

Hardy's idea of the Immanent Will is informed in general by the materialistic and deterministic thinking of nineteenth-century science and in particular by Darwin's theory of natural selection. In Hardy as in Darwin, the sufferings of the individual are inconsequential in relation to the natural laws governing the differentiation and survival of species. Although individuals cannot control or direct the impersonal operations of this Will, it is sometimes possible to observe and acknowledge the ways it manifests itself in the world. Through a process of what he called "evolutionary meliorism," Hardy believed, the unconscious workings of the Immanent Will might eventually be brought to consciousness. Hardy concludes the end of his epic drama *The Dynasts* (1903, 1906, 1908) by suggesting that mankind will either "darkle to extinction swift and sure" as a result of the Will's unconscious workings or else receive "deliverance offered from the darts that were, / Consciousness the Will informing, till it fashions all things fair!" Until that time, which may or may not ever come, man must endure the casual dispensations of this impersonal force, which usually entail pain and suffering, only to be extinguished by death.

The success of Hardy's Immanent Will theory in poetic works like *The Dynasts* and "The Convergence of the Twain" (1912) is due in large part to the fact that Hardy uses historical material (the Napoleonic Wars, the sinking of the *Titanic*) to illustrate the implacable workings of the Immanent Will. The contingencies of historical events become in his poetry the expression and result of a necessity dictated by the Immanent Will. "The Convergence of the Twain" clearly illustrates how the Will manifests itself in what seems to be a literal coincidence. In the poem, the iceberg and the *Titanic* come together "bent / By paths coincident / On being anon twin halves of one august event." The equipoise of the poem and its elements (iceberg and luxury liner, impersonal nature and hubristic technology, sea worms crawling on opulent mirrors) are both balanced and climactically brought together by "the Immanent Will that stirs and urges everything," which is invoked in the fulcrum-like middle stanza. Of course, there is really nothing chancy about such a coincidence for Hardy; he uses the cataclysmic convergence of the ship and the mountain of ice to illustrate the "consummation" of a necessity preordained and determined by the inexorable Immanent Will.

Hardy explicated the idea of the Immanent Will in overtly philosophical terms in his later poetry, though its influence can be felt in much of the earlier work, the prose as much as the poetry. Gillian Beer observes about Hardy's novels:

In reading Hardy's work, we often find a triple level of plot generated: the anxiously scheming and predictive plot of the characters' making; the optative plot of the commentary, which often takes the form "Why did nobody" or "had somebody . . . ," and the absolute plot of blind interaction and "Nature's laws."[9]

It is this final level of plot that exemplifies in novelistic terms what Hardy in his later poetry called the Immanent Will at work in the world. The "absolute plot" governing the life and, more often than not, bringing about the extinction of Hardy's protagonists is informed by scientific laws in a deterministic universe and so is very different from the absolutism of a providentialist plot ordered and authored by God.

It is helpful to distinguish between Aristotelian coincidence (the intersection of two or more causal series in an event of some consequence) and a distinctively aleatory kind of chance in Hardy's poetry. Hardy's poetic treatment of chance—what he usually calls "haps," as in "the neutral-tinted haps and such" of "He Never Expected Much" (1928)—does not necessarily evidence the operations of an Immanent Will at work in the world as does the coincidence of Titanic and iceberg in "The Convergence of the Twain." Consider for instance the well-known poem "Hap," one of the first poems Hardy published after abandoning the novel form. This poem was actually written in 1866 but it was not published until 1898. The fact that it was written long before Hardy decided to abandon novel writing does not minimize its significance for my argument. I am concerned here not with the chronology of Hardy's thinking about chance but with the formal constraints on his treatment of the subject in narrative, which can be clarified by comparing his novelistic interest in chance to his thematizations of it in his lyric poetry. And "Hap" is the most explicit and programmatic treatment of the subject in Hardy's work, prose or poetry.

Hap

If but some vengeful god would call to me
From up the sky, and laugh: "Thou suffering thing,
Know that thy sorrow is my ecstacy,
That thy love's loss is my hate's profiting!"

Then would I bear it, clench myself, and die,
Steeled by the sense of ire unmerited;
Half-eased in that a Powerfuller than I
Had willed and meted me the tears I shed.

But not so. How arrives it joy lies slain,
And why unblooms the best hope ever sown?
—Crass Casualty obstructs the sun and rain,
And dicing Time for gladness casts a moan. . . .
These purblind Doomsters had as readily strown
Blisses about my pilgrimage as pain.

(Vol. 19, p. 6)

This poem articulates Hardy's economy of chance: the speaker would stoically submit to his suffering if only the Power required to slay his joy and make his gladness moan were somehow yielding a return on the expenditure of energy, the "profiting" of some vengeful god's hate. This dreadful prospect is still preferable to suffering with no cause, purpose, or origin.

The first two stanzas of "Hap" express Hardy's usual way of considering chance with their invocation of a malicious divinity who wills its victims' pain and disappointment. But this version of Hardy's inverted Providence is in the conditional form—"*if* there were such a god *then* I would bear the suffering"—and the poem's negation of a benevolent divine will is itself negated: "But not so." Out of this Nietzschean double negation emerges the only suggestion in Hardy's mordant *oeuvre* that chance might offer pleasure as well as pain, that it might create possibilities as well as thwart aspirations: "These purblind Doomsters had as readily strown / Blisses about my pilgrimage as pain." This affirmation of a possibly blissful chance (which is almost obscured by the imagery of wilting and the sound of moans and the dispensations of "Doomsters") is perhaps Hardy's distanced acknowledgment that the "hap" of "haphazard" is the etymological root of "happy."

With this one dimly registered exception, the two terms "hap" and "happy" for Hardy are not cognate but polar opposites: as Gillian Beer comments, "Happiness and hap form the two poles of Hardy's work." Such happiness as there is in the novels is only an experience of the moment, intense, evanescent, frequently lyrical; and it is inevitably extinguished as it gives way to the formidable and inexorable machinations of plot. "Happiness does not share in the powers of narrative," Beer writes. "Indeed it is almost at odds with narrative, because it is at odds with succession."[10] Beer does not elaborate on the intimate alignment of "hap" with Hardy's narrative project. Hap is in fact always *mis*hap in Hardy's novels; he consistently uses chance in narrative to deny, invert, and negate the traditional religious and metaphysical affiliations of the narrative form he inherited.

Hardy affirms chance to repudiate a providentialist understanding of the world but denies chance in the implacable operations of the Immanent Will. The sense of an Immanent Will at work in the plotting of the novels is often sketchy and contradictory, however; and this is the case not just because Hardy only completely elaborated his theory of the Immanent Will after abandoning the novel form. There are formal constraints that problematize the idea of such a force directing and determining the course and outcome of fictional narratives. Hardy's attempt to replace the Divine Will with the Immanent Will in his novels does not necessarily or adequately account for the seemingly arbitrary dispensations of the authorial will in relation to the world it supervises.

Both Hardy's poetry and his novels disclaim a providential agency at work in the world; but Hardy's poetic treatment of coincidence and chance manages to do and say and be more than just an inversion or denial of a providential order. Granted, the adjective "purblind" applied to the dicing Doomsters in "Hap," like the characterization of the Immanent Will as "the Great Foresightless" in *The Dynasts*, denies the power and efficacy of Providence, which means, literally, foresight.* But the Immanent Will of "The Convergence of the Twain" and *The Dynasts* and the doubly negated affirmation of the aleatory in "Hap" provide a way of understanding coincidence and chance that does not simply signify the absence, indifference, or malice of a Supreme Being. In the novels, however, the meaning and importance of coincidence and chance are inescapably determined by the providential framework they are designed to negate and invert. In "Hap"'s terms, there is indeed a "Powerfuller" one who foresees

---

*Here are the first few lines of the "After Scene" that concludes *The Dynasts*, spoken by the Spirit of the Years: "Thus doth the Great Foresightless mechanize / In blank entrancement now as evermore / Its ceaseless artistries in Circumstance / Of curious stuff and braid, as just foreshown" (Hardy, *Works*, vol. 21, p. 251).

and wills novelistic happenstance: the "Crass Casualty" and "Dicing Time" that torment Michael Henchard and Tess Durbeyfield and Jude Fawley are plotted by Thomas Hardy.

Chance in James

Henry James developed a narrative method for which the problematics of chance do not necessarily constitute, as they do for George Eliot and Thomas Hardy, a critique of the providential tradition. In the James novel, chance events more often than not reveal the blind spot that both limits and organizes the presiding perspective. The chance experience reveals and dramatizes what had previously and resolutely been left unsaid in the narrative. Since narrative discretion—dictated for the most part by a character's point of view—structures the story from the very beginning, the aleatory aspects of an experience tend to be aestheticized and assimilated to James's notion of organic form.* What might seem like a forced coincidence or an authorial infelicity in the more panoramic and panoptic Victorian novel becomes in James's perspectival fiction an explicit dramatization of a (usually erotic and/or monetary) force already implicitly at work in and affecting the form of the narrative.

I want eventually to examine what is probably the most striking and famous example of chance in James's fiction, the scene in *The Ambassadors* (1903) where Strether finally realizes the nature of the relationship between Chad Newsome and Madame de Vionnet when he runs into them out boating together during his holiday in the country. But first I want to look briefly at several scenes from earlier novels in order to show how this chance occurrence in *The Ambassadors* fits into a larger pattern that runs throughout James's fiction, only becoming (like so much else) more self-conscious and artistically wrought in the later works. The crisis of *Daisy Miller* (1878) comes when Winterbourne, walking home one moonlit evening and responsive to "the sense of the romantic in him," decides that the interior of the Roman Colosseum on such a night "would

---

*See Henry James, *Theory of Fiction*, for a helpful compilation of James's reflections about his theory of the novel. For the idea of characterological perspective, see chapter 12, "Point of View," pp. 234–56; for his notion of organic form, see chapter 13, "Form and Structure," pp. 257–67.

well repay a glance." There he is shocked to discover Daisy Miller and Mr. Giovanelli alone together. This unchaperoned intimacy suddenly and effectively resolves Winterbourne's ambivalence about Daisy as he realizes, finally, "[s]he was a young lady about the *shades* of whose perversity a foolish puzzled gentleman need no longer trouble his head or his heart. That once questionable quantity *had* no shades— it was a mere black blot."[11] In *The Portrait of a Lady* (1881) Isabel Archer similarly intrudes on a moment of revealing intimacy, though the encounter is not so much a matter of chance as Winterbourne's moonlit discovery of Daisy Miller and her "cicerone." Entering the drawing room on silent feet, Isabel discovers her husband, Gilbert Osmond, with Madame Merle at a time when "their colloquy had for the moment controverted itself into a sort of familiar silence." Osmond is seated while Madame Merle is standing, an uncharacteristic informality on his part that adds to the unprecedented impact of the scene on Isabel. "Their relative positions, their absorbed mutual gaze, struck her as something detected."[12] This is the first intimation she has of the cunning and calculation at work in her husband's involvement with Madame Merle. As we are later told, this striking tableau makes her realize how completely the two have taken advantage of her innate responsiveness to experience in order to implement their own self-serving designs: "The sense of accident indeed had died within her that day when she happened to be struck with the manner in which the wonderful lady and her own husband sat together in private."[13] This accidental intrusion reveals to her that, in her dealings with Osmond and his former mistress, nothing has happened by accident. In *The Princess Casamassima* (1886) Hyacinth Robinson also happens to witness a scene that suddenly and disturbingly reveals an intimacy of which he was formerly unaware. Seeing the princess and Paul Muniment get out of a cab late at night, talk on her doorstep, then enter her house together, Hyacinth Robinson "felt his heart beat insanely, ignobly. He couldn't tell why." At that moment he had "a very exact revelation of the state of feeling of those who love in the rage of jealousy."[14] Like the speaker of Shakespeare's sonnets, Hyacinth sees the two people he cares for most in the world, and who he brought together, form a connection in relation to which he is an outsider.

Each of these moments in earlier novels has a structure similar to

that of the uncanny chance encounter that brings Strether, Chad, and
Madame de Vionnet together in *The Ambassadors*. All of these scenes
come late in their stories, and they represent a major crisis of perception (and, eventually, self-perception) for the protagonist. In each instance the vision revealed by chance to the observer exposes the blind
spot that has been determining the perspectival limits of that character for most of the novel. The chance observation opens the eyes
of Winterbourne, Isabel Archer, Hyacinth Robinson, and Strether to
an intimacy they were formerly not able, or just as likely, resolutely
refused, to see. Such blind spots circumscribe not just the characters'
point of view but also the material and focus of the narrative. Unlike,
say, the treatment of the heroine's notorious blind spots in *Emma*,
where Austen occasionally supplements Emma Woodhouse's limited
vision with the comparatively unimaginative, empirical, and chasten-
ing perspective of Mr. Knightley, James's narratives do not provide
explicit indications of or correctives to the limitations that structure
characterological point of view. Like the blind spots associated with
the physiology of the eye, the blind spots in James's narratives are
not simply areas in the visual field that could in principle be comprehended with a shift of focus. The blind spot, a small blankness just
below the horizontal plane, is intrinsic to the workings of the ocular
organ and constitutive of the visual field; it both limits and makes
possible any and all visual perception. The observers of the scenes
mentioned do gradually manage to take in the meaning and implications of the intimacy they witness, but in each case (with the likely
exception of Winterbourne) this entails the collapse of their entire
worldview.

The chance incident that disabuses the James hero or heroine of
the formative blind spot stages a kind of primal scene wherein the
intimate intercourse intruded upon and observed by the naive consciousness is primarily discursive, with only secondary sexual connotations.* A primal scene in psychological terms refers to a child's
witnessing of a sexual act, an event that plays a traumatic role in
his or her subsequent sexual development. The moments of conver-
sational intimacy witnessed by Winterbourne and Isabel Archer and
Hyacinth Robinson and Lambert Strether reveal, represent, and in

---

*Leo Bersani briefly considers several of these moments, though he assimilates the
thematics of vision they represent to masochism rather than to the primal scene. See
A Future for Astyanax, pp. 133–36.

a sense repeat a sexual intimacy; and the descriptions of the observed couple's interactions are fraught with sexual suggestiveness.*
It is "their relative position, their absorbed mutual gaze" that makes Isabel Archer take notice of Osmond and Madame Merle's rapport. Hyacinth Robinson feels that "[t]here was something inexpressibly representative to him in the way that friend had abruptly decided to re-enter the house, after pausing outside with its mistress. . . . The movement repeated itself innumerable times to his inward sense, suggesting to him things he couldn't bear to learn." [15] And as Strether observes Chad and Madame de Vionnet in their boat, he senses "that they were expert, familiar, frequent—that this wouldn't at all events be the first time. They knew how to do it, he vaguely felt." [16] All of these primal scenes dramatize the focal characters' traumatic encounter with a sexual relationship and their anguished realization of a sexual history in relation to which they are both excluded and, somehow, disturbingly implicated.

The operations and effects of narrative blind spots in James's fiction, which are dramatically exposed in powerfully condensed moments having the character of a primal scene, do not yet explain why and how these moments always occur by chance. In order to pursue this question, I want to turn now to the most pronounced and striking instance of chance in James's fiction. In the comparatively short Book Eleventh of *The Ambassadors*, James emphatically calls attention to the chance nature of the encounter between Strether, Chad, and Madame de Vionnet: Strether ventures into the country on a whim; the station at which he disembarks was "selected almost at random" (p. 245); and his rambling visit is one of leisured divagation. Further, the entire scene is framed in explicitly aesthetic terms. Thinking of a painting of a French landscape by Lambinet he almost purchased in Boston, Strether regards the charm of his rural adventure as through "the little oblong window of the picture-frame" (p. 245). He is delighted to discover how well the countryside and its inhabitants live

---

*If the illicit activities of Paul Muniment and the princess are sexual and not just political (James is rather discreet on this point), the scene Hyacinth witnesses would in fact be the beginning of such a relationship. The import of Daisy Miller's unchaperoned outing with Mr. Giovanelli in that early novel seems to exist almost entirely in the domain of the social, so likewise does not necessarily indicate an illicit liaison. Edith Wharton's 1934 short story "Roman Fever" is more explicit, taking for granted the fact that couples went to the Colosseum for just that purpose.

up to his fancied anticipation, shaped as it is by "the background of fiction, the medium of art, the nursery of letters" (p. 245):

The oblong gilt frame disposed its enclosing lines; the poplars and willows, the reeds and river—a river of which he didn't know, and didn't want to know the name—fell into a composition, full of felicity, within them; the sky was silver and turquoise and varnish; the village on the left was white and the church on the right was grey; it was all there, in short—it was what he wanted. (p. 247)

The pleasant scenery seems to consist in harmonious lines, pigment, brushwork, and varnish; and the colorful French rustics remind him of Maupassant (p. 248).

The day and its scenic pleasures, associated with a painting and with fiction, become as well a play: "For this had all day been at bottom the spell of the picture—that it was essentially more than anything else a scene and a stage, that the very air of the play was in the rustle of the willows and the tone of the sky" (p. 253). The play that merges with the picture is the drama Strether has just been living in Paris, negotiating between the staid expectations of Woolett, Massachusetts, and the exhortation to "live!" urged on him by Paris and the Parisians. As Strether reviews in his mind the characters and action of that drama, which he finds reflected in his country ramble, "[n]ot a single one of his observations but somehow fell into a place in it; not a breath of the cooler evening that wasn't somehow a syllable of the text" (pp. 253–54). The drama of Strether's experiences in France is condensed in and identified with a framed picture, which he experiences as a pure aesthetic event.

When Strether sees a boat approaching on the river, it seems "exactly the right thing": "It was suddenly as if these figures, or something like them, had been wanted in the picture, had been wanted more or less all day, and had now drifted into sight, with the slow current, on purpose to fill up the measure" (p. 256). Earlier in the day, all the details of his rural adventure had not exceeded the framed aestheticism of Strether's appreciation: "The frame had drawn itself out for him, as much as you please" (p. 252). But when he recognizes with a start the two boaters, that frame and the romanticized picture it sets off threaten to crack from side to side. When Strether first sees the boaters, he observes: "The air quite thickened, at their approach, with further intimations; the intimation that they were expert, familiar, frequent—that this wouldn't be the first time. They knew how to do it, he vaguely felt" (p. 256). The immediate referent of Strether's vague assessment "They knew how to do it" is the couples' rowing and boating skills, but it of course suggests other forms of worldly knowledge and experience. The intimations of intimacy in this scene bring Strether to acknowledge for the first time the sexual rapport between Chad and Madame de Vionnet.

Strether has learned how to turn experience into an aesthetic event from the cultured Europeans, Madame de Vionnet in particular. She as usual takes the lead in the awkward moments of their mutual recognition. Trying to make the best of their embarrassing situation, she remarks

the charming chance they had, the others, in passing, ordered some food to be ready, the charming chance that he had not eaten, the charming chance, even more, that their plans, their hours, their train, in short, from *là-bas*, would all match for their return together to Paris. The chance that was the most charming of all, the chance that drew from Madame de Vionnet her clearest, gayest "*Comme cela se trouve!*" was . . . the word given him by their hostess in respect to his carriage for the station, on which he might count. It settled the matter for his friends as well; the conveyance—it was all too lucky!—would serve for them; and nothing was more delightful than his being in a position to make the train so definite. (pp. 259–60)

Madame de Vionnet's aestheticizing instincts cannot quite transform this distressing chance encounter into a charming moment. As Strether eventually realizes, such aestheticism is designed not just to give pleasure but to deceive: "there had been simply a *lie* in the charming affair" (p. 262). Madame de Vionnet's effusive "appreciation" of chance only reveals what all of its "charm" is trying to conceal, that Chad and Madame de Vionnet in fact have not made any arrangements for their return to Paris because they planned to spend the night together.*

*As David Lodge points out in "Strether by the River," a careful analysis of the language in this part of *The Ambassadors*, the shift from aesthetic appreciation to a recognition of deceit is conveyed in the descriptive details of the recognition scene: Madame de Vionnet's pink parasol, "formerly a purely pictorial element, is now a device of deception—'shifting as if to hide her face' " (pp. 200–201). About this meeting, Lodge comments: "The encounter between Strether and Chad and Madame de Vionnet on the river is an event of pure chance. Yet it occurs to no reader of *The Ambassadors*, I suspect, to question the artistic propriety of James's reliance on coincidence at so crucial a point in the action; and it is worth inquiring why this should be so" (p. 205). His explanation for such readerly complaisance (about which I am myself suspicious) centers on the way this scene fits into a larger image pattern of water and boats running throughout the novel.

"It was too prodigious, a chance in a million" (p. 257). The suggestions of theater and fiction continue in the characters' rather uncomfortable response to "the prodigy of their convergence" (p. 261): "it was as queer as fiction, as farce, that their country could happen to be exactly his" (p. 257); they all remark on "the general *invraisemblance* of the occasion" (p. 259); Strether even worries that Chad and Madame de Vionnet might perhaps be "secretly suspecting him of having plotted this coincidence, taking such pains as might be to give it the semblance of an accident" (p. 259). But of course it was not Strether who plotted this coincidence, which (as even the characters who experience it remark) strains a sense of verisimilitude.

By repeatedly calling attention to its own fictionality, this scene in *The Ambassadors* lays bare in a startlingly naked way how James's perspectival plotting makes use of chance in order to realize his aesthetic ends. The characters' own observation about "the general *invraisemblance* of the occasion" does not simply defuse a reader's possible objections to such a forced coincidence. Plots based on criteria of verisimilitude have managed to assimilate and recuperate unlikely events by an old and venerable strategy: unlikely things *do* happen in life, this form of justification claims, and the inclusion of such an incident only makes the plot more "life-like." Aristotle states in the *Poetics*: "The Improbable one has to justify either by showing it to be in accordance with opinion, or by urging that at times it is not improbable; for there is a probability of things happening also against probability."[17] But the improbability of this coincidence in *The Ambassadors* does not simply constitute an exception that proves the rule of verisimilitude; rather, it makes absolutely explicit and self-conscious the usual workings of verisimilitude vis-à-vis chance. By pushing plausibility to the breaking point, James exposes the way seemingly aleatory experience is *always* being assimilated to aesthetic design by novelistic notions of the probable.

Despite the fact that Strether's impulse to go touring is called "artless" (p. 245), all the elements of his country ramble contribute to or themselves constitute an aesthetic experience: "The oblong gilt frame disposed its enclosing lines." By locating the aestheticizing impulse in Strether and suggesting that he is responsible for the framing effect organizing the narrative depiction of this scene, James makes this coincidence seem to emerge out of his character's own fictional expectations: "What it all came to had been that fiction and fable *were*, inevitably, in the air" (p. 262). Inasmuch as the chance nature of the meeting is *de trop* then, Strether is framed for what might otherwise seem a narrative indiscretion on James's part.

In James's economy of novelistic form, an excursion like Strether's holiday in the country, an interlude of vagrancy and indulgence, is not allowed to dissipate under the impetus of its own vague and undirected responsiveness to pleasure. Strether may take a vacation, but the Jamesian laws dictating that all narrative material must contribute to the integrated wholeness of the work do not. Likewise the experience of chance, which might seem to pose a challenge to James's ideas of novelistic decorum (verisimilitude, for example), instead works (is put to work) to reveal the integrity and comprehensiveness of the artistic vision. The revelation of Chad and Madame de Vionnet's affair effectively demolishes the frame of reference for Strether's naive and aestheticizing view of things as he finally sees the (to him) sordid sexual truth deceptively hidden under so much charm. But from James's point of view, the disclosure of the lovers' sexual secret only completes and makes explicit the frame of reference that has been structuring the presentation of narrative material from the beginning. The "wild extravagance of hazard" (p. 350) that brings Chad and his mistress floating up to the waiting and confounded Strether does indeed complete the picture—James's picture—by dramatizing a truth that Strether's formerly so elastic aestheticizing perspective can no longer accommodate.

Such Jamesian chance encounters as have been discussed here constitute primal scenes not just because in them a naive consciousness interrupts and observes a kind of intercourse that brings to light a hitherto unacknowledged sexual intimacy. The primal scene is always a fantasy about the origins of the individual. Of course, in psychological terms, the scenes witnessed by Strether and Winterbourne and Isabel Archer and Hyacinth Robinson do not really offer any insights into their own conception. But in terms of narrative structure, the primal scene—especially as staged in *The Ambassadors*, which is so self-conscious about its aesthetic implications—does indeed dramatize the origins of these characters, and it does so in a manner that is not restricted to the psychologistic perspective of the fiction's focal consciousness. The primal scene that occurs as if by chance in the James novel offers a revealing insight into the way his characters are conceived by exposing the aesthetic framing that makes the character and her or his story possible in the first place.

In James's fiction the chance encounter dramatically brings the frame of the presiding perspective into play, revealing what had formerly constituted the border or limit of the focal character's cognitive and experiential awareness. This is certainly no violation of the aesthetic principles mandated by James's commitment to characterological point of view or his notion of organic form in the novel; the frame is an integral part of the aestheticizing process, and its fortuitous disclosure dramatizes the inextricable intertwining of chance with novelistic perspective in James's formal aesthetic. And that aesthetic was foundational for the modern novel.

Reference Matter

Notes

Introduction

1. See Welsford, *The Fool*, especially chap. 3, "Origins: the Fool as Mascot and Scapegoat," pp. 55–75.
2. Leavis, *Great Tradition*, p. 223.
3. Lyotard, *Postmodern Condition*.
4. *Mallarmé: the Poems*, pp. 254–55.

Chapter One

1. Heisenberg, *Physics and Beyond*, pp. 131–2.
2. Ibid., p. 139.
3. See Bailey, *Greek Atomists and Epicurus*, p. 51.
4. Quoted ibid., p. 85.   5. Aristotle, *Physics*, p. 243.
6. Ibid., p. 244.   7. Ibid., p. 243.
8. Ibid., p. 246.
9. See Steven M. Cahn, "Chance," in *Encyclopedia of Philosophy*, vol. 2, p. 73.
10. Quoted in Bunge, "What Is Chance?," p. 214.
11. See for instance Peirce, *Chance, Love, and Logic*, and William James, "Dilemma of Determinism."
12. Cahn, "Chance," p. 74.
13. Quoted in Bunge, "What Is Chance?," p. 218.
14. Mill, *System of Logic*, bk. 3, chap. 17, sec. 2.
15. Quoted in Bunge, "What Is Chance?," p. 211.
16. Marx, *Difference*, p. 77.
17. Lucretius, *Nature of the Universe*, p. 67.
18. Bailey, *Greek Atomists and Epicurus*, p. 320.
19. Lucretius, *De Rerum Natura*, vol. 1, p. 88.
20. See Bailey, *Greek Atomists and Epicurus*, pp. 347–50.
21. These examples are mentioned in P.H. De Lacy, "Epicurus," *Encyclopedia of Philosophy*, vol. 3, p. 4.
22. Monod, *Chance and Necessity*, pp. 112–113.
23. Ibid., p. 118.

24. Ibid., pp. 118–19.

25. The following exposition of chance in quantum theory is informed by "Causality and Indeterminism in Physical Theory," chap. 10 of Nagel, *Structure of Science.*

26. Bohm, *Causality and Chance*, p.86.

27. In this regard see ibid., pp. 84–89.

28. See Nagel, *Structure of Science*, p. 296.

29. Ibid., p. 316.

30. Heisenberg, *Physics and Beyond*, p. 104.

31. Einstein, *Born-Einstein Letters*, p. 149, letter dated 7 Sept. 1944.

32. Derrida, "My Chances/Mes Chances."

33. Lacan, "Seminar," p. 72.

34. Lacan, *Four Fundamental Concepts*, p. 52.

35. Ibid., p. 54.   36. Ibid.

37. Ibid., p. 56.   38. Ibid., p. 54.

39. L. 1080 in the Greek text of Sophocles' *Oedipus Tyrannus*, p. 142.

40. Lacan, "Seminar," p. 60.

41. Watt, *Rise of the Novel*, pp. 82, 83. Page references to this work will henceforth appear in parentheses after the quotations.

42. Lukacs, *Theory of the Novel*, p. 88.

43. The following critical overview of responses to *Robinson Crusoe* is informed by "Robinson Crusoe and Friday," chap. 5 of Hulme's *Colonial Encounters*, pp. 174–222.

44. See Starr, *Defoe and Spiritual Autobiography*, and Hunter, *Reluctant Pilgrim.*

45. McKeon, *Origins of the English Novel*, p. 120. Page references to this work will henceforth appear in parentheses after the quotations.

46. Quoted ibid., p. 121.

47. Defoe, *Robinson Crusoe*, p. 129. Page references to the 1972 Oxford edition will henceforth appear in parentheses after the quotations.

48. Watt, "*Robinson Crusoe* as a Myth," quoted in Hulme, *Colonial Encounters*, p. 179.

49. See Viner, *Role of Providence*, pp. 4–16.

50. Tillotson, *Works*, vol. 3, pp. 98–99.

51. Hulme, *Colonial Encounters*, p. 177.

52. Ibid.

53. Aristotle, *Poetics*, p. 1465.

54. Starr, *Defoe and Spiritual Autobiography*, p. 126.

Chapter Two

1. Eliot, *Letters*, vol. 5, p. 102.

2. Dickens, *Letters*, vol. 3, p. 124; quoted in Vargish, *Providential Aesthetic*, p. 38.

3. Vargish, *Providential Aesthetic*, p. 2.

4. Ibid., p. 6.

5. Darwin, *Origin of Species*, pp. 173–74.

6. Quoted in Hull, *Darwin and His Critics*, pp. 65–66.

7. Eliot, trans. [as Marian Evans], Ludwig Feuerbach, *Essence of Christianity*, p. 188.

8. Aquinas, *Summa Contra Gentiles*, bk. 3, chaps. 90–94.

9. Eliot, *Silas Marner*, p. 17.

10. Beaty, *"Middlemarch" from Notebook to Novel*, pp. 74–75.

11. Eliot, *Letters*, vol. 5, p. 168.

12. Garrett, *Victorian Multiplot Novel*, p. 164.

13. Carroll, "*Middlemarch* and the Externality of Fact," p. 82.

14. Eliot, *Letters*, vol. 5, p. 175.

15. Haight, *George Eliot*, p. 66.

16. Ibid., p. 319.

17. Eliot, *Middlemarch*, p. 591. Page references to the 1986 Oxford edition will henceforth appear in parentheses after the quotations.

18. Hertz, "Recognizing Casaubon," pp. 75–96.

19. Ibid., p. 79.

20. Ibid., pp. 78, 85.

21. Levine, "Determinism and Responsibility," p. 272.

22. Hertz, "Recognizing Casaubon," pp. 85, 78.

23. Eliot, *Silas Marner*, p. 265.   24. Ibid., p. 269.

25. Eliot, *Daniel Deronda*, p. 3.   26. Ibid., p. 309.

27. Garrett, *Victorian Multiplot Novel*, p. 160.

28. See in this regard Christ, "Aggression and Providential Death."

29. Eliot, *Felix Holt* (1980 Oxford edition), p. 332.

30. Eliot, *Felix Holt* (Penguin edition), p. 511.

31. Hertz, "Recognizing Casaubon," p. 85.

32. Furst and Skrine, *Naturalism*, p. 16.

33. See for instance Chevrel, *Naturalisme*; Bowlby, *Just Looking*; Michaels, *Gold Standard*; Mitchell, *Determined Fictions*; and Baguley, *Naturalist Fiction*.

34. Furst and Skrine, *Naturalism*, p. 18.

Chapter Three

1. Karl, *Joseph Conrad*, p. 174n.

2. In this regard see Derrida, "My Chances/*Mes Chances*," pp. 5–6.

3. Henry James, "New Novel," p. 202.

4. Ibid., p. 203.

5. *The Secret Agent: A Simple Tale*, vol. 13 of Conrad, *Works*, p. 31.

6. Barthes, "Introduction to Structural Analysis," p. 94.

7. Freud, *Psychopathology*, pp. 257–58.

8. Freud, "Delusion and Dream," p. 9.

9. Freud, *Psychopathology*, p. 257.

10. Ibid.

11. Lacan, "Seminar on 'The Purloined Letter,' " p.72.

12. Derrida, "Purveyor of Truth," pp. 31–113.

13. Derrida, "My Chances/*Mes Chances*," p. 10.

14. Siegle, *Politics of Reflexivity*, p. 68.

15. *Chance: A Tale in Two Parts*, vol. 2 of Conrad, *Works*, p. 376. Page references to the Canterbury Edition will henceforth appear in parentheses after the quotations.

16. Karl, *Joseph Conrad*, p. 713.

17. Moser, "Conrad's Later 'Affirmation,' " p. 151.

18. Ibid., p. 150.

19. See in this regard D. A. Miller, *Narrative and Its Discontents*.

20. Laplanche and Pontalis, "Fantasy and the Origins of Sexuality," p. 10.

21. Conrad, *Secret Agent*, pp. 238–48.

22. Derrida, "My Chances/*Mes Chances*," p. 15. Page references to this essay will henceforth appear in parentheses after the quotations.

23. Laplanche and Pontalis, "Fantasy and the Origins of Sexuality," p. 11.

24. See Conrad, *Personal Record*, pp. 22–26.

25. Freud, "The 'Uncanny,' " p. 157.

Chapter Four

1. Ellmann, *James Joyce*, p. 649.

2. Joyce, *Portrait of the Artist as a Young Man*, p. 253.

3. Quoted in Ellmann, *James Joyce*, p. 204.

4. Joyce, *Exiles*, p. 112.

5. Ibid., p. 114.

6. Quoted in Ellmann, *James Joyce*, p. 501.

7. Joyce, *Portrait of the Artist as a Young Man*, p. 217.

8. Rader, "Exodus and Return"; see especially pp. 165–67.

9. Quoted in Ellmann, *James Joyce*, p. 501.

10. Rader, "Exodus and Return," pp. 158, 156.

11. Gifford and Seidman, *"Ulysses" Annotated*, p. 33.

12. Ibid., p. 514.

13. See Rader, "Exodus and Return," especially pp. 159–60, for a complete discussion of Murphy as ghost.

14. Gifford and Seidman, *"Ulysses" Annotated*, p. 265.

15. See Ellmann, *James Joyce*, p. 438.

16. Rader, "Exodus and Return," p. 164.

17. Derrida, *Dissemination*, p. 48.

18. Hayman, "Stephen on the Rocks."

19. Joyce, *Selected Letters*, pp. 280–81. The letter was originally in Italian; the translation is Ellmann's.

20. *Oxford English Dictionary*, vol. 5, p. 500.

21. Jakobson, "Two Aspects of Language."

22. Joyce, *Portrait of the Artist as a Young Man*, p. 35.

23. Rader, "Logic of *Ulysses*," p. 572.

24. See for instance Gallagher and Laqueur, *Making of the Modern Body*.

25. Gifford and Seidman, *"Ulysses" Annotated*, p. 544.

26. See Sedgwick, *Between Men*, for a discussion of homosocial and homoerotic male bonds.

27. "Canto XLV," in Pound, *Cantos*, p. 230.

28. Ellmann, *James Joyce*, p. 438.

29. *Oxford English Dictionary*, vol. 11, entry for "T," p. 1; entry for "tittle," p. 81.

Conclusion

1. Tillotson, "Wisdom of Being Religious," in his *Works*, vol. 1, pp. 346–47.

2. Stoppard, *Travesties*, pp. 53–55.

3. For these three attempts to define postmodernism, see Hassan, "Postface 1982: Toward a Concept of Postmodernism," in his *Dismemberment of Orpheus*, pp. 259–271; Jameson, "Postmodernism and Consumer Society"; and Lyotard, *Postmodern Condition*.

4. For an illuminating discussion of the proper name in Wilde's play, see Fineman, "Significance of Literature."

5. For an interesting discussion of antonomasia in the work of Jacques Derrida, see Ulmer, *Applied Grammatology*, pp. 44–45.

6. Cage, *Writing Through Finnegans Wake*, n.p.

7. Ibid.

8. Joyce, *Portrait of the Artist as a Young Man*, p. 215.

9. Lucretius, *De Rerum Natura*, vol. 3, p. 34.

Appendix

1. Howe, *Thomas Hardy*, pp. 90–93.

2. *Tess of the D'Urbervilles*, vol. 1 of Thomas Hardy, *Works*, p. 300. Page references to the Wessex edition will henceforth appear in parentheses after the quotations.

3. Entry for May 1865, quoted in Florence Hardy, *Life of Thomas Hardy*, p. 48.

4. Edmund Gosse, review in *Cosmopolis*, January 1896, pp. 60–69; reprinted in Cox, *Thomas Hardy*, p. 269.

5. Quoted in Millgate, *Thomas Hardy*, p. 382.

6. In the "General Preface to the Novels and Poems," written for the 1912 Wessex edition; included in Thomas Hardy, *Personal Writings*, p. 48.

7. Thomas Hardy, *Personal Writings*, p. 39; also quoted in Beer, *Darwin's Plots*, p. 245.

8. J. Hillis Miller, *Thomas Hardy*, p. 14. My general exposition of Hardy's "Immanent Will" is informed by Miller's discussion.

9. Beer, *Darwin's Plots*, p. 240.

10. Ibid., p. 246.

11. *Daisy Miller*, pp. 85–86, in Henry James, *Novels and Tales*, vol. 18.

12. *Portrait of a Lady*, vol. 2, pp. 164–65, in Henry James, *Novels and Tales*, vol. 3.

13. Ibid., vol. 2, pp. 322–23.

14. *The Princess Casamassima*, vol. 2, pp. 323–24, in Henry James, *Novels and Tales*, vols. 5–6.

15. Henry James, *The Princess Casamassima*, vol. 2, pp. 347–48.

16. *The Ambassadors*, vol. 2, p. 256, in Henry James, *Novels and Tales*, vols. 21–22. Page references to the New York edition will henceforth appear in parentheses after the quotations; all citations are from the second volume.

17. Aristotle, *Poetics*, p. 1486.

Works Cited

Aristotle. *Physics*. Trans. R. P. Hardie and R. K. Gaye. In *The Basic Works of Aristotle*, ed. Richard McKeon, pp. 213–394. New York: Random House, 1941.

———. *Poetics*. Trans. Ingram Bywater. In *The Basic Works of Aristotle*, ed. Richard McKeon, pp. 1453–87. New York: Random House, 1941.

Baguley, David. *Naturalist Fiction: The Entropic Vision*. Cambridge, Eng.: Cambridge University Press, 1990.

Bailey, Cyril. *The Greek Atomists and Epicurus: A Study*. Oxford: Clarendon, 1928.

Barthes, Roland. "Introduction to the Structural Analysis of Narratives." Trans. Stephen Heath. In *Image, Music, Text*, pp. 79–124. New York: Hill and Wang, 1977.

Beaty, Jerome. *"Middlemarch" from Notebook to Novel: A Study of George Eliot's Creative Method*. Urbana: University of Illinois Press, 1960.

Beer, Gillian. *Darwin's Plots: Evolutionary Narrative in Darwin, George Eliot, and Nineteenth-Century Fiction*. London: Routledge and Kegan Paul, 1983.

Benstock, Shari. "*Ulysses* as Ghoststory." *James Joyce Quarterly* 12, no. 4 (1975): 396–411.

Bersani, Leo. *A Future for Astyanax: Character and Desire in Literature*. Boston: Little, Brown, 1976.

Bloom, Harold. *Poetry and Repression*. New Haven, Conn.: Yale University Press, 1976.

Bohm, David. *Causality and Chance in Modern Physics*. London: Routledge and Kegan Paul, 1957.

Bohr, Neils. *Atomic Theory and the Description of Nature*. New York: Macmillan; Cambridge, Eng.: The University Press, 1934.

Bowlby, Rachel. *Just Looking: Consumer Culture in Dreiser, Gissing, and Zola*. New York: Methuen, 1985.

Bunge, Mario. "What Is Chance?" *Science and Society* 15, no. 3 (1951): 209–31.

Cage, John. *Writing Through Finnegans Wake*. Tulsa: University of Oklahoma Press, 1978.

Carroll, David. "*Middlemarch* and the Externality of Fact." In Ian Adam, ed., *This Particular Web: Essays on "Middlemarch,"* pp. 73–90. Toronto: University of Toronto Press, 1975.

Chevrel, Yves. *Le naturalisme*. Paris: PUF, 1982.

Christ, Carol. "Aggression and Providential Death in George Eliot's Fiction." *Novel* 9 (Winter 1976): 130–40.

Conrad, Joseph. *Complete Works*. Canterbury edition. 26 vols. Garden City, N.Y.: Doubleday, Page, 1924.

——— . *A Personal Record*. New York: Harper and Brothers, 1912.

Cortázar, Julio. *Hopscotch*. Trans. Gregory Rabassa. New York: Pantheon Books, 1966.

Cox, R. G., ed. *Thomas Hardy: The Critical Heritage*. London: Routledge and Kegan Paul; New York: Barnes and Noble, 1970.

Curle, Richard. *The Last Twelve Years of Joseph Conrad*. New York: Russell and Russell, 1968.

Dante Alighieri. *Inferno*. Trans. John D. Sinclair. New York: Oxford University Press, 1976.

——— . *Paradiso*. Trans. John D. Sinclair. New York: Oxford University Press, 1976.

Darwin, Charles. *The Origin of Species by Means of Natural Selection: or, The Preservation of Favored Races in the Struggle for Life*. London: Penguin Books, 1968.

Defoe, Daniel. *The Life and Strange Surprizing Adventures of Robinson Crusoe*. Ed. J. Donald Crowley. Oxford: Oxford University Press, 1972.

Derrida, Jacques. *Dissemination*. Trans. Barbara Johnson. Chicago: University of Chicago Press, 1981.

——— . "My Chances/*Mes Chances*: A Rendezvous with Some Epicurean Stereophonies." Trans. Irene Harvey and Avital Ronell. In William Kerrigan and Joseph H. Smith, eds., *Taking Chances: Derrida, Psychoanalysis, and Literature*, pp. 1–32. Baltimore, Md.: Johns Hopkins University Press, 1984.

——— . *The Post Card: From Socrates to Freud and Beyond*. Trans. Alan Bass. Chicago: University of Chicago Press, 1987.

——— . "The Purveyor of Truth." Trans. Willis Domingo et al. *Yale French Studies* 52 (1975): 31–113.

——— . "Ulysses Gramophone: Hear Say Yes in Joyce." In Bernard Benstock, ed., *James Joyce: The Augmented Ninth; Proceedings of the Ninth International James Joyce Symposium, Frankfurt, 1984*, pp. 27–75. Syracuse, N.Y.: Syracuse University Press, 1988.

Dickens, Charles. *Bleak House*. Harmondsworth, Eng.: Penguin Books, 1976.

——— . *David Copperfield*. Harmondsworth, Eng.: Penguin Books, 1966.

————. *Great Expectations*. Harmondsworth, Eng.: Penguin Books, 1965.

————. *The Letters of Charles Dickens*. Vol. 3. Ed. Walter Dexter. London: Nonesuch, 1938.

————. *Nicholas Nickleby*. Harmondsworth, Eng.: Penguin Books, 1978.

————. *Oliver Twist*. Harmondsworth, Eng.: Penguin Books, 1966.

Einstein, Albert. *The Born-Einstein Letters: Correspondence Between Albert Einstein and Max and Hedwig Born from 1916 to 1955, with Commentaries by Max Born*. Trans. Irene Born. New York: Walker, 1971.

Eliot, George. *Daniel Deronda*. Ed. Graham Handley. Oxford: Clarendon; New York: Oxford University Press, 1984.

————. *Essays by George Eliot*. Ed. Thomas Pinney. New York: Columbia University Press, 1963.

————. *Felix Holt, the Radical*. Harmondsworth, Eng.: Penguin Books, 1975.

————. *Felix Holt, the Radical*. Ed. Fred C. Thomson. Oxford: Clarendon; New York: Oxford University Press, 1980.

————. *The George Eliot Letters*. Vol. 5. Ed. Gordon S. Haight. New Haven, Conn.: Yale University Press, 1955.

————. *Middlemarch: A Study of Provincial Life*. Ed. David Carroll. Oxford: Clarendon; New York: Oxford University Press, 1986.

————. *Romola*. In *The Works of George Eliot*, Cabinet edition, vols. 19–20. Edinburgh: William Blackwood, 1878–85.

————. *Scenes of Clerical Life*. Ed. Thomas A. Noble. Oxford: Clarendon; New York: Oxford University Press, 1985.

————. *Silas Marner: The Weaver of Raveloe*. In *The Works of George Eliot*, Cabinet edition, vol. 3, pp. 1–273. Edinburgh: William Blackwood, 1878–85.

————, trans. [as Marian Evans]. Ludwig Feuerbach, *The Essence of Christianity*. New York: Harper and Row, 1957.

Ellmann, Richard. *James Joyce: New and Revised Edition*. Oxford: Oxford University Press, 1982.

Encyclopedia of Philosophy. 8 vols. Ed. Paul Edwards. New York: Macmillan, 1967.

Fineman, Joel. *Shakespeare's Perjured Eye: The Invention of Poetic Subjectivity in the Sonnets*. Berkeley: University of California Press, 1986.

————. "The Significance of Literature: *The Importance of Being Earnest*." *October* 15 (Winter 1980): 79–90.

————. "The Sound of O in *Othello*: The Real of the Tragedy of Desire." *October* 45 (Summer 1988): 76–96.

Ford, Ford Madox. "Conrad on the Theory of Fiction." In Marvin Mudrick, ed., *Conrad: A Collection of Critical Essays*, pp. 167–77. Englewood Cliffs, N.J.: Prentice-Hall, 1966.

French, Marilyn. *The Book as World: James Joyce's "Ulysses."* Cambridge, Mass.: Harvard University Press, 1976.

Freud, Sigmund. *Beyond the Pleasure Principle.* Trans. James Strachey. London: Hogarth, 1950.

————. "Delusion and Dream in Jensen's *Gradiva.*" Trans. James Strachey. In *The Standard Edition of the Complete Psychological Works of Sigmund Freud*, vol. 9, pp. 7–93. London: Hogarth, 1959.

————. "Family Romances." Trans. James Strachey. In Sigmund Freud, *Collected Papers*, vol. 5, pp. 74–82. New York: Basic Books, 1959.

————. "Fragment of an Analysis of a Case of Hysteria." Trans. James Strachey. In Sigmund Freud, *Dora: An Analysis of a Case of Hysteria*, Philip Rieff, ed., pp. 21–144. New York: Collier Books, 1963.

————. *The Interpretation of Dreams.* Trans. James Strachey. New York: Avon Books, 1965.

————. *The Psychopathology of Everyday Life.* Trans. Alan Tyson. New York: W. W. Norton, 1965.

————. "The 'Uncanny.'" Trans. Alix Strachey. In Sigmund Freud, *On Creativity and the Unconscious: Papers on the Psychology of Art, Literature, Love, Religion*, Benjamin Nelson, ed., pp. 122–61. New York: Harper and Brothers, 1958.

Furst, Lillian R., and Peter N. Skrine. *Naturalism.* London: Methuen, 1971.

Gallagher, Catherine, and Thomas Laqueur, eds. *The Making of the Modern Body: Sexuality and Society in the Nineteenth Century.* Berkeley: University of California Press, 1987.

Garrett, Peter K. *The Victorian Multiplot Novel: Studies in Dialogic Form.* New Haven, Conn.: Yale University Press, 1980.

Genette, Gérard. *Narrative Discourse: An Essay in Method.* Trans. Jane E. Lewin. Ithaca, N.Y.: Cornell University Press, 1980.

Gifford, Don, with Robert J. Seidman. *"Ulysses" Annotated: Notes for James Joyce's "Ulysses."* Berkeley: University of California Press, 1988.

Hacking, Ian. *The Emergence of Probability: A Philosophical Study of Early Ideas About Probability, Induction, and Statistical Inference.* Cambridge, Eng.: Cambridge University Press, 1975.

Haight, Gordon S. *George Eliot: A Biography.* New York: Penguin Books, 1985.

Hardy, Florence Emily. *The Life of Thomas Hardy, 1840–1928.* Hamden, Conn.: Archon Books, 1970.

Hardy, Thomas. *Thomas Hardy's Personal Writings: Prefaces, Literary Opinions, Reminiscences.* Ed. Harold Orel. Lawrence: University of Kansas Press, 1966.

————. *The Works of Thomas Hardy in Prose and Verse.* Wessex edition. 18 vols. London: Macmillan, 1920.

Harvey, W. J. "Chance and Design in *Bleak House*." In John Gross and Gabriel Pierson, eds., *Dickens in the Twentieth Century*, pp. 145–57. Toronto: University of Toronto Press, 1962.

Hassan, Ihab Habib. *The Dismemberment of Orpheus: Toward a Post-modern Literature*. 2nd edition. Madison: University of Wisconsin Press, 1982.

Hayman, David. "Stephen on the Rocks." *James Joyce Quarterly* 15, no. 1 (1977): 5–17.

Heisenberg, Werner. *Nuclear Physics*. New York: Greenwood, 1969.

———. *The Physical Principles of the Quantum Theory*. Trans. Carl Eckart and Frank C. Hoyt. Chicago: University of Chicago Press, 1930.

———. *Physics and Beyond: Encounters and Conversations*. Trans. Arnold J. Pomerans. New York: Harper and Row, 1971.

Herring, Phillip F. *Joyce's Uncertainty Principle*. Princeton, N.J.: Princeton University Press, 1987.

Hertz, Neil. "Recognizing Casaubon." In Neil Hertz, *The End of the Line: Essays on Psychoanalysis and the Sublime*, pp. 75–96. New York: Columbia University Press, 1985.

Hornback, Bert G. *The Metaphor of Chance: Vision and Technique in the Works of Thomas Hardy*. Athens, Ohio: Ohio University Press, 1971.

Howe, Irving. *Thomas Hardy*. New York: Macmillan, 1967.

Hull, David L. *Darwin and His Critics: The Reception of Darwin's Theory of Evolution by the Scientific Community*. Cambridge, Mass.: Harvard University Press, 1973.

Hulme, Peter. *Colonial Encounters: Europe and the Native Caribbean, 1492–1797*. London: Methuen, 1986.

Hunter, J. Paul. *The Reluctant Pilgrim: Defoe's Emblematic Method and Quest for Form in "Robinson Crusoe."* Baltimore, Md.: Johns Hopkins University Press, 1966.

Jakobson, Roman. "Two Aspects of Language and Two Types of Aphasic Disturbances." In Roman Jakobson and Morris Hall, *Fundamentals of Language*, pp. 67–96. The Hague: Mouton, 1975.

James, Glenn, and Robert Clarke James, eds. *Mathematics Dictionary*. 4th edition. New York: Van Nostrand Reinhold, 1976.

James, Henry. "The New Novel, 1914." In Henry James, *The Art of Fiction and Other Essays*, pp. 181–214. New York: Oxford University Press, 1948.

———. *The Novels and Tales of Henry James*. New York edition. 26 vols. New York: Charles Scribner's Sons, 1907–1909.

———. *Theory of Fiction: Henry James*. Ed. James E. Miller, Jr. Lincoln: University of Nebraska Press, 1972.

James, William. "The Dilemma of Determinism." In William James, *Essays in Pragmatism*, ed. Alburey Castell, pp. 37–64. New York: Hafner, 1948.

Jameson, Fredric. *The Political Unconscious: Narrative as a Socially Sym-
    bolic Act.* Ithaca, N.Y.: Cornell University Press, 1981.
––––––. "Postmodernism and Consumer Society." In Hal Foster, ed., *The
    Anti-Aesthetic: Essays on Postmodern Culture,* pp. 111–125. Port Town-
    send, Wash.: Bay Press, 1983.
Jenkin, Fleeming. "The Atomic Theory of Lucretius." *The North British
    Review* 48 (June 1868): 211–42.
Joyce, James. *Exiles.* New York: Viking, 1951.
––––––. *Finnegans Wake.* New York: Viking, 1959.
––––––. *A Portrait of the Artist as a Young Man.* Harmondsworth, Eng.:
    Penguin Books, 1976.
––––––. *Selected Letters.* Ed. Richard Ellmann. New York: Viking, 1975.
––––––. *Ulysses: The Corrected Text.* Ed. Hans Walter Gabler. New York:
    Vintage Books, 1986.
Karl, Frederick R. *Joseph Conrad: The Three Lives.* New York: Farrar,
    Straus and Giroux, 1979.
Knoepflmacher, U. C. *George Eliot's Early Novels: The Limits of Realism.*
    Berkeley: University of California Press, 1968.
Kosinski, Jerzy. *Being There.* New York: Harcourt, Brace, Jovanovich, 1970.
Lacan, Jacques. *The Four Fundamental Concepts of Psychoanalysis.* Trans.
    Alan Sheridan. New York: W. W. Norton, 1981.
––––––. "Seminar on 'The Purloined Letter.'" Trans. J. Mehlman. In J.
    Mehlman, ed., *French Freud: Structural Studies in Psychoanalysis* (*Yale
    French Studies* 48 [1972]: 38–72).
Laplanche, Jean, and J.-B. Pontalis. "Fantasy and the Origins of Sexuality."
    International Journal of Psychoanalysis 49 (1968): 1–18.
Leavis, F. R. *The Great Tradition: George Eliot, Henry James, Joseph
    Conrad.* New York: New York University Press, 1964.
Levine, George. *Darwin and the Novelists: Patterns of Science in Victorian
    Fiction.* Cambridge, Mass.: Harvard University Press, 1988.
––––––. "Determinism and Responsibility in the Works of George Eliot."
    PMLA 77 (1962): 268–79.
––––––. *The Realistic Imagination: English Fiction from Frankenstein to
    Lady Chatterley.* Chicago: University of Chicago Press, 1981.
Lodge, David. "Strether by the River." In David Lodge, *Language of Fic-
    tion: Essays in Criticism and Verbal Analysis of the English Novel,* pp.
    189–213. New York: Columbia University Press, 1966.
Lucretius Carus, Titus. *De Rerum Natura: Libri Sex.* Ed. and trans. H. A. J.
    Munro. 3 vols. Cambridge, Eng.: Deighton Bell; London: George Bell,
    1893.
––––––. *The Nature of the Universe.* Trans. Ronald Latham. Harmonds-
    worth, Eng.: Penguin Books, 1951.

Lukacher, Ned. *Primal Scenes: Literature, Philosophy, Psychoanalysis.* Ithaca, N.Y.: Cornell University Press, 1986.

Lukács, Georg. *The Theory of the Novel: A Historico-philosophical Essay on the Forms of Great Epic Literature.* Trans. Anna Bostock. Cambridge, Mass.: M.I.T. Press, 1971.

Lyotard, Jean-François. *The Postmodern Condition: A Report on Knowledge.* Trans. Geoff Bennington and Brian Massumi. Minneapolis: University of Minnesota Press, 1984.

McGee, Patrick. *Paperspace: Style as Ideology in Joyce's "Ulysses."* Lincoln: University of Nebraska Press, 1988.

McKeon, Michael. *The Origins of the English Novel, 1600–1740.* Baltimore, Md.: Johns Hopkins University Press, 1987.

Mallarmé, Stephane. *Mallarmé: The Poems: A Bilingual Edition.* Trans. Keith Bosley. Harmondsworth, Eng.: Penguin Books, 1977.

Marx, Karl. *The Difference Between the Democritean and Epicurean Philosophy of Nature.* Trans. and included in Norman D. Livergood, *Activity in Marx's Philosophy.* The Hague: Martinus Hijhoff, 1967.

Michaels, Walter Benn. *The Gold Standard and the Logic of Naturalism: American Literature at the Turn of the Century.* Berkeley: University of California Press, 1987.

Mill, John Stuart. *A System of Logic, Ratiocinative and Inductive.* New York: Harper and Brothers, 1846.

Miller, D. A. "Discipline in Different Voices: Bureaucracy, Police, Family, and *Bleak House.*" In D. A. Miller, *The Novel and the Police,* pp. 58–106. Berkeley: University of California Press, 1988.

———. *Narrative and Its Discontents: Problems of Closure in the Traditional Novel.* Princeton, N.J.: Princeton University Press, 1981.

Miller, J. Hillis. "Narrative and History." *English Literary History* 41 (Fall 1974): 455–73.

———. *Thomas Hardy: Distance and Desire.* Cambridge, Mass.: Harvard University Press, 1970.

Millgate, Michael. *Thomas Hardy: A Biography.* Oxford: Oxford University Press, 1982.

Mitchell, Lee Clark. *Determined Fictions: American Literary Naturalism.* New York: Columbia University Press, 1987.

Monod, Jacques. *Chance and Necessity: An Essay on the Natural Philosophy of Modern Biology.* Trans. Austryn Wainhouse. New York: Vintage Books, 1972.

Moser, Thomas. "Conrad's Later 'Affirmation.'" In Marvin Mudrick, ed., *Conrad: A Collection of Critical Essays,* pp. 145–65. Englewood Cliffs, N.J.: Prentice-Hall, 1966.

Nagel, Ernest. *The Structure of Science: Problems in the Logic of Scientific*

Explanation. New York: Harcourt, Brace, and World, 1961.

Nettels, Elsa. *James and Conrad*. Athens: The University of Georgia Press, 1977.

Newsom, Robert. *Dickens on the Romantic Side of Familiar Things: "Bleak House" and the Novel Tradition*. New York: Columbia University Press, 1977.

———. *A Likely Story: Probability and Play in Fiction*. New Brunswick, N.J.: Rutgers University Press, 1988.

Nietzsche, Friedrich. *The Portable Nietzsche*. Trans. Walter Kauffmann. New York: Viking, 1954.

Oxford English Dictionary. 12 vols. Ed. James A. H. Murray. Oxford: Clarendon, 1933.

Paley, William. *Natural Theology: or, Evidences of the Existence and Attributes of the Deity, Collected from the Appearances of Nature*. Boston: Gould and Lincoln, 1854.

Patey, Douglas Lane. *Probability and Literary Form: Philosophic Theory and Literary Practice in the Augustan Age*. Cambridge, Eng.: Cambridge University Press, 1984.

Peirce, Charles Sanders. *Chance, Love, and Logic*. Ed. Morris R. Cohen. New York: Harcourt, Brace, 1923.

Pettersson, Torsten. *Consciousness and Time: A Study in the Philosophy and Narrative Technique of Joseph Conrad*. Abo, Finland: Abo Akademi, 1982.

Pollard, William G. *Chance and Providence: God's Action in a World Governed by Scientific Law*. New York: Scribner's, 1958.

Pound, Ezra. *The Cantos of Ezra Pound*. New York: New Directions Books, 1979.

Rader, Ralph W. "Exodus and Return: Joyce's *Ulysses* and the Fiction of the Actual." *University of Toronto Quarterly* 48 (Winter 1978–79): 149–71.

———. "The Logic of *Ulysses*; or, Why Molly Had to Live in Gibraltar." *Critical Inquiry* 10 (June 1984): 567–79.

Schorske, Carl E. *Fin-de-Siècle Vienna: Politics and Culture*. New York: Vintage Books, 1981.

Sedgwick, Eve Kosofsky. *Between Men: English Literature and Male Homosocial Desire*. New York: Columbia University Press, 1985.

Senn, Fritz. "Joyce the Verb." In Morris Beja and Shari Benstock, eds., *Coping with Joyce: Essays from the Copenhagen Symposium*, pp. 25–54. Columbus: Ohio State University Press, 1989.

———. *Joyce's Dislocations: Essays on Reading as Translation*. Ed. John Paul Riquelme. Baltimore, Md.: Johns Hopkins University Press, 1984.

Serres, Michel. *Hermes: Literature, Science, Philosophy*. Trans. Josue V.

Harari and David F. Bell. Baltimore, Md.: Johns Hopkins University Press, 1982.

———. *The Parasite*. Trans. Lawrence R. Schehr. Baltimore, Md.: Johns Hopkins University Press, 1982.

Shuttleworth, Sally. *George Eliot and Nineteenth-Century Science: The Make-Believe of a Beginning*. Cambridge, Eng.: Cambridge University Press, 1984.

Siegle, Robert. *The Politics of Reflexivity: Narrative and the Constitutive Poetics of Culture*. Baltimore, Md.: Johns Hopkins University Press, 1986.

Sophocles. *Oedipus Tyrannus*. Vol. 1 of *Sophocles: The Plays and Fragments*. Ed. and trans. R. C. Jebb. Cambridge, Eng.: Cambridge University Press, 1893.

Starr, G. A. *Defoe and Spiritual Autobiography*. Princeton, N.J.: Princeton University Press, 1965.

Sterne, Laurence. *Works*. 7 vols. Oxford: Basil Blackwell; Boston: Houghton Mifflin, 1926–27.

Stoppard, Tom. *Travesties*. New York: Grove, 1975.

Thomas Aquinas, Saint [Thomas of Aquino]. *The Summa Contra Gentiles*. Trans. the Dominican fathers. London: Burns, Oates, and Washbourne, 1923.

Thomas, Brook. *James Joyce's "Ulysses": A Book of Many Happy Returns*. Baton Rouge: Louisiana State University Press, 1982.

Thompson, Michael. *Rubbish Theory: The Creation and Destruction of Value*. Oxford: Oxford University Press, 1979.

Tillotson, John. *Works*. 10 vols. London: J. F. Dove, 1820.

Ulmer, Gregory L. *Applied Grammatology: Post(e)-Pedagogy from Jacques Derrida to Joseph Beuys*. Baltimore, Md.: Johns Hopkins University Press, 1985.

Vargish, Thomas. *The Providential Aesthetic in Victorian Fiction*. Charlottesville: University Press of Virginia, 1985.

Viner, Jacob. *The Role of Providence in the Social Order: An Essay in Intellectual History*. Philadelphia: American Philosophical Society, 1972.

Warner, William Beatty. *Chance and the Text of Experience: Freud, Nietzsche, and Shakespeare's "Hamlet."* Ithaca, N.Y.: Cornell University Press, 1986.

Watt, Ian. *The Rise of the Novel: Studies in Defoe, Richardson, and Fielding*. Berkeley: University of California Press, 1957.

———. "*Robinson Crusoe* as a Myth." *Essays in Criticism* 1 (1951): 95–119.

Welsford, Enid. *The Fool: His Social and Literary History*. Gloucester, Mass.: P. Smith, 1966.

Welsh, Alexander. *George Eliot and Blackmail*. Cambridge, Mass.: Harvard University Press, 1985.

Wharton, Edith. "Roman Fever." In Edith Wharton, *"Roman Fever" and Other Stories*, pp. 9–24. New York: Scribner's, 1964.

Woolf, Virginia. *The Waves*. Harmondsworth, Eng.: Penguin Books, 1931.

Young, Alan. *Dada and After: Extremist Modernism and English Literature*. Manchester: Manchester University Press; Atlantic Highlands, N.J.: Humanities Press, 1981.

Index

In this index "f" after a number indicates a separate reference on the next page, and "ff" indicates separate references on the next two pages. A continuous discussion over two or more pages is indicated by a span of numbers. *Passim* is used for a cluster of references in close but not consecutive sequence.

Literary realism (Michael McKeon), 33–36, 42–43, 45
Lodge, David, 171n
Lucretius, 3, 5, 21–22, 23, 28, 56, 79, 99, 150n, 152–53; *De Rerum Natura*, 152. *See also* Epicurus
Lukacher, Ned, 105n
Lukács, Georg, 32
Lyotard, Jean-François, 7, 147

McGee, Patrick, 132n
McKeon, Michael, 31, 33–35, 36, 40–44
Mallarmé, Stephane, 8–9
Marx, Karl, 20, 30n
Maupassant, Guy de, 170
Mesostic, 149–50
Metaphor, in *Ulysses*, 137ff
Metaphysics, 4–5, 16, 19, 63
Metonymy, 39, 61, 137f
Mill, John Stuart, 19
Miller, D. A., 83n
Miller, J. Hillis, 66–67, 161
Milton, John, 76
Modernism, 3–14 *passim*, 76ff, 79, 84, 157, 174
Moira, 30–31, 127–28. *See also* Fate
Monod, Jacques, 24–25
Moral sympathy, in George Eliot, 12, 48, 68, 74
Moser, Thomas, 92f

Nagel, Ernest, 27
Narcissus, 119–20
Narrative, *see under* Chance: and narrative
Naturalism, 12, 73–74, 79–80, 85, 100, 154
Naturalization, of chance and writing, in *Ulysses*, 129, 139–143
Natural selection, theory of, 7, 24f, 48–49, 81, 162. *See also* Darwin, Charles; Evolution, theory of

Natural theology, 49
Necessity, *see under* Chance: vs. necessity
Nettels, Elsa, 76n
Newsom, Robert, 44n, 54n
Nietzsche, Friedrich, 4n, 16, 67, 164
Novel, rise of the, 6, 11, 31–45, 150n

Oedipus, 30–31, 82, 94
Old Maid, 103–4
Onomastics, 136n
Origins, in George Eliot, 68–70, 73
Overdetermination, 29n, 81
Oxford English Dictionary, 68, 136

Paley, William, 49n
Parable, 130, 154; in George Eliot, 57–63 *passim*, 66f, 71
Parasite, 63, 70, 73, 130
Particle theory, vs. wave theory, 26, 78
Paternity, consubstantial vs. transubstantial, 12, 110–21 *passim*, 133–44 *passim*
Patey, Douglas Lane, 44n
Peirce, Charles Sanders, 18
Perspective, in the novel, 76–77, 86–88, 157, 166, 174
Pettersson, Torsten, 77n
Picaresque, 10n
Planck, Max, 80
Pleasure principle, 29, 153
Poe, Edgar Allan, 73n, 83
Point of view, *see* Perspective, in the novel
Pollard, William G., 37n
Pontalis, J.-B., 94, 105
Positivism, 50, 82
Postmodernism, 10, 13, 147
Pound, Ezra, 143
Power-knowledge, 5, 63, 153
Pre-Socratics, 10, 30n

Library of Congress Cataloging-in-Publication Data

Monk, Leland.
  Standard deviations : chance and the modern British novel / Leland Monk.
    p.   cm.
  Includes bibliographical references and index.
  ISBN 0-8047-2174-2 (alk. paper) :
    1. English fiction—20th century—History and criticism.
  2. English fiction—19th century—History and criticism.   3. Fate and
  fatalism in literature.   4. Chance in literature.   I. Title.
  PR888.F35M66   1993
  823'.809—dc20   92-38358
                                                                  CIP